THE SEEKER
D. S. MEREZHKOVSKIY

THE SEEKER
D. S. MEREZHKOVSKIY

by

Charles
C. Harold Bedford

THE UNIVERSITY PRESS OF KANSAS
Lawrence/Manhattan/Wichita

Library of Congress Cataloging in Publication Data

Bedford, Charles Harold, 1929-
    The seeker : D. S. Merezhkovskiy.

    List of Merezhkovskiy's works: p.
    Bibliography: p.
    Includes index.
    1. Merezhkovskii, Dmitrii Sergeevich, 1865-1941—
Religion and ethics. I. Title.
PG3467.M4Z63   891.7'8'4209   74-28496
ISBN 0-7006-0131-7

Acknowledgments

I am indebted to the editors of *The Slavonic and East European Review* for permission to employ, in somewhat altered form, the texts of two articles—"D. S. Merezhkovsky: the Forgotten Poet" (December 1957) and "Dmitry Merezhkovsky, the Third Testament and the Third Humanity" (December 1963). The former serves as the basis of chapters 2 and 3; the latter as the basis of chapter 8 and the concluding section of chapter 6. Chapter 7 is an expansion of an article, "Dmitry Merezhkovsky, the Intelligentsia, and the Revolution of 1905," which appeared in volume 3 of *Canadian Slavonic Papers* (1959). I am especially grateful to Professor Temira Pachmuss of the University of Illinois for permission to examine the Merezhkovskiy archives in her possession. Her kindness stands in marked contrast to a much-delayed refusal to my request to have access to the Merezhkovskiy archives in the U.S.S.R. My gratitude is also extended to the Canada Council and the University of Toronto for grants-in-aid of research, which contributed to the completion of this work.

My deepest appreciation, however, is reserved for the long-suffering members of my family: my young daughters, Kristina and Melanie, who have displayed a patience, forbearance, and even quietness beyond their years; and my wife, Hannele, for her never-failing understanding, encouragement, and Finnish *sisu*, the last frequently called upon to serve for two.

All translations from Russian and French sources are my own. In translating excerpts from Merezhkovskiy's poems, I have endeavored to retain the metric pattern—and, in a few instances, the rhyme—of the original.

Preface

Dmitriy Sergeevich Merezhkovskiy was one of the most prolific authors of the modern period. Poetry, the novel, the drama, religious-philosophical tracts, essays: these were the genres that served as the means for the expression of his views on the problem that he considered most vital not only in the contemporary world, but in mankind as a whole—the discovery and practice of true Christianity. Nor was he alone in such striving. Soren Kierkegaard's treatises on the state of Christendom and the need to return to a more elemental and more existential form of Christianity had already begun to effect a change of outlook among numerous theologians and religious thinkers of various sects.

Nineteenth-century discontent with the increasing secularization of life in the Christian nations of Europe could not but increase as industrialization brought with it into the twentieth century ever more rapid strides in man's scientific knowledge and technological accomplishments. Man was becoming, in his own mind, the center of the universe, either in Nietzsche's terms as a superman who should be free from all constraints or in Marx's view as an atheistic unit in a collective mankind. Even man's growing consciousness of himself in the era of Sigmund Freud, Carl Jung, Alfred Adler, and their progeny contributed to the trend. The revitalizing of a fragmented Christendom was essential as a counterbalance; it found expression in the writings of such Russian religious thinkers as Fedor Dostoevskiy, Vladimir Solov'ev, Vasiliy Rozanov, Nicholas Berdyaev, and Serge Bulgakov; in the neo-Catholic movement in France during the early years of the twentieth century; and in the more recent upsurge of ecumenical sentiments, which have given birth to practical, though as yet insufficient, results. Merezhkovskiy was among the first in Russia at the turn of the century to devote his energies almost exclusively to the search for a form of Christianity that would be more in keeping with man's contemporary and future life—moreover, a Christianity that would be ecumenical in the fullest sense.

Contents

1

Formative Years

It is possible, when discussing the literary and philosophical productions of some authors, to pay but scant attention to their early lives. In the case of Dmitriy Sergeevich Merezhkovskiy such a procedure would be deleterious, or at best misleading, for it would result in an incomplete understanding of Merezhkovskiy the author and religious thinker; it has led, in certain instances, to an unfair appraisal of his literary career as a whole. Merezhkovskiy's early life is of special importance as part of the conditioning process that prepared him to accept or evolve much that he put forward in his later writings. Certain of his religious concepts, his attitude toward state power, and his attitude toward the lower classes, as well as his aristocratic outlook, are the fruits of influences that acted upon him in childhood and adolescence, leaving indelible traces on his mind.

Merezhkovskiy was extremely proud of his ancestry, for it placed him above the common herd. He begins his autobiographical sketch in *Russian Literature of the Twentieth Century* with the asseveration that his great-grandfather was one Fedor Merezhki, *voyskovoy starshina* in the city of Glukhov.[1] Thus, Merezhki was of Cossack stock, and in particular of the officer or gentry class, since *voyskovoy starshina* was a rank in Cossack regiments equivalent to that of lieutenant colonel. His son Ivan Fedorovich left the Ukraine for St. Petersburg towards the end of the eighteenth century and, as a Russian *dvoryanin,* received a junior rank in the noted Izmaylovskiy Regiment. It was he who russified the family name to Merezhkovskiy. There is little further information available about Ivan Fedorovich, other than that he was transferred to Moscow, where he served during the War of 1812 and where he presumably settled afterwards, for it was in Moscow that his son Sergey Ivanovich was born in 1821.

Sergey Ivanovich was destined to make a brilliant career in the civil service. At the age of eighteen he received his first post in the administration of Orenburg Province; subsequently he held more responsible positions in various provinces, finally moving to St. Petersburg as an assistant department head, and later as department head, in the Court Department. In 1853 he married Varvara Vasil'evna Chesnokova, daughter of a high-ranking official in the St. Petersburg police department. At the time of the birth of Dmitriy Sergeevich, Sergey Ivanovich had reached the highest rank in the service, that of privy councillor, a position from which he retired in 1881 after the assassination of Alexander II. Sergey Ivanovich and his family, therefore, were members of the society in the highest echelon of the bureaucracy, and they moved, moreover, in court circles. This aspect of his early life may have contributed to Merezhkovskiy's later sense of superiority, his spiritual "aristocratism," which became a prominent part of his outlook on life during his Symbolist period.

Sergey Ivanovich and Varvara Vasil'evna raised a large and apparently discordant family. Dmitriy Sergeevich Merezhkovskiy— who was born in St. Petersburg at his parents' summer residence, one of the palace buildings on Elagin Island, on 14 August 1865[2]—was the youngest of six sons. While he could not claim the dubious distinction of being the youngest member of the family, only one of his three sisters was junior to him. Merezhkovskiy was to complain later that "there was little happiness in childhood."[3] He attributed both the unhappiness and the eventual dissolution of the family to his father, claiming that he failed to provide the spiritual bond which alone could unite such a large group.[4]

It is perhaps unfortunate, though not unexpected, that any evaluation of Sergey Ivanovich's character must be based on Merezhkovskiy's personal recollections, which are echoed to some degree by Merezhkovskiy's wife, Zinaida Gippius, in her regrettably rather unreliable biography of her husband. Yet it is a tribute to Merezhkovskiy that his references to his father are made without acrimony and that the degree of impartiality he reaches permits him to indicate his father's virtues as well as his failings. Merezhkovskiy ascribes the unhappiness of his childhood and adolescence to his father's misdirected sense of values. Sergey Ivanovich was quite rich, but he did not believe in wasting money, especially on frivolities. In his autobiographical poem *Octaves of the Past (Starinnye oktavy)*, Merezhkovskiy cites a number of incidents to bear out such a contention. For the sake of economy the majority of the household furnishings were draped in dust covers, which were removed only when guests were invited.[5] More forceful is the scene in which Merezhkovskiy's mother is berated in the child's presence for having bought him an inexpensive toy.[6] The object of life for Sergey Ivanovich was not the attainment of happiness; life was a sorrowful task, the burden of which he bore without a murmur or a smile. He spoiled his life for money, since he considered no rank or order a just reward for his work and since he had faith only in capital and rents. It is interesting to note that Merezhkovskiy stresses that his father was striving not for personal aggrandizement, but for the benefit of the family. He thought only of his children, and it was from a sense of duty to them that Sergey Ivanovich devoted his life to this task.[7]

While he was willing to amass wealth for his family, Sergey Ivanovich considered love (the externals of it, at any rate) a harmful indulgence. For years he tormented his wife by his interference in the management of the household and the raising of the children. An official from his youth, he was strict and businesslike in all things. Even his home—a two-story government building on the Znamenskiy Embankment, facing the Summer Garden and flanked by the Summer Palace of Peter I and the Troitskiy Cathedral—reflected his character; in it there reigned eternal order and an officelike spirit. His love for his children did not permit him to make himself their equal, for he could not understand and did not like their laughter and games. As a result of his moroseness and severity the children were afraid to disturb him in any way. Merezhkovskiy presents as an example an episode in which he spilled a bottle of ink in his father's study and then, trembling with fear, cowered in bed to await the outcome of his father's wrath.[8]

The excessive strictness and severity of paternal authority, which verged on the absolute in the Merezhkovskiy household, had a profound effect on Merezhkovskiy's psychological development. In maturity it resulted in his reaction against any manifestation of authority, whether temporal or spiritual, that might constrain his personal freedom. His rebellious attitude towards Russian autocracy, indeed towards any form of government, as well as his rejection

3

of Russian Orthodoxy and any other denomination of "historic Christianity," though justified by intellectual argumentation and fully in keeping with the spirit of the times, may in part have derived from the all-pervading force of the father image in Merezhkovskiy's early life.

Of no less consequence was the impression left on Merezhkovskiy by his mother. Fortunately for the children, Varvara Vasil'evna's nature was a contrast to that of her husband. Although she submitted to his will on most matters, she never failed to intercede with her husband on behalf of the children, in spite of the fact that such intercession resulted in anguish and suffering for herself and (if Merezhkovskiy's assertion is true) in the illness that persisted throughout her life.[9] Dmitriy, the youngest son, became her favorite; and an unusually strong love grew up between them. "All the strength of Merezhkovskiy's love was concentrated from his childhood on one point: his mother,"[10] Gippius comments. *Octaves of the Past* leaves no doubt as to the validity of this statement. There are repeated references to her protecting him from his father's anger; to the effect that her physical presence had on him, particularly when nightmares left him in a state of terror; to her helping him with his homework, so that he felt her charm in his books and "found poetry in the rules of cube roots."[11] A contributing factor to the dependence of Merezhkovskiy on his mother and to his idealization of her was her rushing to his bedside from abroad when he suffered a severe attack of diphtheria at the age of seven or eight.[12] Merezhkovskiy's dependence on Varvara Vasil'evna did not abate after he had reached manhood, for it was she who prevailed upon Sergey Ivanovich to permit the marriage of their twenty-three-year-old son to Zinaida Gippius and to grant the young couple an allowance. Nor did Merezhkovskiy's idealization of his mother diminish after her death. "If there is any good in me, I owe it to her alone,"[13] he wrote in 1914. In *Octaves of the Past* it is she who is his goddess, his muse; their great love is what will save him; and it is because of her that death arouses no fear but would be welcomed.[14] Above all, Merezhkovskiy's devotion to his mother was to manifest itself in his formulation of the concept of the Divine Mother as the third member of the Trinity.

One other woman also had an influence on Merezhkovskiy during his childhood. This was his nurse. Just as Pushkin owed much to his nurse, who told him Russian folk tales which he later put to excellent use in his poems, so Merezhkovskiy, during his career as a writer of both poetry and prose, revealed evidence of the stories his nurse had told him. In this instance it was not folk tales, but popular accounts and legends of the lives of saints and their struggles with demons. Some of his earlier poems, including "The Prophet Jeremiah" (*Prorok Ieremiya*), "Archpriest Avvakum" (*Protopop Avvakum*), and "Francis of Assisi" (*Frantsisk Assisskiy*), could easily have had their origin in the stories he heard as a child. To claim that his later works on St. Augustine, St. Paul, Joan of Arc, and others were direct outgrowths of his nurse's legends would be to infringe upon credulity; nevertheless, it is quite probable that his interest in the lives of saints, which persisted throughout Merezhkovskiy's life, was derived from these tales. Even his firm conviction in the existence of the devil as a living entity may have had its source in this legacy of folk literature. Merezhkovskiy reveals his childish impressionability and imaginativeness in his description of the reaction that his nurse's stories, no doubt very lurid ones, had upon him:

> With trembling seized, and curiosity,
> I heeded nurse; then full of wondrous dreams,
> The icon lamp aflicker, all night in bed
> From fear the Pater Noster oft I said.[15]

Mother, father, nurse: these were the three persons who most deeply affected Merezhkovskiy during his childhood. Perhaps it was the disparate characters of his brothers and sisters, as well as differences in age, that prevented his assimilating much from them. That they were of little importance is clearly brought out in *Octaves of the Past*, for Merezhkovskiy does not even trouble to reveal the names of all of them, though he does indicate the main characteristics of a few. Merezhkovskiy himself comments that there was little affection between the nine children.[16] Only from his mother did he receive love, and only to her did he return his.

Merezhkovskiy was a lonely child. His mother was frequently away from home, at times for extensive periods, accompanying her husband. Sergey Ivanovich was obliged to travel on official business, either to the south of Russia or abroad, on many occasions in the company of members of the imperial court.[17] The children were then left in the care of Amaliya Khristianovna, a Baltic German towards whom Merezhkovskiy could evoke no emotion other than pity, despite her devotion to the children.[18] It is to these periods of separation from his mother that Merezhkovskiy refers when he writes:

E'er lonely, I grew up in the cold house,
Not knowing love, morose as a young wolf;
I feared the countenance, the speech of others;
I fled from visitors and shunned my brothers.[19]

His loneliness, which continued throughout his life, was thus partly due to his own preference, perhaps arising from a shyness which led him to avoid people, or perhaps from a simple desire to find solitude, in which he could withdraw into himself without being disturbed. He was, by his own admission, a dreamer who created a fairy-tale world in the gloomy quarters on Znamenskiy Street.[20]

In the summers spent on Elagin Island he found freedom and happiness, and his dreams were pleasant ones. Here he lost himself in the realm of books; so much so that he would often forget about his mother, he remarks almost guiltily.[21] Gustave Aimard and Jules Verne became his favorite authors, and Robinson Crusoe his idol. His imagination quickly adapted these romances to himself; the fields of Elagin were transformed into a wilderness or pampas, and in the palms on the terrace of the house he expected to see tigers or hippopotami. He constantly read books from the library, and his childish fantasy had no peace. He was in perpetual agitation to discover something new, so that every pit and passage in the outbuildings held amazing secrets for him. He played with his brothers at climbing on the roof; he longed to go higher, while his brothers were afraid. Yet for the most part he preferred to be away from people, to be free. To this end he built a "nest" in the branches of a tree, where he could read and dream all alone.[22] To what degree Merezhkovskiy expects his reader to see beyond the literal imagery in this section of *Octaves of the Past* is not clear, but perhaps he wishes to imply that even as a child he was different from his brothers and his fellowmen in his individualism, in his desire for solitude, and in his unique striving for the more exalted, which is expressed by means of the climbing episode. In any case, his recollections of Elagin Island are fond ones, and the trees he climbed in order to be apart did exist; Zinaida Gippius adds testimony in her biography of Merezhkovskiy: "He loved Elagin Island greatly, and on many occasions he related to me how he spent the summer there in childhood, and he even showed me the trees that he climbed with a book, in order to be alone."[23]

With the end of summer there was an end of happiness and freedom, a return to the dull winter dwelling, to the confinement of the city and, as the years passed, to that of school as well. Merezhkovskiy studied in the Third Classical Gymnasium, where, he claimed, the education was geared to suit the needs of the official class of Russian society.[24] He had now entered the second stage in his contact with authority, which he was to oppose so vehemently later. He was subject, as were his classmates, to boredom occasioned by the pedantry of his German pedagogues and to fear inspired by the unjust, cruel treatment of the students which was perpetrated by certain masters. Prominent among the latter was the teacher of algebra, a Russian against whom Merezhkovskiy, in protest, waged "a vain mutiny."[25] There is no need to dwell further on Merezhkovskiy's opinions about his schooling, beyond saying that he did benefit from it, as far as his later career as a writer was concerned. The 1870s and 1880s were the era of the most severe classicism in Russian education, and it is due to this fact that Merezhkovskiy received such a solid basis of knowledge of the language, literature, and life of the ancient Greeks and Romans, thus developing the keen interest in antiquity that was to appear in his works.

Unhappy at home as a teen-ager, unhappy at school, and no less unsociable and shy than as a boy, Merezhkovskiy formed no friendships. He did, as he remarks, come closer to one schoolmate, Evgeniy Solov'ev, a future critic and publicist, than to anyone else. It was not that Solov'ev and he were similar, but rather that they were different: Solov'ev was already a skeptic, while Merezhkovskiy was something of a mystic.[26] Indeed, Merezhkovskiy asserts that a tendency toward mysticism, inherited from their parents, was the only trait common to the utterly dissimilar characters of the Merezhkovskiy children.[27] While little documentation may be added to Merezhkovskiy's statements, it is significant that Sergey Ivanovich turned to spiritualism after his wife's death.[28]

Only the eldest son, Konstantin, rebelled against the family way of life. He cast aside a potentially brilliant career in the civil service by entering the Faculty of Natural Science at St. Petersburg University. Konstantin's faith in science and his lack of belief in the existence of God, as well as his sympathy towards the terrorists, evoked many arguments between him and his father. A particularly violent quarrel broke out as a result of Konstantin's jubilation over the acquittal in April 1878 of Vera Zasulich, who had attempted to assassinate F. F. Trepov, the police commissioner of St. Petersburg. Konstantin was expelled from his father's house; but it must be said, in

Sergey Ivanovich's favor, that he acceded to Varvara Vasil'evna's entreaties to grant his son an allowance of one hundred rubles a month.[29]

Konstantin also played a part in Merezhkovskiy's development. It was he who explained the wonders of science to his youngest brother and who expounded theories, most notably the teachings of Darwin and Spencer, which were unclear to the boy. Although Merezhkovskiy felt that his brother was wrong in many things, he was deeply disturbed, for Konstantin, as he laughed at the devil and God, destroyed everything in which the boy believed. Frightened as he was by what Konstantin revealed to him, Merezhkovskiy was still attracted to the danger of the final step, and for the first time his mind was full of unchildish thoughts.[30] Bitter doubts assailed him, and he was confused by the "devil of science." No longer did church ritual arouse sweet mystery in his soul; now there was only fear, for even the holy-oil lamps appeared to shine with an unfriendly light. He continued to pray before retiring, by force of habit; but in the dark he wrestled with his growing doubt as to the existence of God. He listened avidly to the discussions about God that took place every Saturday, when a learned priest visited his father. Yet the seed of doubt grew in the boy's mind; he withdrew into himself, afraid to utter his "shameful thoughts."[31]

Merezhkovskiy's first religious crisis, reached during his thirteenth year, came to an end during the summer of 1878. With the summer there was the customary return to Elagin Island, where the freshness of the air, the familiar ponds and groves, and the children's games dispelled the boy's fears. Nature called him, and his only worry in church was whether the service would end soon. He began to feel that he loved the world with a love that was different from God's love, and he considered himself a pagan.[32]

It was in the autumn of that year that Merezhkovskiy visited the Crimea for the first time. Sergey Ivanovich had long sought his wife's permission to take young Dmitriy on one of his business trips to the south. Merezhkovskiy was immediately enthralled by the scenic beauties of the Crimea, but most of all by the charm of Hellas, which he found to pervade the region, offering him inspiration. It was here, he recalled later, in the groves of the "mighty pagan Pan," that he composed his "first unskillful verse."[33] However, he hid these first creations from others. He had come to know the poets at an early age, and now he was inspired by the romantic

Pushkin of the 1820s, who was full of Byronism and rebellion. His own verses—those of a thirteen year old about maidens, harem beauties, nightingales, and roses—appeared to him to be filled, like Pushkin's "Fountain of Bakhchisaray" *(Bakhchisarayskiy fontan)*, with heavenly voluptuousness.[34] His attempts to conceal his talents were of no avail, for his fellow students quickly learned of his secret and, after much coaxing, would prevail upon him to read his poems at student gatherings.

It was at about this time that Merezhkovskiy also began to exhibit a critical faculty. He often argued with the other boys about books and authors, revealing erudition and originality of judgment, as well as a thoughtfulness and seriousness far beyond his age. For his first critical essay, on the subject *The Tale of Igor's Campaign (Slovo o polku Igoreve)*, he received the coveted *pyaterka*, the highest mark possible.[35] Merezhkovskiy's relating of this incident in 1914 must not be taken solely as an indication of inordinate pride, though such an accusation may well be justified, but as Merezhkovskiy's recognition that from an early age he revealed propensities towards literary criticism.

Yet one cannot but feel that two incidents in Merezhkovskiy's life as a secondary-school student, both of which involved the assistance of his father, were of great importance in his developing into a literary figure and social critic. The first was an outgrowth of an interest, shared by Merezhkovskiy and his fellow students, in Molière. A club was formed for the purpose of reading and discussing the works of the French dramatist. However, at this period when subversive societies and terrorist activities were increasing, student gatherings were not regarded favorably by the police, and the club was forced to disband. It was not an exaggeration, perhaps, when Merezhkovskiy wrote that but for his father's influence he would have been arrested and exiled.[36] For the first time Merezhkovskiy came into direct confrontation with the power of the state, which curtailed his personal freedom. The final stage in his experience with external authority was thus reached during Merezhkovskiy's youth.

The second event was the result of Sergey Ivanovich's pride in his son's literary endeavors. Sergey Ivanovich had recently met Fedor Mikhaylovich Dostoevskiy, had mentioned his son's verse to him, and had arranged for young Merezhkovskiy to visit the great author. Shortly before Dostoevskiy's death in 1881 the encounter took place. Merezhkovskiy read some of his poems, and Dostoevskiy is reputed to have criticized them in the following words: " 'Weak . . . bad . . . worthless,' he said at last; 'in order to write well, one must suffer, suffer.' "[37] Such harsh criticism from a literary personage of Dostoevskiy's stature, indeed the first member of the literary society whom he had met, might have caused many a fifteen year old with literary pretensions to blanch and to cast away his pen. But Merezhkovskiy was nothing if not doggedly determined in the attainment of his goals. He did not abandon poetry, nor did he shun the literary world of St. Petersburg.

In 1881, shortly after his meeting with Dostoevskiy, Merezhkovskiy became acquainted with Semen Yakovlevich Nadson, then a junker at the Pavlovskiy military school and already, despite his youth, one of the influential poets of his day. Merezhkovskiy felt an unusually strong attraction to Nadson, whom he came to "love like a brother."[38] Their frequent meetings and discussions on various subjects—in particular on death and religion—as well as the reading of Nadson's poems, exerted a strong influence on Merezhkovskiy during his late teens. The majority of his earliest published verses, which are to be found in various journals, including *Zhivopisnoe Obozrenie* (Pictorial Review), *Otechestvennye Zapiski* (Notes of the Fatherland), and *Severnyy Vestnik* (Northern Herald), clearly exhibit his orientation towards Nadson's examples.

Even before his initial encounter with Nadson, indeed prior to his meeting with Dostoevskiy, Merezhkovskiy had had a poem accepted for publication. He erroneously dates his entry into print as 1882, with a poem published in *Zhivopisnoe Obozrenie;*[39] but as S. A. Vengerov points out in a footnote, Merezhkovskiy's first poem appeared in 1881. Merezhkovskiy had barely turned sixteen when, after much delay and with many technical faults, the literary collection *Response (Otklik)* was released to the public in September 1881. A collection of short stories, poems, and articles of literary criticism, it was conceived by the students of St. Petersburg as the first of a series of such volumes in which their own compositions could be published, interspersed with a small number of contributions by established writers, presumably to attract a wider audience. It is not unreasonable to assume that Merezhkovskiy later regarded *Response* as a parochial undertaking of limited merit, in spite of any value it may have had for aspiring talents, and not a true entering into the literary life of the time. Perhaps he also recognized his poem contained in it to be immature, as compared to what was to follow. Certainly "Narcissus" *(Nartsis)*, a reworking of the legend of the handsome Greek youth, does not warrant comment. It is significant only to the degree that it reveals Merezhkovskiy's attraction to classical antiquity both as subject matter and as the means for delivering a message to the modern world. "Narcissus," therefore, stands as the earliest example of the trend that was to be subordinated for a time to Populist themes, was later to compete with them, and was ultimately to dominate his compositions.

Merezhkovskiy's participation in the literary and intellectual world of St. Petersburg developed rapidly, thanks to his friendship with Nadson. It was Nadson who introduced him to Aleksey Nikolaevich Pleshcheev, a civic poet who was secretary of *Otechestvennye Zapiski*. Pleshcheev, in turn, brought Merezhkovskiy into the home of Karl Yul'evich Davydov, the noted cellist who was also director of the St. Petersburg Conservatory. Davydov's wife, Aleksandra Arkad'evna, the future editor and founder of the journal *Mir Bozhiy* (God's World), held a literary salon, which attracted such outstanding men of letters as the novelist Ivan Aleksandrovich Goncharov and the poets Apollon Nikolaevich Maykov, Yakov Petrovich Polonskiy, and Minskiy (the pseudonym of Nikolay Mikhaylovich Vilenkin).[40] The fact that Merezhkovskiy "neither liked nor understood music" did not harm his relationship with the Davydovs.[41] Indeed, he must have become a favored member of their group, for in the summer of 1886 he accompanied the Davydovs on a trip to Paris and Switzerland, where they spent some time with the consumptive Nadson, who was undergoing treatment at Beatenberg.[42] Although this was his first journey outside Russia, Merezhkovskiy was already an ardent traveler. The south of Russia was his first love, with the Crimea and the Caucasus the destinations of most of his trips. During the course of these wanderings about southern Russia he met the sectarian Vasiliy Kirillovich Syutaev, and through talks with Syutaev he first became interested in Lev Nikolaevich Tolstoy's *Confession (Ispoved')*.[43]

Throughout this period Merezhkovskiy was constantly seeking a philosophy on which to base his existence. Perhaps it was the influence of his brother Konstantin's earlier conversations with him that induced him, on completing his secondary-school education, to enter the Historical-Philological Faculty of St. Petersburg University, where he studied philosophy from 1884 until 1888. The positivists—Spencer, Comte, Mill, and Darwin—attracted him, as they had Konstantin; but, as Merezhkovskiy averred later, his personal religious tendencies did not permit him to accept their views.[44] Of greater influence were the contacts he had with Gleb Ivanovich Uspenskiy and Nikolay Konstantinovich Mikhaylovskiy, with whom he became acquainted, together with Vsevolod Mikhaylovich Garshin and Vladimir Galaktionovich Korolenko, after the founding of *Severnyy Vestnik* by Anna Mikhaylovna Evreinova in 1885.

Merezhkovskiy regarded Mikhaylovskiy and Uspenskiy as the earliest teachers with whom he had serious discussions on the religious sense of life. He even became fired up for a time with Uspenskiy's advice that he should seek the answer to this problem in the outlook of the people. Almost immediately Merezhkovskiy set out on a trip down the Volga and Kama rivers and through Orenburg and Ufa provinces, walking through the villages and talking with the people, gathering and writing down his impressions. Almost convinced, he decided that, upon finishing his university studies, he would go among the people and become a village teacher.[45] His intention was not fulfilled, for by 1888 new influences were beginning to be felt in Russia, in general, and in Merezhkovskiy, in particular.

Populism was not to be the driving force in his life, although it was of great importance during his formative years. It added to his childhood opposition to authority, more specifically now to the social and state structure in Russia. In its way, it contributed to his desire to benefit humanity and to his ambition to set himself up as a prophet and a leader. Thus, despite its socialist aims, Merezhkovskiy's early attraction to Populism did not succeed in abating his sense of personal importance and his aristocratic egotism. The antipathies, sympathies, and outlook developed during his childhood and early youth were never to leave him. Indeed, they were to become more pronounced, though somewhat altered, as the years passed.

2

The Populist Phase

During the first few years of his literary career, the period in which he was associated with the Populists, Merezhkovskiy was exclusively a poet; and even after his advent into the realm of prose about the beginning of the 1890s, poetry still remained his principal outlet. It was only after 1895 that prose gained the ascendancy; and while poems appeared occasionally, the final three volumes of verse that Merezhkovskiy published were primarily compilations of selections taken from earlier collections, which were arranged to suit his ideas of the time.

From the beginning of his life in art Merezhkovskiy was a controversial figure, but never more so than in the realm of poetry. Contemporary opinions of him ranged from Ivanov-Razumnik's considering him a "cold corpse" exhibiting "dead mastery" (as revealed in Merezhkovskiy's repetition of the attributes "dead" and "sepulchral"),[1] to Andrey Belyy's reference to him as being "all sparks, all fire."[2] He was rebuked for taking his style and epithets from other sources, especially from Pushkin; and only one critic, Aleksandr Dolinin, realized that the similarities between Merezhkovskiy's style and Pushkin's were not the result of conscious imitation, but of an inner resemblance between the two poets.[3] While Dolinin did not explain the reasons for this opinion, he was intrinsically right. Later, Merezhkovskiy was to say that Pushkin was the synthesis of the two elements that were constantly in conflict within Merezhkovskiy himself—Christianity and paganism.[4] Although Merezhkovskiy had not yet formulated this concept, the duality was present in him, and it is reasonable to assume that he strove towards this unconsciously desired synthesis.

Merezhkovskiy did not admit that he was under Pushkin's influence, except in his more youthful poetry; nor did he consider himself to be unoriginal in style, stating on one occasion:

> The critics will assuredly rebuke us
> For daring rhymes, the tone, the choice of themes.[5]

He was right in assuming that the critics would attack him for the tone and themes of his poems, but he was mistaken when speaking of his boldness in rhyme. Contrary to his expectations, the majority of critics found his measures stereotyped and uniform and his rhymes uninteresting. Yet some admitted, and justly so, that Merezhkovskiy's verses give the impression of great elaboration. They also conceded that his poems were harmonious, if somewhat affected, that he made good use of assonance, and that he was a connoisseur of the rise and fall of periods. "Tidy" and "elegant" best express the impression created by his verse.

Merezhkovskiy should not be assailed unduly, as he was by some of his contemporaries, because he was lacking in poetic flights and because he, like Evgeniy Boratynskiy and Valeriy Bryusov, allowed mind, not feeling, to govern his creations. Merezhkovskiy's creed was not "art for art's sake," but "art for a purpose." For him, literature—whether in the form of a poem, an essay, a drama, or a novel—was only a vehicle for the propagation of ideas. This led to a certain coldness in his poetry; and many of his coevals consequently condemned him for lack of sincerity, simplicity, and cordiality. Although it is impossible to refute these conclusions categorically, they cannot be accepted without qualification. Despite Merezhkovskiy's constant change of outlook and his refutation of views that he held at different times, he was undoubtedly sincere at the moment when he uttered those ideas: the problems that he dealt with were too close to his heart (and his mind) to be regarded lightly. Zinaida Gippius bears witness to the tenacity with which Merezhkovskiy held to his beliefs when she writes: "When he had taken something into his head, it was difficult to talk him out of it."[6] To complain that he lacked simplicity is absurd, for Merezhkovskiy was complexity personified: his whole literary endeavor, both in its diversity of forms and in its content, testifies to this fact. The third charge—lack of cordiality—is perhaps the most justifiable of the three. Merezhkovskiy made little attempt to attract people to himself, thus he had few intimate friends. Consequently, he could hardly be expected to exude cordiality in his poetry.

Harsh criticism of Merezhkovskiy's poetic talents has not been limited to the period in which he was composing his verse. More recently it has been written that he "was indeed not made to be a poet, and, having had the wisdom to understand this, soon devoted himself to the novel."[7] This, too, is a misleading statement. Merezhkovskiy's fame may rest on his novels, but he did not entirely give up the writing of poetry, although after 1905 it indeed became extremely rare. Nor is the assumption that he himself realized that he was not made to be a poet responsible for the decline of his interest in poetry. As he emerged into maturity, Merezhkovskiy discovered that prose, whether in the form of novels or critical articles, provided him with a vehicle that was much more suitable for the expression of his views than did poetry, with its limiting confines. As for the quality of his verse, it was not of a lower caliber than that composed by his fellow poets of the 1880s and 1890s, and in many cases it was decidedly superior.

The most cursory glance at the poetic compositions of Minskiy is enough to establish the fact that they are far colder and more ponderous in rhythm than those of Merezhkovskiy, that in intellectual content, to echo R. Poggioli's summation of him, Minskiy's verses reveal him to be a camp follower at the outset and a straggler at the end of his career[8]—a derogation that is inapplicable to Merezhkovskiy. As for K. M. Fofanov—whose sense of musicality reminds one of the Russian master Andrey Belyy—uniformity, disharmony, and unevenness (M. Slonim asserts that the unevenness is extreme)[9] are so pronounced in his work as a whole that they fail to be offset by those poems in which genuine inspiration is evident. Most assuredly, Merezhkovskiy may not be compared favorably either with his talented predecessors Maykov, Polonskiy, Tyutchev, and Fet, or with the poets who were to rise to prominence, many following him into the Symbolist camp, at the beginning of the twentieth century. Although when overshadowed by Belyy, Aleksandr Blok, Vyacheslav Ivanov, and others, Merezhkovskiy shrinks into a poet of the second or third rank, nevertheless, though it be but faint praise, Merezhkovskiy must be conceded a position of poetic prominence in that era of hiatus at the end of the nineteenth century when Russian literature was beginning the process of revitalization.

Merezhkovskiy's poetry, therefore, should not be dismissed lightly. Valeriy Bryusov was right when he emphasized the impossibility of separating Merezhkovskiy's literary activity into the individual spheres of poetry, criticism, fiction, and so on.[10] Such a division into genres destroys the cohesion of Merezhkovskiy's intellectual progression:

> From positivism and positive ethics to the exalting of his *ego*, to "mangodhood"; from the pagan cult of the personality to the mystic, to "godmanhood"; from the religion of Christ Who Has Come to the teaching of the Christ Who Is to Come and, further, to the religion of the Holy Trinity, to the Church of John: all this is one path, invariably rushing forward, in which there are unexpected transitions, but nowhere a turning back.[11]

This sentence is a valid summation of Merezhkovskiy's work up to the time when it was written; it would be no less apt if it were to be extended and applied to the continued evolution of his thought. It is thus necessary to examine Merezhkovskiy's works as a whole, and his verse as an integral part of this whole. Without a knowledge of it, it is impossible to understand his later work fully, for it was on the basis of his poetical creation that the entire structure of his more mature period was raised. One finds in his verse the majority of themes, as yet in their infancy, that he developed and enlarged upon later. It is in his poetry, too, that one is able to discern Merezhkovskiy himself, with all his longing and striving, more clearly than in any other phase of his literary career.

When he entered the literary arena, the leading school of prose and poetry was that of Populism, but Populism in its faded, dying form. Populism had developed during the 1860s and 1870s as a social movement that centered its attention on the people, their suffering, and their future. P. L. Lavrov's views on the debt owed by the privileged classes to the toiling masses, who were barred from enjoying the benefits of culture, found fertile soil in the stricken consciences of many members of the gentry and other elements of the intelligentsia, who eagerly seized upon the slogan "go to the people" and then began to devote their energies to educating and to raising the standard of living of the peasantry. At first nonpolitical, the idealistic socialism of the Populists gave birth during the 1870s to the parties of Zemlya i Volya (Land and Freedom) and Narodnaya Volya (the People's Will). The latter group preached terrorism and the assassination of leading conservatives in an attempt to weaken the existing government and to arouse the latent revolutionary tendencies in the people. The culmination of this doctrine was the assassination of Alexander II in 1881, a deed that failed to produce the result desired. The ensuing repression put an end to active revolutionism, though the Populists continued to be the strongest group among the intelligentsia until the 1890s.

The movement had readily found expression in literature during the 1860s under the leadership of Nikolay Alekseevich Nekrasov and Mikhail Evgrafovich Saltykov-Shchedrin, who adhered to the doctrines of Populism as formulated by its leading theoretician, N. K. Mikhaylovskiy.[12] It was largely through their extolling of the virtues of the people, both workmen and peasants, but primarily the latter, that the myth of the *muzhik* was eventually created. The peasant became the ideal, a symbol, the paragon of native wisdom, kindliness, and patience. Tolstoy added to the growing image in his depiction of Platon Karataev in *War and Peace*; and Dostoevskiy, with his mystic slavophilism, lent further support to the idealization of the masses by the intelligentsia.

During the early 1880s the Populist school of poetry continued to be the foremost one. However, since Nekrasov's death in 1878 it had degenerated into the civic poetry of Nadson, Minskiy, and other minor poets, who unceasingly recognized Nekrasov as their forerunner and master, but who had lost the vigor and daring that were felt in his poetry. They continued to express Populist themes and ideals, but their writings were primarily melancholy expressions of impotence in the face of the social evils that they saw around them but could not combat. Nadson, who enjoyed the greatest popularity, appealed to the radical youth of the 1880s. His language was theirs: he spoke in generalities, and he was idealistic, melancholy, and individualistic. Merezhkovskiy was but one of the many who were attracted to Nadson and to the school that he represented. It is not surprising that his close contacts with members of the group and his friendship with Nadson convinced him that he shared their views and ideals and should express them in civic verse.

Merezhkovskiy extolled the virtues of the people. He called them unknown heroes who suffered but stood firm to the end and who struggled and fell honorably on the battlefield of life without demanding a reward.[13] He proclaimed that their unnoticed labor was holy and should be recognized as a saintly relic. He advised the poet to go among the crowd as a friend; to heed the people's words and groans; to share their misfortunes, joys, and sorrows; and, above all, to learn to know and to love the simple folk.[14] One should do this not merely because the people are holy in themselves, but also because in them is the foundation of a future world, each generation building on the other like coral in the sea.[15] There was an even more important reason for the poet to go to the masses. Merezhkovskiy felt that only there could one find the meaning of existence:

You will not find the beauty and the sense of life
In happy and entrancing dreams, or colors mere
And flashes bright; but in the thorns of suffering's strife,
In poverty and toil, simplicity severe.
Forever inexhaustible, like nectar gold,
And quenching in a sumptuous way your breast's great thirst,
Rewarding your distressing task a thousandfold,
The holy poetry from gloomy life so cold
In radiant, mighty stream will then begin to burst.[16]

In this worshiping of the people and this desire to help them and to share their lot, Merezhkovskiy expressed the views of the Populists. He also shared many other themes with Nadson. Both wrote of melancholy, of loneliness, of longing, of grief, of death, of nature, of boredom, and of the banality and triviality of life. When Nadson died, in 1887, it was not unjustifiably concluded that Merezhkovskiy would assume Nadson's role as the leader of the civic poets.

Merezhkovskiy, however, proved this opinion to be completely false. Even during his Populist phase there were signs that he was more than a civic poet like Nadson, despite the apparent similarities in subject matter and mood. Merezhkovskiy did not limit himself exclusively to the themes of civic poetry; he also dealt with loftier subjects. In the oriental legends "Sakyamuni" *(Sak'ya-Muni)* and "The Sacrifice" *(Zhertva)*, for example, he upheld the virtues of mercy and self-sacrifice for others (not just for "the people" in the Populist sense of the word); and in the long poem on the persecution of Archpriest Avvakum he praised the willingness of a man to suffer for his convictions.

Yet the most notable difference between Merezhkovskiy and the civic poets was the courage and the self-confidence that flashed from time to time even in the midst of his more despondent utterances. He exclaimed that he had not given way under the burden of life, but would measure his strength against it and struggle with it. He refused to submit and to lie at life's feet, humbled and weeping. Instead, he would parry life's blows with laughter and scorn; for the greater the misfortunes and griefs that beset him and the deeper the wounds, the greater would be his victory.[17] The world was made for youth, which is blessed and strong, like the gods, and fearless in the face of life. To youth he called out:

> Away, fear! One must revel in dream,
> And not think what tomorrow may bring;
> One must live and must love with whole heart,
> And surrender to powerful spring.[18]

A further epicurean note was sounded in his poetry. This was not a rebellion against life, but a rebellion of his youth against the very ideals that he and his civic friends were expressing. He wondered if these were really what he wanted from life, and decided that they were not. From deep within him there came forth long-subdued desires, the desires of youth:

> I want to revel in creation and in knowledge;
> I want spring days, an azure sky, and coloration;
> I want the senseless merriment of feast's libation;
> I want from tender lips the breath's sweet scent,
> And laughter, too, and wine, and youthful melodies,
> Pale lily of the valley, purple sun's descent—
> All the wondrous music of earth's harmonies;
> I want—and am not shamed by such a thirst for rapture.[19]

Merezhkovskiy soon understood that Populism was alien to him, yet he continued to regard highly those who could follow such a path. The rest, like himself, were worthless dreamers, always alone and thus little more than living corpses.[20] He longed to offer something to the people; but overcome by doubts and suffering, he compared himself to the masses and wondered:

> What will I give the people now?
> They're filled with such devout belief;
> But I no happiness avow,
> Nor freedom, to my soul's deep grief.[21]

He exclaimed that he dared not go to the people, to teach them his sufferings, for he would lead them only to the same end as his own—to perdition:

> Might I conceivably not poison
> Their childlike minds with searing doubt?

19

Then they, in impotent dismay,
Will comprehend life's nothingness;
Minds chilled, in deathly gloom astray,
They will, like me, feel torment's stress;
And hopeless, with sharp mockery,
They'll gaze into the depth of sky;
Before earth's deathless mystery,
With curse, their frailty will decry.[22]

He also observed, with despondency, that he was not heeded by the people. No one, it seemed, was interested in the mournful thoughts of a poet who proffered nothing that had not been voiced by his predecessors; even his last heartrending sob would fail to move the extinguished heart of the crowd.[23] No matter how inspired or inflamed by faith the poet or prophet who preached such exalted virtues and humanitarian principles as love, freedom, and equality to the hungry masses, he would be met only with laughter and scorn.[24] The poet—that is, Merezhkovskiy—was thus rejected.

He now understood that his approach to the people had been wrong. He had wanted to contemplate the human race as an entity, and he had declared his willingness to suffer and to die for it. He realized, however, that not heroic deeds but simple, everyday activities were demanded of him. He should not regard and love humanity as a whole, but should love each individual in it. This was a task for which he was neither prepared nor equipped:

I wait for freedom, heart and soul;
I love the people as a whole;
But mankind asks of me instead,
Beneath the sky of sullen day,
To see and love each lowly head
Among the infinite array.
It matters not who faces me—
A cripple or a worthless lout—
The man in him must I make out.
With my frail soul it cannot be;
Together with its thorny crown
Such heavy bonds I can't embrace:
Before this feat of grim renown
No hero I—but craven base.[25]

Merezhkovskiy bewailed this weakness. He complained bitterly of his attempts to love other people and of his inability to do so. Despite his longing to approach them, he concluded that he was a stranger to others and decided that he was closer to nature than to man. The epitome of this sentiment is contained in a poem of 1887, in which he gave voice to all the despair that was in his soul:

Though I yearn to love people, I have not the strength.
In their midst I am alien; much closer than friends
Are the stars and the sky, chill horizon, dark-blue,
And the deathly still sorrow of wasteland and wood.
Never boring for me is the sighing of trees;
Into darkness of night I can peer until dawn,
And o'er something so sweetly and senselessly weep,
As if wind be my brother, my sister the wave,
And the damp earth the mother who gave birth to me.
Yet I cannot just live with the wave and the wind,
And I dread to love no one throughout my whole life.
Can it be that my heart is eternally dead?
Grant the strength to me, Lord, all my brothers to love![26]

His inability to love and the realization that he had nothing to offer to the people convinced him that he was insincere, that he had not really wanted to hear the groans of the masses and to share their sufferings:

What can you to a long-exhausted world impart?
To whom direct your song of paltry misery?
Your useless verse is but a lie and blasphemy:
Your senseless, unavailing lyre then break apart!
You did not want to fight and suffer with the people,
Not once supply an answer to their supplication;
And yet you dare, you fool, to term yourself
A poet—a sacred appellation![27]

He was somewhat harsh on himself, for earlier he had been sincere in his desire to be of assistance to the masses. Now he understood that he was unsuited to this task. His adherence to the Populist belief in the virtues of the peasantry and his adherence to the civic ideal of service to the people were at an end.

The question of love, which was largely responsible for Merezhkovskiy's turning away from Populism, was raised time and time again throughout his writings. Yet it is his poetry which discloses most readily the struggle that occurred in the writer himself. In this early phase of his literary career Merezhkovskiy's attitude and relation toward love are apt to prove most confusing to his readers. According to his own admission, he could not love, while at the same time he was unable not to love. This was one aspect of the duality of his nature.

In the first instance, Merezhkovskiy was referring to what we might term Christian love, that is, the doctrine of "love thy neighbor," which involves boundless humility and absolute self-sacrifice for others. He was incapable of giving himself up to this kind of love, for he did not possess the virtues necessary for such selflessness. On the contrary, he was exceedingly proud, and there was even a trace of aristocratism in his considering himself a stranger among people. This was the love that was impossible for him to attain, that he longed for, and that he complained of lacking.

Although decidedly wanting in the ability to experience deep affection, Merezhkovskiy could love, as his almost inordinate attachment to his mother demonstrates.[28] He could also experience love for a woman. In May 1888, after presenting his dissertation on Montaigne, Merezhkovskiy went to the Caucasian resort of Borzhomi. Here he was well received by the young intellectuals, for his fame had spread to the provinces in connection with that of the recently deceased Nadson. He immediately became the center of the little group, which included Zinaida Gippius. Gippius was not particularly attracted to Merezhkovskiy at first, nor did she have a high opinion of his poetry. Furthermore, their meetings were little more than incessant quarrels. Yet by the end of the summer they considered it quite natural that they should marry,[29] even though, according to Gippius, their attachment "had other bases than any blinding passion."[30] This statement, incidentally, should not be taken as justification for belief in the unfounded, but still pervasive, rumor that Merezhkovskiy was impotent. Several entries in Gippius's unpublished diaries quite clearly indicate the falsity of such hearsay.[31] In September, Merezhkovskiy returned to St. Petersburg in order to obtain the consent of his parents and an allowance from his father. Once this difficult task had been accomplished, Merezhkovskiy hastened to Tiflis, where Gippius and her family were spending the winter, and there, on 8 January 1889, the wedding took place.[32] Two days later they journeyed via Moscow to St. Petersburg, to make their first home in an apartment on Vereyskaya Street.

In his poetry Merezhkovskiy never referred to the question of sexual love; that was reserved for later works and was used in a different context. His two cycles of love poems, which are full of com-

22

plaints, remain cold and haughty, like their composer. Although Merezhkovskiy could love, it is evident that he was unable to plumb the depths of love, to give himself up to another and to lose himself in another. He concluded that this was a universal failing, that fate decreed love to be fleeting.[33] The tragedy of love, as he saw it, was that the souls of two persons could never merge and become one:

> Another's heart is another world,
>   To it there is no path!
> Not even with a loving soul
>   Can we an entry make.
>
> .   .   .   .
>
> In your own prison, in yourself,
>   You are, unhappy man,
> In love, in friendship, and in all,
>   Eternally alone.[34]

In a later poem Merezhkovskiy revealed the reason for this inability to lose oneself in another—pride:

> There is no guilt for anyone:
> The one who cannot vanquish pride
> Will be forever solitary;
> The one who loves must be a slave.
>
> While striving after bliss and good,
> Enduring agonizing days,
> Alone are we, always alone:
> I lived alone, alone shall die.[35]

This last line testifies most strongly to the power that pride wielded over him.

It was his pride, too, which lay at the root of his fear of love—a subconscious fear perhaps, but a fear that led him to try to destroy love in himself. He considered love to be suffering and grief, whether in its transitory nature, or as the result of a woman's toying with one's heart, or as enmity and as a duel. This last point was made in the second cycle of love poems, written a few years after Merezhkovskiy's marriage to Gippius; it was undoubtedly the literary expression of the tribulations that beset these two unyielding, strong-willed characters, whose countless clashes resulted in heated arguments before and after their wedding.

Love also held the terrors of enslavement. Merezhkovskiy knew that it was possible to fall under the sway of a loved person, so that one's will was lost completely. For an extremely proud man who exulted in his freedom, this prospect was not appealing, and he expressed his opinion of love as slavery in no uncertain terms.

In his fear of love and his desire to stamp it out in himself, Merezhkovskiy resembled the heroes of two of his narrative poems, Sergey Zabelin in "Vera" and Boris Kamenskiy in "Death" *(Smert').* Both these young men succumb to love. Both are rational, scientifically minded individuals who believe only in concrete facts and fear the consequences of such a nebulous sentiment as love; and they struggle violently to throw off its hold on them—Kamenskiy by enjoying epicurean pleasures and Zabelin by further study in the sciences. Merezhkovskiy, in revolt himself, attempted to replace love with things of this world: nature, youth, freedom, and art.[36] This was all to no avail; for like his heroes, he himself succumbed. While love was unacceptable to Merezhkovskiy, freedom without it was even worse. Although he succeeded in removing love from his soul, he was not satisfied and exclaimed:

A loveless freedom is a gloomy dungeon's thrall;
If I could only love again with senseless anguish
And suffer, as I did before, and weep and languish,
My life and joy and peace—I would surrender all.[37]

Ultimately Merezhkovskiy was forced to concede, ungraciously, that he, like everyone else, was a slave to love, although he still called out in despair for the strength not to love:

I lack profound insensitivity:
I love my native land and also God;
I love my love; all bitterness with meekness
I suffer in the name of happiness.
For me is duty fearsome, love disturbing.
I am too weak, alas, to live at will.
Is freedom really unattainable,
And man a slave until his very death?[38]

Merezhkovskiy himself supplied the answer to this question:

There is no freedom, and no pardon;
We all are born to slavery;
Condemned are all of us to death,
To tribulations, and to love.[39]

Neither complete impassivity nor all-consuming passion: this was Merezhkovskiy's tragedy of love, to be forever halfway between the two extremes. It caused him, on the one hand, to revile love, to seek escape from it, and, on the other, to praise it and to deify it. Love in the latter instance became omnipotent, one of the prime movers of the universe. It need not be merely love between the sexes or love of one's neighbor or the broad love of humanity, but should, and did for Merezhkovskiy, also include the love of all nature—such an all-embracing love as that of St. Francis of Assisi. Love in each or all of its forms was capable of working miracles. It was love that illumined the earth[40] and produced peace in a battle-torn world.[41] It was love, too, that could overcome the fear of death[42] and resurrect the symbolically dead Sergey Zabelin, so that he could slough off his moroseness, doubts, and complaints and emerge a new and useful man.[43] Love could even transcend death, Merezhkovskiy revealed in the triumphant cry of Imogena—"You are mine, mine forever!"—as she and her lover plunge to their deaths.[44] It was this concept of love the all-powerful that Merezhkovskiy was to develop further in his subsequent works.

The importance of love in Merezhkovskiy's outlook upon the world and life is therefore not to be minimized. Indeed, it is central to his whole development as a writer and as a religious and social thinker. He had taken his first steps along his literary path under the banner bearing the inscription "love for the people." His apperception that his humanitarian love could not be directed toward individuals, whether through a sense of superiority or through pride, was one of the major reasons, if not the primary cause, for his rapidly abandoning the civic ideals of the Populists and for his turning to the aestheticism and sexuality of the Symbolist movement, which had already developed in Western Europe.

3

The Symbolist Mood

Merezhkovskiy's movement into the Symbolist camp was not marked by a sudden, unexpected transition. The very features of his early verse that set him somewhat apart from his fellow civic poets were, in fact, precisely those that were to come to the fore gradually and that were to dominate him during his second literary phase. The Symbolist mood had been held in abeyance only temporarily by his desire to benefit the people. Once he had conceded that he was unable to serve the masses (which he could not regard as a collection of personalities), once he had begun to recognize that he himself was different from other men, and, most significant of all, once he had wearied of reiterating the unavailing, hackneyed pronouncements of the Populists, there was no dam to retard the flow of the second, opposing current within him. Having formerly turned his face outwards to the world, Merezhkovskiy now rejected the world and withdrew into himself, into his own individuality.

Within the framework of the problem of Merezhkovskiy and love, reference has been made to his loneliness. He was by no means unique in this, for loneliness appears to have been a factor common to his age. Nadson and the civic poets experienced it, as did the Symbolists to an even greater degree shortly afterwards. One contemporary critic, E. Anichkov, expressed the opinion that "symbolist" and "decadent" were inappropriate terms for the members of the Symbolist movement, that they should have been called "solitaries" (*odinokie*) instead.[1]

Merezhkovskiy's earliest realization of this trait in his character led him to complain bitterly about it, to regard it as a serious failing, as indeed it was. Even in some of his later poems he revealed the same sentiment and a certain amount of self-pity. However, under the influence of the Western decadents Verlaine and Baudelaire, who were "solitaries" as well as extreme individualists, Merezhkovskiy's latent aristocratism came to the surface, little by little producing a change in his view of loneliness. Traces of aristocratism and a praising of his isolation are to be found in his verse as early as 1885. In the poem "He Sat on a Granite Rock" *(On sidel na granitnoy skale)* he decided that he was not an ordinary person, who could be obedient to inexorable heaven and who could forget himself in the desire for wealth, in the embrace of a prostitute, in drink, or in love. Moreover, he had already begun to translate Baudelaire. The last three quatrains of Baudelaire's "Chant d'automne" were rendered into Russian in 1884 under the title "Autumn" *(Osen')*; they were followed in 1885 by "L'Invitation au voyage," which Merezhkovskiy entitled "From Baudelaire" *(Iz Bodlera)*. As Western Symbolist attitudes appealed to him ever more strongly and as his aristocratic and individualistic outlook took a firmer grip on him, he ceased to consider loneliness a curse, proclaiming instead that it was a most desirable and praiseworthy trait. With pride bordering on arrogance he wrote:

> I am a stranger to mankind;
> I have small faith in earthly virtue;
> I measure life with my own measure:
> A different, undirected beauty.[2]

Loneliness now seemed to him to be his last and only friend, the "angel" of his childhood, who alone could lull and soothe him.[3] Loneliness was even more—it was happiness and protection:

> There is great joy in that all people hate you
> And good consider evil,
> And pass you by, and having termed you foe,
> Do not remark your tears.

> There is great joy in being ever an exile
> And, like the ocean's wave
> Or cloud in sky, a solitary rover
> Without a single friend.[4]

His new conception of loneliness offered him a defense, so that he was able to bear the attacks of his critics not only with indifference

27

but also with joy. The highest point of this aristocratism was reached a few years later in his declaration "I love God and myself as one."[5]

While such assertions have their source primarily in Merezhkovskiy's sense of personal worth, they also spring in part from his seeking escape from the tedium that pervaded his whole being and that in turn was engendered by the banality and the emptiness of life as he saw it. He was convinced that the feeling of tedium was universal, that it was the product of the age in which he lived:

> We are the children of sad times,
> Of darkness and of unbelief.[6]

It was an age of iron, of machines, and of the preponderance of the bourgeoisie. Although he regretted the physical indications of middle-class supremacy—the factories around Moscow, their chimneys rising up to the heavens, casting a blight on the blue, mysterious distance;[7] the railways, which speeded up mass transportation, but were beset with minor irritations for one of Merezhkovskiy's temperament, and which were in no way comparable to the romantic *troyka*[8]—he was far more concerned about the spiritual transformations that had occurred, the change in the very guiding principles of man. Love and faith, he claimed, had been replaced by anger, hatred, and bloodshed; the phrase "might is right" was in full accord with men's actions.[9]

Life was filled, not with great and inspiring deeds, but with cares and griefs brought on by the struggle for everyday existence. Its effects were visible in the worker who passed silently and morosely along the street, preoccupied with his enigmatic thoughts. It was equally apparent in the girl dancing with abandon in a Paris bistro, her face a lifeless mask; yet she possessed a certain charm, something *fin de siècle*. Every onlooker could recognize his own daughter in her, so universal was the condition.[10] Merezhkovskiy further perceived that it was necessary for people to delude themselves. Each day brought with it new shame, additional suffering, and greater boredom; yet everyone attempted to convince himself that happiness existed and, above all, that he himself was happy. Mankind sought distraction in love, drink, feasting, and merrymaking, thereby vainly hoping to find relief from ever-present sorrows:

> But monstrous grief is growing in the souls of all:
> How long will this feast last; how long endure this laughter?
> Which path is yours; where are you going, age of iron?
> Or is there aim no more, and you hang over a chasm?[11]

This self-deception was all the more pitiful, because everything was transitory. The most outstanding expression of these sentiments is found in "The Song of the Temple Dancers" *(Pesn' bayader)*, which, in later editions, was entitled "Buddha" *(Budda)*. While the temple dancers sang of joy, hope, and happiness and while they praised life and love, Buddha-Merezhkovskiy heard different words. These foretold the destruction of the world and the death of all living things:

No salvation! Glory, joy,
Even love and beauty, too,
Disappear, as in bad weather
Does the brightest rainbow's hue.[12]

Instead of the dancers' song about the mitigation of suffering and sorrow he heard that thousands of men were doomed to perish from passions and grief. And finally he heard that everything was deception:

Our delights are momentary,
Like deceptive dreams are they.
Or like foam spray in the ocean,
Like the moon's glow on the sea.[13]

Yet mankind, he observed, could not do without such delights but rushed voluntarily after the vision presented by the deceptive dreams.

For a brief period Merezhkovskiy continued to portray in his poems the life he saw about him. His two narrative poems "Vera" and "Death" are commonplace tales of ordinary people in contemporary society, in which Merezhkovskiy made the tedium strongly felt. Its impact is even greater in "A Family Idyll" *(Semeynaya idilliya)*; for here, in a series of sketches, Merezhkovskiy dwelt on the petty jealousies, quarrels, worries, and cares of family life and everyday existence. He was aware of the fact that his readers most certainly would not appreciate such trivial themes, and he forestalled complaints by arguing his conviction that the poet should reveal life as it is.

These poems were written at a time when Merezhkovskiy had grown accustomed to life and had reconciled himself to it, if not wholly, then at least to the extent that he could speak of it calmly and write:

Thus life by trifles is made dreadful;
There is no struggle and no torment,
But only with unending boredom
And quiet horror is it filled.
It seems, then, that I do not live
And that my heart has ceased to beat,
And only when I am awake
I see this never-changing dream.[14]

Like Nadson, who had also discovered the emptiness of life, Me-rezhkovskiy had formerly been overcome by its corrosive banality and tedium. Many of the poems of his Populist period, as we have seen, were devoted to his bewailing the griefs, sufferings, doubts, boredom, and weariness that life, composed of these same elements, aroused in him. Equally poignant were his cries of longing for escape, for peace and rest from the thoughts that tormented him. He cursed the day for waking him from the forgetfulness of night, and he called on night to soothe him:

Do come to me, o night; extinguish all my thoughts!
I have great need of dusk, and of a calm caress:
Bright light is hateful to the eyes of a sick soul.
I am most fond of somber and mysterious tales.

Do come, do come, o night; extinguish now the sun![15]

Then even night increased his burden, and he sought escape elsewhere. For a time he found it in nature, and spring was able to destroy the despair, replacing it with happiness.[16] Only in nature, in the presence of waves, sky, and clouds, could he find a moment of respite, in which suffering, hope, love, and recollection were dulled in his seething breast.[17] Yet soon nature could no longer soothe him, for he perceived both the indifference of nature to man and the cruelty that also existed in nature:

Here, even here, alas! there is not peace and rest:
Before me even here, in forest depths, there is
    Of monstrous war the self-same slaughter
    And malice of enfrenzied foes![18]

The last refuge, the only nirvana, was death. Death should therefore not be regarded as a horror; on the contrary, it was to be desired and welcomed; for while it put an end to life's fleeting joys and hopes, it also ended life's sufferings and cares. Man should ob-serve the fall of petals and the paling of the sunset in order to witness the calm and the beauty of death in nature, for death was the final gift of a benign nature:

> People, you should learn from her,
> Our divine preceptress, how to die,
> So that with a meek, triumphant smile
> You would meet your end without a murmur.[19]

And Merezhkovskiy's ultimate word of advice on death:

> If you must, then most humbly return,
> When you die, to your heavenly homeland;
> Both from death and from life you must learn
> Not to fear either dying or living.[20]

Merezhkovskiy realized, of course, that although he himself was unable to find peace, there were those who were able to do so in service to the people, in science, or in faith and God. He envied such fortunate individuals, particularly the last, and he did not try to dissuade them from their beliefs:

> O, I do deeply envy him
> Who does believe with all his soul:
> Not lonely is his heart, like mine,
> By grief exhausted, as is mine,
> Before death's certain mystery:
> My friends, who can believe, believe!
> No, do not be ashamed of tears
> And holy prayers and revelations:
> He who has borne with faith life's burden
> Was happy in the midst of torments.
> But we — in all the gifts of earth
> How little happiness we found.[21]

Merezhkovskiy was well aware of the advantages of belief in a higher entity; he had long been seeking such a faith. As he had been raised in a Christian environment, he naturally regarded Christian doctrine favorably and considered Christian ideals to be sacred. Yet he was aware of the anomaly that these ideals were not preponderant in the Christian society of Europe. The jubilant cry "Christ is risen" took on an aspect of hypocrisy, even of sacrilege, and could arouse no response in him; for it represented the triumph of brotherly love, peace, and humility, whereas the very opposite was true. The world, as Merezhkovskiy saw it, was full of blood, tears, and hatred.[22] He was further confused by God's permitting such discord to exist in the world that He had created, which was now bowed before Him in despair.[23]

The inscrutability of God's truth and ways increased Merezhkovskiy's doubts and led him to rebel against what he considered God's injustice to man. He found it an incomprehensible paradox that God permitted evildoers to live in peace and contentment, to prosper and multiply, while He simultaneously inflicted severe punishments and torments on the good, who obeyed His laws and who had done nothing to warrant such harsh treatment. He was not willing to accept such an unjust God, before Whom one should bow down in fear, without daring to voice complaints or to seek redress.[24]

Merezhkovskiy contemplated other factors which caused him to move away from the Christian Church. Most important of all was his belief that the Church no longer followed Christ's teachings:

> At first she truly loved Me,
> But failing in her vows,
> My bride did then betray Me
> And did abandon Me.
>
> . . . .
>
> She is in flesh's power;
> Forgetful of her Lord,
> She did disdain My gifts,
> Rejected too My summons.[25]

He even found traces of idolatry replacing the spirit of Christ's Church with its humble prayers. During a visit to Capri in 1891 he witnessed a festival in honor of St. Constantius; the processions, the merrymaking, the carrying of a statue of the saint through the streets seemed more reminiscent of the worship of a pagan god than the veneration of a Christian saint.[26]

Merezhkovskiy was dissatisfied with this aspect of the Christian Church and with certain other doctrines that had become prominent. Among them was the ascetic concept that true Christianity lay in a renunciation of the world, in the chastising of the flesh, and in the consigning of everything beautiful and joyful to the realm of the devil. Merezhkovskiy was convinced that this was directly opposed to what Christ taught. He was just as certain that St. Francis of Assisi embodied the true conception of Christianity, for he realized that beauty was of God and that one should be joyful in God. Yet the Church, while hypocritically willing to make use of St. Francis for its own ends, did not believe in his teachings.[27]

Such a conviction could not fail to add fuel to Merezhkovskiy's growing anticlerical sentiments, especially since he had always been (and would remain throughout his life) deeply conscious of the beauties of nature. He even evolved a concept of God in nature, but as the following poem entitled "God" *(Bog)* reveals, it was not a pantheistic belief:

My God, I offer thanks to Thee
For suffering my eyes to see
The world, Thy temple everlasting,
And night and billows and the dawn.
Let fearful torments threaten me, —
I thank Thee for that very moment,
For all that with my heart I knew,
And which the stars impart to me.
I feel Thee everywhere, O Lord —
Both in the silence of the night,
And in the most remote of stars,
And in the depths of my own soul.
I longed for God — and did not know;
I still did not believe, but, loving,
While I denied it with my mind,
I felt Thy presence with my heart,
And Thou revealed Thyself to me;
Thou art the world. All things art Thou.
Thou art the heavens and the sea;
Thou art the voice of storms, the ether;
Thou art the poet's thought, the star.
Thus, while I live, I pray to Thee.
I love Thee; I am filled with Thee.
And when I die, I'll merge with Thee,
Just as the stars blend with the dawn.
I wish this life of mine to be
A never-ending praise to Thee.
To Thee for midnight and for dawn,
For life and death — I render thanks.[28]

Nature occupied a significant place in Merezhkovskiy's life and works. He felt an affinity with it, and the beauty he saw in it was almost a cult with him. In his poems he described all the visible aspects of nature, treating it sympathetically, so that his descriptions of it, whether in poetry or in prose, are among the best pages of his writings. Yet there was more in his love of nature than the attraction of its scenic beauty. He found in it elements that he esteemed, probably because they were lacking in himself: harmony, calm, freedom, power, and imperturbability. Nature became virtually an entity, beyond the reach of man and his troubles:

> We have not been able to darken
> With evil or murderous hate
> The heavens' magnificent chamber,
> The charm of the flowering earth.[29]

Thus nature was revealed as God's temple; and the two, God and nature, became inseparable.

Merezhkovskiy was simultaneously in the throes of two irreconcilable principles, which were represented for him by Christianity and Olympian paganism—death and life. Christ crucified, His hands pierced with nails and His brow wreathed with thorns, offered torment and death. But this was his brother, his God, before Whom he bowed unwillingly, for Christ had joyfully accepted suffering and death for him:

> Lord, my belief is in Thee, let me repudiate life,
> Grant that I may in love's name die now, together with Thee.[30]

The Olympians, on the other hand, were the antithesis of torment; they refused to recognize it, hiding their gaze from it. They offered light, beauty, and life, the most precious of all gifts. Merezhkovskiy was torn between the two extremes, and his cry of indecision was echoed in his poetry:

> Where are you, truth? — Here in death, in celestial love and
>   in torments,
> Or, o you shades of the gods, in your terrestrial beauty?
> As in this temple divine, in the soul of mankind there disputes
> Joy everlasting and life, endless enigma and death.[31]

It was the solution of this problem—how to reconcile one with the other—that was to occupy the greater portion of Merezhkovskiy's religious works, including his trilogy of novels.

For a moment, he saw only that Olympian Rome had perished, and after it Christian Rome, for faith had died:

> Now are we wandering, hearts filled with grief, in antiquity's
>   ruins.
> O, will we surely not find faith of such strength that again
> We may unite on the earth all generations and nations?

34

Where then art Thou, unknown God; where art Thou, Rome
   of the future?[32]

This "unknown God" was to become the object of Merezhkovskiy's
religious quest—an "unknown God" in whom he hoped to unite the
two elements that existed within himself.

Merezhkovskiy's first attempt to discover where truth lay led him
to Symbolism and to Nietzsche, whose doctrines were spread into
Russia during the 1880s. Minskiy was the first to follow the new
trend in Russia with his book *By the Light of Conscience (Pri svete
sovesti)*, and Merezhkovskiy was not far behind, for his second collection of poetry, *Symbols (Simvoly)*, the first symbolist work in Russian
literature, shows a marked tendency towards Nietzscheism.

Merezhkovskiy's religious dilemma was the culminating factor
in an already impressive list of qualities, some of which were very
similar to those revealed in Nietzsche and the Western decadents,
and which attracted him to them. There were his aristocratism, his
love of beauty, and his predilection for the attributes of Greek and
Roman antiquity. There was also his desire to flee from the toils of
the tedium, the emptiness, and the mediocrity of life; and the only
escape appeared to be offered by Nietzscheism. Then, too, there
were his longing for life and his renunciation of an unjust, fear-
inspiring God, a God proffering only suffering and death, while
denying beauty and life. All other means had failed Merezhkovskiy;
Nietzscheism and decadence revealed themselves as the last resort.

Merezhkovskiy turned to aestheticism, as if by the expedient of
overlooking them he could deny and thereby overcome the problems
that beset him. For a time, at least, he was successful. All references
to social problems and complaints against tedium were absent from
his poems of this period. No longer was there any praising of the
people, but in its place such statements as:

In the midst of fools triumphant
Do I walk, rejected, homeless.[33]

The ideal became all-important. Whatever the ideal might be
was of no concern; it was belief in an ideal that was essential. In
Merezhkovskiy's words,

But faith in an ideal is now the only faith
Remaining to us from the general destruction;
It is the final God; it is the final temple.[34]

35

Merezhkovskiy's ideal was beauty: the eternal, cold beauty of the Venus of Melos, indifferent to the sufferings of humanity, yet ruling over it forever; beauty filled with might and power, able to calm chaos and to conquer death.[35] No matter how perfidious and treacherous it might appear, no matter how cursed it might be, beauty could not be anything but pure and innocent, the very hope of the world.[36]

Classical antiquity provided Merezhkovskiy with the subject matter for his verse, as it was to attract the majority of Russian Symbolists, most notably Bryusov and Ivanov. By delving into antiquity and selecting his themes from Greek and Roman sources—the voluptuousness of Leda; the fearless, joyful life of ancient Pompeii before its destruction; and the rebellious might of the Titans—Merezhkovskiy was able to avoid contemporary problems. He was lavish with his praise of the past, for he considered pagan Rome to be holy; and although it had perished centuries before, its invincible spirit still prevailed:

> If everywhere in the world the spirit of man were to fall,
> Then would the hallowed stones of the Rome of antiquity
>   clamor:
> "Mortal, immortal thy spirit; man is the equal of gods."[37]

This is one of the earliest evidences of Merezhkovskiy's having adopted Nietzsche's concept of superman. Like Nietzsche, Merezhkovskiy set himself up above good and evil. He sang of extremes, and by doing so, he avoided the mediocrity that he detested:

> More than happiness, goodness, and even thyself,
> Love thou life — there is nothing superior on earth.[38]

He advocated that one should live in great and cold beauty. Man should be fearless and not believe in the possibility of human good and evil, but should conquer all with gay, carefree laughter, which is the most valuable crown of life:

> Children's laughter and gods'
> Above evil and storm,
> Like the azure, this laughter
> Is above all the clouds.[39]

Sin was permitted, provided that one was intrepid in sin. Indeed, Merezhkovskiy declared that the greatest sin of all was despondency:

The only feat in life is gladness;
The only truth in life is laughter.[40]

He denounced all bigots and called for bacchanalian joys, for un-
ashamed nudity, and for the beauties of the body. Thus

We drink life's nectar to the dregs,
Just like the gods in heaven's vault,
And death we vanquish by our laughter
With Bacchus's frenzy in our hearts.[41]

There was nothing to fear in death, any more than there was in
life. The same horrors and mysteries existed in both, for death and
life were equal abysses. Good and evil, the secrets of the grave and
of life, were paths leading to the same goal: it did not matter which
path one followed. There need be no fear at all, for

You are your God; you are your neighbor.
O, be yourself your own Creator;
Be the abyss above, below,
Your own beginning and your end.[42]

It was the expression of such seemingly amoral and even sacri-
legious sentiments that induced certain of his contemporaries and
still later critics to brand Merezhkovskiy a decadent and to place him
in the company of Bryusov and Fedor Sologub.[43] This is a categoriz-
ing that is as superficial as it is incorrect. Not only are these "evidences" of Merezhkovskiy's decadence not overly numerous, but they
were also stated over a relatively short space of time. They may more
correctly be regarded as an indication of an overreaction on Merezhkovskiy's part—an extolling of man's *ego*, of the individual's need
for total freedom—after his rejection of the socialism of the Populists. Of more significance is the fact that they reveal the preliminary
stage in Merezhkovskiy's search for faith: the conflict between himself and God—his sense of worth as a man and his need to submit to
the dictates of a superior being.

Like Nietzsche before him, Merezhkovskiy maintained the conviction that it was necessary to destroy utterly the old in order to
create a new life.[44] He was certain that this new life would arrive in
the future, and he proclaimed that it was man's duty to prepare for
it; yet, he averred, the majority of his contemporaries neglected to
consider the needs of future generations:

But drunkenness has passed; died out
Blind valor's fire; the goblet drained;

No drop of moisture is there left
To wet your children's burning lips.

Like the last fragrance of the chalice,
We live but as a shadow's shadow,
And fearfully we contemplate
By what things will our scions live.[45]

The few who were preparing for the future life, among them Merezhkovskiy himself, were

Much too premature precursors
Of too slowly coming spring.[46]

Consequently, they were not destined to see the new age for which they had labored; only its dawn would cast its light upon them:

We — above the step's abyss,
Sons of darkness — wait the sun;
We shall see the light and perish,
Shadowlike, in its bright rays.[47]

They would hand their lyre to future prophets as, dying, they greeted the rising sun:

We perish, victims of atonement.
There will come other generations.
But on that day, before their court,
May curses not be heaped on us;
Remember only this, my brothers,
How much great suffering we bore!
New radiance of coming faith,
To you, from those who perish, greetings![48]

Merezhkovskiy was not to be alone for long in the expression of such sentiments. The concept of the poet as being ahead of his time, conscious of a needed change in the future, and striving toward that longed-for goal was to become common property of future Russian Symbolist poets. From Bryusov, who egotistically compared himself and his like thinkers to "the crest of a rising wave" (*greben' vstayushchey volny*),[49] to Belyy, with his apocalyptic utterances, and Ivanov, with his belief in mystical anarchism as the ideal of the future, Symbolist writers hailed themselves as seers, prophets, and agents in the ultimate transformation of the world into a more perfect state.

Less egotistic than Bryusov's, Merezhkovskiy's regarding of himself as a precursor of a new era reflects rather his reawakening sense of duty to humanity, if not to the present generation then to a future one. He could not keep his own natural tendencies in abeyance. No matter how much he claimed that man was his own God or how extravagantly he praised sin, he could not prevent himself from being drawn to forces outside himself—to mankind and to God. In anger he confessed:

> My soul and Thou — we are alone, both Thou and I,
> Forever face to face, o Thou, my greatest Foe.
> To Thee each sigh and step of mine direct themselves
> In day's brief light and grave's eternal mystery;
> And while in violent murmur for this life I curse Thee,
> Still do I know that Thou and I are but the same.
> To Thee I cry, as did Thy son: my God, my God,
> Why hast Thou forsaken me?[50]

Still striving for truth, Merezhkovskiy was unable to consider God his enemy for long. Disenchanted with the efficacy of what he had preached as the solution of his problem, he realized that he wanted a calm life and a calm death and that he needed God's assistance in order to resist the temptations that beset him. Nevertheless, he continued to assert:

> I love the stench of earthly joys,
> When on my lips are prayers to Thee —
> Both sin and evil do I love;
> I love the insolence of crime.[51]

Such an admission may seem strange from one seeking a pure love and humility from God. Yet it is but a further indication of Merezhkovskiy's ever-present dilemma, his duality: his longing for the things of the world and of the flesh, while at the same time desiring the things of heaven and of the spirit.

The clamor of bacchanalian singing, the fury of the impassioned dance, and the ringing of bold laughter palled on him. The opposite became the ideal: silence became holiness, and especially the silence of nature:

> Undiscovered mystery
> In the forest depths; all over
> Silence most exceptional.[52]

God's spirit calmed the earth, taught peace to nature, and put an end to the wild destructive storms that captured the heart of youth. The heavens, far above all earthly storms, remained eternally silent. Thus, Merezhkovskiy concluded:

> God is not in words, not in prayers,
> Not in death-bearing fire,
> Not in destruction and battles;
> God is in silence.[53]

This statement marks the culmination of Merezhkovskiy's poetic career. He had passed from civic poet to Symbolist and finally to religious thinker, or rather his religious bent had come to dominate his being and his writings. Poetry was too constraining to permit the fullest expression of his ideas. Consequently, he turned to the novel and the essay, which were to win for him greater renown than his poetic compositions. It was also in the realm of prose that he was to formulate his religious and social concepts. These were but the results of his striving ever upwards. It was his poetry which revealed the striving itself and which served as the cornerstone of the monolithic structure that he created with his pen.

4

The New Idealism

Merezhkovskiy's initial essays into the realm of prose coincided with two important events in his early life: his marriage to Zinaida Gippius and his turning to Symbolism. His first two articles of literary criticism—"An Old Question Regarding a New Talent" *(Staryy vopros po povodu novogo talanta)*, on Chekhov, and "Flaubert in His Letters" *(Flober v svoikh pis'makh)*—were published in *Severnyy Vestnik* in the two months preceding his wedding, November and December 1888. From then until 1896, the year in which his last collection of new poems and the independent edition of his first novel were published, Merezhkovskiy contributed two to four articles a year to a number of journals, including *Severnyy Vestnik, Russkoe Obozrenie* (Russian Review), *Trud* (Labor), *Russkaya Mysl'* (Russian Thought), *Teatral'naya Gazeta* (Theatrical Gazette), and *Vestnik Inostrannoy Literatury* (Herald of Foreign Literature). The fact that Merezhkovskiy published his compositions in such an array of journals, representing widely divergent editorial policies, is of no little significance. It indicates that he was unwilling to ally himself with the policies of a specific journal; no less does it reveal that at the very outset of his career, just as in later years, he found it extremely difficult to have his works accepted by the periodical press.

These were years of intense activity for the young writer and his bride. In St. Petersburg they participated in the meetings of various literary circles and salons, in particular the Literary Society, and counted among their closest acquaintances those with whom Merezhkovskiy had been associated earlier: Minskiy, the Davydovs, Pleshcheev, Baroness Varvara Ivanovna Üxküll (of whom all the young poets were enamored),[1] the Moscow lawyer Prince A. I. Urusov, and the St. Petersburg lawyer and poet S. A. Andreevskiy. In spite of the many social engagements, the major portion of their day was devoted to work, although Merezhkovskiy insisted on a certain amount of exercise.[2]

It was not until the spring of 1891 that Merezhkovskiy and Gippius made their first trip abroad. Italy was their objective, with Warsaw and Vienna stopping places on their journey. In Venice the Merezhkovskiys came across Chekhov and A. S. Suvorin. Merezhkovskiy had already arranged that his second collection of poems, *Symbols*, should be published by the latter. This was considered by the intelligentsia of the time to be a serious blunder, for Suvorin was notoriously antiliberal.[3] It was an "error" that Merezhkovskiy was not to make on a second occasion.

In addition to Venice, the Merezhkovskiys also visited Bologna, Florence, Rome, Naples, and Capri. The trip was not primarily a holiday, for it was Merezhkovskiy's purpose to engage in research in each city, increasing his knowledge of the periods of history that he intended to treat in his novels. While he was interested in the fourth century for his first novel, *The Death of the Gods: Julian the Apostate (Smert' bogov: Yulian Otstupnik)*, he could not but be impressed by the striking evidences of the Italian Renaissance; and it is more than likely, as Gippius points out, that he conceived the idea of his second historical novel, *The Gods Resurrected: Leonardo da Vinci (Voskresshie bogi: Leonardo da Vinchi)*, at that time.[4] A series of "Italian novellas" as well as numerous poems were assuredly a more immediate result of this and a subsequent trip to Italy during the spring and summer of 1892.

The return journey to Russia at the end of the latter visit to Italy was also profitable for Merezhkovskiy. In the course of the voyage by sea he and Gippius visited Corfu, Athens, and Constantinople. Merezhkovskiy's interest in classical antiquity was intensified thereafter, and he embarked on a series of translations of the tragedies of Aeschylus, Sophocles, and Euripides, as well as Longus's *Daphnis and Chloe*. The quality of his translations was such that some of them came to be widely used in the schools.[5] Furthermore, his impressions of the Acropolis, the Parthenon, and the former Byzantine cathedral of St. Sophia were embodied in poems and articles written soon after.

Once again in St. Petersburg, Merezhkovskiy continued his activities in various literary societies. Of importance at this period was his meeting Volynskiy (pseudonym of Akim L'vovich Flekser), who, after the change in management of *Severnyy Vestnik*, became assistant editor of that journal. Merezhkovskiy's acquaintance with Volynskiy had grown sufficiently close by 1894 for Volynskiy to accompany the Merezhkovskiys on their next trip to Italy. As a result of their friendship, Merezhkovskiy was able to prevail upon Volynskiy to publish *Julian the Apostate*, which had already been rejected by *Vestnik Evropy* (Herald of Europe) because of its religious tendencies.[6] The novel appeared in the first six issues of *Severnyy Vestnik* for 1895, but with many alterations and omissions demanded by Volynskiy. It was shortly afterwards, perhaps because of Volynskiy's intransigence, that Merezhkovskiy and Volynskiy had their first break. Nevertheless, in the course of the next few years Merezhkovskiy published a number of his Italian novellas in Volynskiy's journal, subsequently submitting them to any magazine that would accept them, including *Niva* (Cornfield), *Zhivopisnoe Obozrenie*, and *Vsemirnaya Illyustratsiya* (Universal Illustration).

Merezhkovskiy's first major work of literary criticism, indeed one of his most significant contributions to the further development of Russian literature, was in part made up of articles published from 1888 to 1892. *On the Reasons for the Decline and on New Trends in Contemporary Russian Literature (O prichinakh upadka i o novykh techeniyakh sovremennoy russkoy literatury)*, which appeared in 1893, was a landmark in Merezhkovskiy's life and in the literature of the period; it initiated the Symbolist school in Russia, and at the same time it elevated Merezhkovskiy to the leading position in the Modernist movement.

As the title implies, Merezhkovskiy presents the reader with a significant contemporary analysis of Russian literature and the literary milieu during the 1880s and early 1890s. He also puts forward his concepts of literature as a profound cultural force, which he strove to serve throughout his life, and of the "subjective artistic" method of literary criticism, of which he was ever to remain an exponent. Simultaneously, the work stands as the earliest manifesto of Russian Symbolism, for in it Merezhkovskiy established the primary tenets, all of which were to be accepted to a greater or lesser degree by subsequent Symbolists, even those theoreticians such as Bryusov, Belyy, Blok, and Vyacheslav Ivanov who were later to propound

43

more elaborate systems of Symbolist art and beliefs. Yet all owe a debt to Merezhkovskiy, whose *On the Reasons for the Decline and on New Trends in Contemporary Russian Literature* was the foundation stone of the new literary movement.

Before embarking on an evaluation of contemporary Russian literature, Merezhkovskiy found it expedient to expound, as did V. G. Belinskiy some sixty years earlier in his "Literary Reveries" (*Literaturnye mechtaniya*), his own definition of literature. For Merezhkovskiy, there was a distinction between literature and poetry, and between the poet and the littérateur. "Poetry is a primordial and eternal, an *elemental*, force, an involuntary and spontaneous gift of God."[7] Consequently, it is no less subject to human dominance and control than are any other manifestations of nature. Furthermore, the poetic talent may appear in anyone, in a child or a savage, in Goethe or Homer. Of utmost significance is Merezhkovskiy's statement: "The poet may be great in complete isolation. The force of inspiration does not need to depend on whether the poet is heeded by humanity, or by one or two persons, or indeed by anyone at all."[8] In other words, the poet and poetry do not necessarily have any influence on mankind.

Literature is an outgrowth of poetry and is, moreover, superior to it:

> In essence, literature is the same as poetry, but only that which is considered not from the point of view of the individual creation of individual authors, but as a force that moves whole generations, entire nations, along a certain cultural path, as a succession of poetic phenomena which are transmitted from age to age and are united by a great historic principle.[9]

Literature, then, is a unified body of individual poetic creations, spanning the centuries, which has emerged as a cultural force. In his own time Homer's works were but poetry; only centuries later, during the Golden Age of Greek civilization, did they take on literary as well as poetic consequence, because they were the basis on which arose a school of artists and writers. Since Homer's influence continued throughout the ensuing ages in the Greek world, even as late as the third century A.D. in Longus's *Daphnis and Chloe*, Homer served as the "historic principle" that united all the individual manifestations of poetry into Greek literature. Conversely, classical Greek literature reflected Homer's influence, for "a great literature remains true to its progenitor to its very last breath."[10]

In addition to the unifying principle, literature—like any other manifestation of culture, be it painting, sculpture, or architecture—can only develop if the atmosphere is suitable. The talents that were Ghirlandaio and Verrocchio could have flourished at any time and in any place; but only in Florence in the fifteenth century were conditions such that they could contribute to the emergence of the national spirit in the persons of their pupils Michelangelo and Leonardo da Vinci. Once found, the features of the Florentine Renaissance entered into all its cultural manifestations. This must be the case, for: "On all the creations of truly great cultures, just as on coins, is stamped the visage of one sovereign. This sovereign is the genius of the nation."[11] Merezhkovskiy found an analogous, though lesser, situation in contemporary France. The French national spirit had emerged in the era of Romanticism; the subsequent reaction led literature to the extreme of Naturalism, which in turn was decaying; then, once again, the national genius was making efforts "to find new creative paths, new combinations of the truth of life and the greatest idealism."[12] The atmosphere was again favorable.

Thus Merezhkovskiy postulated his theories on literature. It is based on poetry (individual talent, individual genius); it is a cultural force, which poetry is not. Like any other cultural manifestation, it is an expression of the national spirit; but as a part of the national culture, it can only emerge in a specific atmosphere, when the spark that is the individual genius ignites the waiting, dry tinder that is the national genius. The transformation of poetry into literature, the emergence of the national culture, has occurred in various nations during various epochs: in the Athens of Pericles, the Florence of the Renaissance, the England of Elizabeth I, the Germany of Goethe, the France of the Romantics. It remained for Merezhkovskiy to turn to his own country, to declare and to question: "There is no doubt that in Russia there have been truly great poetic manifestations. But here is the question: has there been in Russia a truly great literature, worthy of standing on a par with other world literatures?"[13]

As R. E. Matlaw has quite rightly observed, Merezhkovskiy was hardly justified in putting forward the contention that literature, as he himself defined it, had not yet emerged in Russia.[14] In his brief examination of Russian literature from Pushkin to his own day, Merezhkovskiy strove to emphasize the lack of all the conditions that he deemed essential for the transformation of poetry into literature. Russian writers had always flourished in isolation one from another;

consequently, the "descent of the national spirit on literature" had never occurred—nor had there been time for it to occur—even though the national spirit was manifested momentarily in one poet or another.[15] Above all, in nineteenth-century Russian literature there was a general desire, most obviously visible in Tolstoy, to escape from culture:

> In Pushkin, who perhaps derived the most daring of his inspirations in the wild gypsy camp; in Gogol' with his mystic raving; in Lermontov's scorn for people and for contemporary civilization in his all-absorbing Buddhistic love for nature; in Dostoevskiy's sickly-proud dream about the role of the *Messiah*, granted by God to the meek Russian people, who are come to redress everything that Europe has done: in all these writers there is the same elemental principle as in Tolstoy — *a flight from culture.*[16]

Literature, which is a cultural force, could not come into being, for each Russian writer refused, consciously or unconsciously, the role of littérateur.

Russia had need of a Goethe, "a representative of universal-historic culture" and Merezhkovskiy's ideal man of letters.[17] Goethe welcomed all new scientific discoveries and strove to come into contact with every cultural phenomenon of all ages and nations. Never would he reject his creations and withdraw into nature, away from culture and science, as did Tolstoy: "He was not afraid that science and culture would estrange him from nature, from the earth, from his native land; he knew that the highest degree of culture is at the same time the highest degree of nationality."[18] Despite its need, Russia would not produce such a representative of the national spirit as long as it had no literature, no cultural force, and as long as it failed to recognize the fact that one nation alone could not bear the weight of the world. Merezhkovskiy might or might not, in his youthful egotism, have conceived of himself as a rival to Turgenev and Lermontov, or as a Russian Goethe. Nonetheless, there is no doubt, as he proceeded to analyze the contemporary situation and to present his views on the new idealism, that he regarded himself to be one of the pioneers in the creation of a great Russian literature.

In his condemnation of the contemporary state of Russian letters and the conditions that continued to prevent the emergence of a national literature, Merezhkovskiy first turned his attention to the publishing enterprises of his time, to the journals, and to the literary circles that had sprung up around them. Throughout he observed the tedium and lifelessness that pervaded the whole of Russian society. An advocate of culture, he could not condone the debasement of the Russian literary language, which he attributed to those who wrote for the journals in faulty imitation of D. I. Pisarev's method of criticism and Saltykov-Shchedrin's particular satiric manner.[19] No less lamentable was the growing ignorance of the "democratic Bohemia," as exemplified by a newspaper account of Ibsen's *Nora* (that is, *A Doll's House*) having first been presented at Weimar when Goethe was director of its theater, and by a reference in another source to Leconte de Lisle as *Graf* (count) de Lisle.[20] He would rather have had total ignorance—that is, lack of education—than incomplete knowledge. The uneducated, who had not lost contact with the people, commanded a pure, beautiful language;

> but in an environment that is semi-ignorant, semieducated, that is already estranged from the people but has not yet attained culture, precisely in that environment from which come all the literary artisans and all the democratic newspaper Bohemia, the language grows still and decays.[21]

Not only were the journals responsible for the debasement of the Russian language, but they also contributed to the abasement of the author. Merezhkovskiy attacked bitterly the system of honoraria, and he regretted the fact that writers sought to be paid for their compositions, which they ought to give freely to the public. He himself was in such an advantageous financial position that he could afford to be a literary aristocrat. Although there may have been periods of monetary shortage in the early years of his married life, as Gippius indicates,[22] Merezhkovskiy nevertheless had a private income, the allowance from his father, which freed him from the need to work for his living and enabled him to consider the monetary rewards of his publications to be other than payment for labor. Indeed, one of Merezhkovskiy's contentions was that honoraria, especially when they lost all idealistic sense and became official pay, were among the major contributing factors to the decline of literature. They led to the deplorable contemporary situation: literature had been given over to the "street crowd," and authors pandered to the taste of the lowest elements of society.[23] Moreover, the petty press fostered this "most degrading form of prostitution" by compelling the author to surrender his freedom and to fetter his inspiration.[24]

Merezhkovskiy was decidedly harsh in his pronouncements concerning Russian literary journals and their editors. In part, at least, his animosity must have been engendered by his own experiences, by his own difficulty in having his works published in the periodical press. For him the editor was "the servant of the crowd,"[25] almost never a littérateur or scholar by vocation. Though possessing qualities that entitled them to respect, editors as a whole were timid conformists who forced new talents into stereotyped forms. Mistrustful of the reading public, enthralled by the crowd (an attitude that Merezhkovskiy could never condone), cowardly and banal in his taste, the editor strove for his ideal: external literary decorum. Yet editors, together with publishers and the system of honoraria, were components of an external force, which was in no way as destructive to literature as the inner forces, particularly criticism.

Merezhkovskiy commented but briefly on Taine's scientific method—which he rejected as being insufficiently worked out, although it might be of value in the future—before turning his attention to the subjective-artistic method, of which he was to be a staunch advocate. Those who had adhered to the latter method in the past—Sainte-Beuve, Herder, Brandes, Lessing, Carlisle, Belinskiy (Merezhkovskiy made no effort to justify his juxtaposition of such disparate individuals)—on occasion gave evidence that the critic might be transformed into an original poet. The reverse might also be true: the poet might become a critic. Merezhkovskiy observed the earliest examples of "critical poetry" in certain epigrams of Goethe and Schiller, in which the poets commented on art and literature. He asserted that "for the subjective-artistic critic, the world of art plays the same role as the world does for the artist."[26] Books are living people, and, like real persons, they arouse in the critic the sentiments of hatred, love, torment, and enjoyment. The subjective-artistic method was a form of poetry—"the poetry of poetry"[27]—because the poet-critic reflected "not the beauty of real objects, but the beauty of the poetic images that reflect these objects."[28] It was a new method of criticism, unknown to the past; it was "the poetry of the idea, a result of the nineteenth century with its boundless freedom of spirit and its unappeasable grief of knowledge."[29] Such criticism possessed a mysterious charm which was not found in the very beauty of which it was but a reflection. Lest this prove an insufficient virtue, Merezhkovskiy pointed out a more "scientific" significance: that the mystery of creation was more readily understood by a poet-critic than by an objectively scientific investigator, for "if an artist reads the work of another artist, there takes place a psychological experiment, which corresponds to the experiment in scientific laboratories when the chemical reaction of one body on another is investigated."[30] One cannot comprehend how the subjective and the intuitive may be termed "scientific," although one may sympathize with Merezhkovskiy for his deeming it essential, in a world oriented towards rationalism and the sciences, to prove the worth of his method by claiming that it is more scientific than the scientific methods of his opponents.

However, Merezhkovskiy himself did not believe that Russian criticism had been scientific or artistic, for Russian critics had been neither real scientists nor real poets: "Russian criticism, with the exception of the best articles of Belinskiy, Ap. Grigor'ev, and Strakhov, some separate essays of Turgenev, Goncharov, and Dostoevskiy, and some brilliant notes scattered in the letters of Pushkin, has always been an antiscientific and antiartistic force."[31] To demonstrate that the tendency had continued into the current period, Merezhkovskiy selected three contemporary critics for specific comment. Through M. A. Protopopov, he attacked publicist-critics who turned literature into a pulpit for their journalistic preaching, delivered political orations, popularized the most basic moral ideas for the uncultured and immature mob, and raised the scholastic question "Is art for life, or life for art?"[32] For Merezhkovskiy, such a question need not be posed:

Such a question does not exist for a living man, for a sincere poet: he who loves beauty knows that poetry is not an accidental superstructure, not an external appendage, but the very breath, the heart of life, without which life becomes more terrible than death. Certainly, art is for life, and certainly, life is for art. One without the other is impossible.[33]

A. M. Skabichevskiy served as an example of the chronicler of literary manners, who was too involved in bourgeois morality and too easily moved by banal tragedy, so that he was ready to praise the most crudely executed work if it possessed the banality of humane feelings. His primary error lay in his misinterpretation of the moral significance of art, which differed from that propounded by Merezhkovskiy:

The highest *moral* significance of art is not at all to be found in touching, moral tendencies, but in the disinterested, incorruptible *truthfulness* of the artist, in his intrepid sincerity. The beauty of the image cannot be untruthful and therefore cannot be immoral; only deformity, only banality in art are immoral.[34]

Finally, Merezhkovskiy deplored the effect of "the plague of literary corruption" on young, beginning writers, such as Volynskiy, who also represented for him the publicist-philosopher turned literary critic.[35] Merezhkovskiy's attitude towards Volynskiy was ambivalent. Most sympathetic in Volynskiy's work as a publicist-philosopher was his non-Russian, his Jewish temperament: his ardent, exalted mysticism; his hatred for the banal side of positivism; his aptitude for the most subtle metaphysical abstractions. Yet in Volynskiy the literary critic, it was this very Jewishness that was detested by Merezhkovskiy, who declared: "The abstract Semitic metaphysics, which is quite appropriate in the philosophical articles of Mr. Volynskiy, strikes his artistic understanding with murderous aridity and futility."[36] Moreover, despite his feigned Russian patriotism, Volynskiy had "absolutely nothing Russian in him";[37] in this respect, he was no less a "corpse" than Protopopov and Skabichevskiy.[38]

Merezhkovskiy feared that the continuation of the conditions that he had treated in the first half of his study of the state of Russian literature would lead to a literary barbarism, which was unworthy of the great Russian writers of the past, and to the death of a national literature. The sole hope for the future was to be found in a new literary trend, which had arisen "directly from the living heart, from the depths of the contemporary general European and Russian spirit."[39] As yet weak but nonetheless alive, the new current of the young literature would grow, strengthen, and ultimately vanquish all that sought to repress it.

It is significant that Merezhkovskiy attempted to find national as well as foreign origins for the new idealism. This is, to be sure, fully in accord with his views on the need for a national culture and a national literature in Russia. Although the new movement that he subscribed to had emerged in France, it could not be a transplant to Russian soil unless that soil had had adequate preparation. It would be more accurate, perhaps, to liken it to the grafting of a different species to an already existing plant, for Merezhkovskiy would undoubtedly have declared that the soil in France and Russia were similar and the plant was growing with difficulty in both countries. Indeed, he commented on the almost universal conflict between materialism and idealism in the nineteenth century; the support of the crowd, which is essentially realistic, for the former; and the resultant artistic materialism, which corresponded to scientific and moral realism: hence the popularity and financial success of the positivist novel of Emile Zola both in France and Russia, as opposed to the proudly accepted poverty of Paul Verlaine, the head of the French Symbolists.

Literary idealism was not a new invention, but a historic, eternal trait. Therefore, the idealism of the French Symbolists represented a return to the past. Moreover, they reflected a characteristic common to the whole generation of the end of the nineteenth century: a feeling of revolt against "suffocating, deathly positivism."[40] Echoing an idea frequently expressed in his poetry of the time, Merezhkovskiy added: "It is quite possible that they [the exponents of the new idealism] will perish, that they will not succeed in doing anything. But others will come and will still continue their task, because this task is *a living one*."[41] Aware of a need for a more authoritative source than the French Symbolists, Merezhkovskiy again drew support for his views from Goethe, who recognized the value of realism but who also thought that the ideal was essential for the higher qualities possessed by man. It was also Goethe to whom Merezhkovskiy turned in stressing that a poetic work must be symbolic. Merezhkovskiy accepted this premise unquestioningly and apparently considered it unnecessary to argue the point further, once he had summoned the prestige of the great German littérateur to his aid.

The nature of the symbol, however, was subject to more detailed examination. First and foremost, "symbols must naturally and involuntarily flow out of the depths of reality."[42] Otherwise, they become dead, unmoving allegory. To demonstrate his meaning, Merezhkovskiy compared Egyptian and Greek frescoes. For him, the former were of interest only as ethnographical relics; whereas the frescoes on the Parthenon, which were both realistic and naturalistic, were pervaded by a feeling of the ideal human culture and thus emerged as a symbol of the free Hellenic spirit. In Merezhkovskiy's opinion, the whole of Greek art was permeated with such symbolism, though he cited but two additional examples: Euripides' Alcestis, a symbol of motherly compassion; and Sophocles' Antigone, a symbol of the religious-virginal beauty of woman's character. The introduction of a lamp in Ibsen's drama *A Doll's House*, though a realistic detail, contains an artistic symbol: the alternation between darkness and light vitally affects the conversation between two characters and produces an effect on "our inner world."[43] The relationship between the symbol and feeling is prominent, and it should be included in Merezhkovskiy's criterion for the symbol, cited above. The symbol must not only proceed from reality, but must invariably affect the sensitivity of the beholder. Merezhkovskiy expressed it in a somewhat different manner:

> *"The uttered thought is a lie."* In poetry what is not stated and glimmers through the beauty of the symbol has a stronger effect on our hearts than what is expressed in words. Symbolism makes the very style—the very artistic substance of poetry—spiritual, transparent, completely translucent, like the delicate sides of an alabaster amphora in which a flame is kindled.[44]

Lest his reader fail to draw an accurate conclusion from his earlier reference to Alcestis and Antigone, Merezhkovskiy explicitly states that characters may be symbols expressing visions that have pursued and accompanied mankind from century to century. The idea contained in such symbolic characters as Faust, Hamlet, and Don Quixote cannot be expressed in words, for "words only define, restrict the idea; but symbols express the unlimited aspect of the idea."[45] Merezhkovskiy thus rejected photographic exactitude and demanded "new, as yet undiscovered worlds of impressionability,"[46] hints of which he ascertained in such writers of the immediate past as Turgenev, Maupassant, Flaubert, and Ibsen. A desire for the novel was therefore to be a characteristic of the future ideal poetry. Merezhkovskiy was careful to indicate his indebtedness to Baudelaire and Poe, by referring to their contention that the beautiful must surprise, must seem unexpected and rare—a trait that was termed "impressionism" by French critics.

Once he had completed the exposition of his arguments, Merezhkovskiy then summarized the key features of Symbolism: "Such are the three main elements of the new art: *mystic content, symbols,* and the broadening of artistic impressionability."[47]

It was clearly important that the literary movement, of which Merezhkovskiy was now the champion, have a foundation in the past, above all in the Russian past. To this end he undertook a brief critical evaluation of the four major representatives of Russian Realism in whom he discovered one or another of those essential features of Symbolism—Turgenev, Goncharov, Dostoevskiy, and Tolstoy. As was invariably the case in his literary criticism, Merezhkovskiy followed the tenets advocated in the earlier section of *On the Reasons for the Decline and on New Trends in Contemporary Russian Literature*. In spite of many apt and perspicacious insights into the persons under discussion, his literary criticism was above all a means for the expression of his own views, while the object of his criticism served primarily as evidence for the justification of those views. Such was his approach to the four Russian authors listed above: to demonstrate that they "with incomparable strength and completeness rendered all three bases of the ideal poetry"[48]—Turgenev and Goncharov in the matter of form, and Dostoevskiy and Tolstoy in mystic content.

Rejecting Turgenev's novels, Merezhkovskiy insisted that the most important and ageless aspect of Turgenev was to be found in his *Poems in Prose (Stikhotvoreniya v proze)*, in "Bezhin Meadow" *(Bezhin lug)*, and in other shorter works, in which he had proven himself to be a master of the semifantastic and had made use of ordinary character types and human banality solely as a means for the presentation of the beauty of the fantastic, that is of the nonrealistic, the ideal. In this feature of his work, Turgenev continued Pushkin's task: "He extended the limits of our *Russian conception of beauty*, conquered whole regions of still unknown sensuality, discovered new sounds, new sides of the Russian language."[49] Moreover, in his ability to arouse in his readers the charm of nature, through his capacity to find the exact combination of words which appeared to be new, Turgenev had proved to be the greatest "magician of the word" in Russian literature,[50] "a great Russian artist-impressionist."[51] Thus, he was the foundation of two criteria of the new ideal art: impressionism and the use of the novel and the unexpected in order to express beauty.

Of the four Realists, Goncharov presented whole characters as living products of history, nature, their times, and their society. Even more memorable in Goncharov was "the supreme beauty of eternal cosmic images,"[52] which rose above the particular to the level of the universal. Goncharov's success was due to the fact that he, together with Gogol', of all Russian authors possessed the deepest aptitude for Symbolism. At this point Merezhkovskiy almost by chance defined Symbolism as "an artistic system of images, under which is concealed an inspired idea."[53] He also aptly described Goncharov's novels as complete architectural structures, the characters, which form parts of the whole, standing out as bas-reliefs or statues: "The characters . . . are only a series of symbols necessary to the poet in order to raise the reader from a contemplation of the particular phenomenon to a contemplation of the eternal."[54] Such was to be Merezhkovskiy's approach to the characters in his own novels and dramas: they were to be symbols which, taken together with additional artistic images, would reveal the universal and Merezhkovskiy's own inspired thought. Undoubtedly he believed, as he remarked concerning Goncharov's works, that as a result they would be ageless. In any case, Goncharov was one of the foremost "artist-symbolists" in contemporary European literature and, as such, one of the foundations on which to erect the edifice of the new ideal poetry.[55]

Merezhkovskiy was much less successful in demonstrating the new mysticism in Dostoevskiy and Tolstoy, for he inadvertently slipped into the juxtaposition of these two authors and his antipathy towards Tolstoy, which he was to treat at such length a few years later in his massive study *L. Tolstoy and Dostoevskiy (L. Tolstoy i Dostoevskiy)*. What stands out most clearly in this short evaluation of Tolstoy's and Dostoevskiy's contributions to the ideal poetry is a feature that Merezhkovskiy attributed to all his contemporaries—the bifurcation within each: in Dostoevskiy, between faith and doubt; in Tolstoy, between creative strength and utilitarian, methodical, almost puritanical preaching. Dostoevskiy's ambivalence led him into the abyss (an oft-repeated image in Merezhkovskiy's compositions), from which he returned triumphant, bearing the eternal truth of life, humility, and faith in man. Such an assertion, together with his argumentation and the statement that Dostoevskiy felt the novelty of the Gospels more deeply than any other contemporary European writer, was enough to justify Merezhkovskiy's claim for Dostoevskiy. Not so was his approach to Tolstoy, which was almost entirely negative: a scornful rejection of Tolstoy's moralistic tracts of the 1880s, concluding with the remark that *Anna Karenina* and the death of Prince Andrey in *War and Peace* were far more valuable to mankind. Unexpected, perhaps, is the exclamation "Thank God, he belongs to us,"[56] and Merezhkovskiy's conclusion that the Russian people therefore has no right to renounce its expectations of a great future. Despite the weakness of his presentation of Tolstoy's role in the development of the new idealism, Merezhkovskiy concluded: "Tolstoy and Dostoevskiy showed Europe a Russian measure of free religious feeling. Their Christianity . . . flowed from the very heart of the people. And only a movement proceeding from the very heart of the people can make literature truly national and at the same time universal."[57]

The latter statement may be regarded as justification for Merezhkovskiy's devoting an entire chapter to the Populist movement in Russian literature. It would also be correct to assume that he included such a disproportionately long analysis because he and certain others, in whom he found the new idealism, had been associated with it. His ambivalent approach, therefore, served as a means for the defense of his own earlier adherence to Populism and as an explicit statement of the reasons for his having abandoned it.

Merezhkovskiy's argumentation was based on his initial assertion that Populism was a mighty literary trend, very close to idealism, to which most critics attributed a utilitarian and realistic character. He differentiated between A. V. Kol'tsov—the paragon of Populist idealism, who fully identified with the people and whose poetry was the expression of the agricultural mode of life of the Russian peasantry—and intellectual Populists, who scorned the eternal ideals of beauty and poetry as being contradictory to active love for the people and who were in fact divorced from those for whom they professed love. The intellectual Populists failed to accept the religiosity of the peasantry, which equated its primary earthly concern, the growing of grain, with the concept of God, for "God gives birth to grain";[58] consequently, they refused to recognize the fact that the deepest, divine basis of the popular philosophy of life was the relationship of God to the necessities of life. By adhering to a lifeless, economic point of view, the intellectuals had lost contact with the living heart of the people. There was but one way to renew the contact: "Only by returning to God will we return to our people, to our great Christian people."[59]

Nekrasov, the greatest of the Populist poets, exemplified both trends within the Populist movement. He all too often held the utilitarian, economic point of view; and his poetry was reduced to the level of cold prose or journalistic satire. Regrettably, this weak facet of Nekrasov overshadowed Nekrasov the great and free poet, the idealist, the mystic: "Nekrasov who believes in the divine and long-suffering image of the crucified God, the purest and holiest embodiment of the popular spirit."[60] In Nekrasov's service to beauty and in his love for the peasantry and his country as something almost divine, Merezhkovskiy found a form of religion. Despite the quantity of the vain, the journalistic, the satirical, the skeptical in Nekrasov as he attacked the evils of his day, the light of the popular evangelical ideal was never extinguished in his soul. It was later Populists who failed to value the eternal aspect of Nekrasov's poetry and who turned his love into pure statistics and political economy, with the result that their writings were "not popular, but *muzhik* literature."[61]

Yet, true love for the people had not been extinguished in Russian literature, but continued to be vital and deep. This was particularly visible in the case of Korolenko, whose short story "Makar's Dream" *(Son Makara)* revealed the author's religious inspiration. "Makar's Dream" was completely unique in young Populist literature; it was "the purest religious legend, childlike, naïve, and deep, like the best legends of past ages."[62] It proved that the spirit of life and the spirit of the Russian people had not yet vanished from the most recent manifestations of Russian literature and that only on the surface was there a decline, numbness, and coldness. Occasionally, by accident and in passing, a Russian poet penetrated into the depths and touched the eternal evangelical ideals of the people.

Merezhkovskiy was less sympathetic to his two preceptors in Populism: Gleb Uspenskiy, who had been afraid to give himself up to inspiration and wrote polemics "under the yoke of the evil of the day,"[63] and N. K. Mikhaylovskiy, who considered idealism a reactionary rebirth of mysticism. They and the Populists as a whole did not comprehend that the Russian peasant combined "God's truth" and "earth's truth" in one, and in going to the people, they sought only the latter—earth's truth.[64] Nevertheless, those who were striving for the rebirth of idealism sympathized most deeply with the ideal of love for the people, which lay behind the external forms employed by Mikhaylovskiy, Uspenskiy, and Nekrasov. But mystic feeling had to be freed once and for all from those forms if it were to attain for humanity the significance that it should have: "One of the most profound sources of universal poetry—love for the people—cannot spring from some utilitarian calculation, or from some politico-economic necessity, but only from a free belief in the evangelical holiness of the people, only from divine idealism."[65]

In the last chapter of his study, Merezhkovskiy wished to show the widespread revival of idealism in his contemporary generation. Garshin, whose recent suicide made a profound impression on Merezhkovskiy, was praised without reservation for his mastery of the short-story form, for his unswerving sincerity, and for his brevity of expression, which resulted from the discarding of details, including psychological motivation and character delineation—thus enabling the reader to empathize more readily with the heroes. Of significance was the symbolism employed by Garshin in all his works: the corpse and the wounded soldier in "Four Days" (*Chetyre dnya*), the palm in "Attalea Princeps," the poppy in "The Red Flower" (*Krasnyy tsvetok*). Merezhkovskiy recognized the duality of Garshin: he observed it in Garshin's combination of the lyric poem in prose (a more "ideal form" than the novel)[66] and the "terrifying realism" of his content.[67] A thoroughly subjective-lyrical writer, Garshin was uninterested in people and knew little about them; but he treated the themes of man and war, the ideals of love and freedom—despairing love and freedom—as they related to himself and his own experience. In the latter, Garshin was a product of the 1860s, unable to reconcile his thirst for God, which he vainly sought to stifle, with the utilitarian theory of earthly happiness and freedom. From this inner conflict developed his thought and the despair that led to his death: "The poet, who had the misfortune to be born in an era and in a country where negation had become a synonym for intellectual independence, was created for faith, and only faith in an *eternal ideal* could have saved him."[68] Garshin made the fatal mistake of rejecting the latter.

Chekhov, although he presented a contrast to Garshin, was rightly judged by Merezhkovskiy to be a product of the same generation. Chekhov, too, turned to the ideal form; but he produced "epic poems in prose" by virtue of his interest in and knowledge of people,[69] his multifarious portrayals of ordinary Russians, and, because of his healthy attitude, his receptivity to the many questions and trends of contemporary life. Above all, in contributing to the development of the new idealism, Chekhov's importance lay in his being a student of Turgenev, an impressionist.

To show the same trend in poetry, Merezhkovskiy selected K. M. Fofanov and Minskiy, whom he considered the most characteristic. Fofanov was, like Garshin, a poet of St. Petersburg, introspectively subjective and unhealthy but sincere. Although Fofanov was not an outstanding poet, Merezhkovskiy regarded him as worthy of inclusion in his brief list of contemporaries because of his propensity towards symbols. While Fofanov was an unconscious talent, little influenced by culture, Minskiy was a poet of thought, who had begun his poetic career under the aegis and limitations of Populism but had since awakened. He exhibited the same tormenting unrest, grief, and impassioned demands of the new idealism as did Garshin, Chekhov, and Fofanov. Minskiy also served Merezhkovskiy as a means for presenting his view that the ideals of the past generation—"Populist realism, civic motifs in art, and questions of social justice"[70]—had not reappeared in the contemporary generation but had entered a broader arena, in which the problems of infinity, death, and God, presented artistically by Tolstoy, Dostoevskiy, and Turgenev and rejected by the Positivists, arose again, though without their former beauty, in tragic nakedness, in philosophical tracts or philosophical lyrics. Yet, beneath the dialectics, which predominated over spontaneous feeling in Minskiy, beneath the denial and the irony, there remained that which thought could not destroy: "grief for the impossible holiness, the hopeless need of faith, the unquenchable thirst for God."[71]

Merezhkovskiy regretted that the public was incapable of comprehending philosophical language, that it either felt or argued but had not learned to think, hence could not attain to "the deepest and most passionate poetry of thought."[72] This was no less true of the critics who could not distinguish rational rhetoric from the inspired idea of the poet-philosopher. Merezhkovskiy had in mind, of course, the critic-publicists, whom he had treated earlier. Poet-critics, however, were beginning to emerge, among them Merezhkovskiy's long-standing friend S. A. Andreevskiy, whose monographs on Russian authors were critical poems in prose in which the poet-critic had penetrated into the inner world of the author. Andreevskiy exhibited the features of the ideal subjective-artistic critic: not only love, which alone permitted the poet-critic to enter into the soul of another poet, but also "the highest cultural tolerance" (a virtue lacking in Merezhkovskiy, it must be added),[73] which raised him above the rivalry of factions and enabled him to respect the moral freedom of another writer. In addition to Andreevskiy, V. D. Spasovich, though in age a member of the older generation, was an idealist, interested—as all critics should be interested—in "how a writer relates to the eternal questions of God, death, love, nature."[74]

Merezhkovskiy could not overlook Vladimir Solov'ev, but surprisingly limited his comments on him to a single paragraph. In fact, he made only one twice-repeated asseveration. Solov'ev exemplified the combination of deep religious feeling and a sincere and great thirst for earthly justice, which had reappeared in the new man after many years in which mysticism was considered a reaction and was overcome by utilitarian, positivistic theories.

Merezhkovskiy concluded his remarks on contemporary literature by reiterating his assertions on the need for love and faith, for otherwise "there is no beauty, no justice, no poetry, no freedom on earth."[75] Everywhere in the nineteenth century the rebirth of the eternal ideal art could be felt, and the contemporary generation was attempting to continue the trend, formidable as that task might be. "We must enter from a period of creative, spontaneous, and elemental poetry into a critical, conscious, and cultural period."[76] The attainment of this goal was inevitable, for the mission was divine: "When God's spirit blows over the earth, no one knows whence and whither it flies. . . . But it is impossible to oppose it. It is stronger than human will and reason, it is stronger than life, stronger even than death."[77]

Thus, in his first major critical work, Merezhkovskiy presented his views on literature and delineated the essential features of the Symbolist movement in Russian literature. Far more significant, however, was the fact that Merezhkovskiy at such an early stage in his career stated explicitly his own exalted goals as a writer and, with typical lack of humility, proclaimed the divine inspiration that was to guide his future course.

5

Christ and Antichrist

Since Merezhkovskiy's early articles appeared at a time when he was still devoting a considerable proportion of his activity to the writing of verse, it is understandable that he would express in his prose the same ideas and problems that were to be seen in his poems. Yet there was a considerable difference between these two forms of literary creation as Merezhkovskiy made use of them. To be sure, he revealed in his prose works the attraction that ancient paganism held for him, and he also exhibited the same inclination towards Christianity that appeared in his later poetic compositions, but with less passionate outbursts and less tendency towards extremes. In short, it was in his prose that Merezhkovskiy laid bare the duality that existed within himself much more fully and coldly, even more rationally, than in his poetry.

Merezhkovskiy's duality should not be treated lightly. It was of the utmost significance, not only in Merezhkovskiy the writer, but in Merezhkovskiy the man. It was the driving force of his life, urging him on in his religious searchings, which were in turn the source from which all his literary activity sprang.

In reference to Merezhkovskiy's poetic creation it has been remarked, in part, why he attempted to abandon Christianity completely and to place his faith in Graeco-Roman, pagan, values. He was trying to escape from the tedium of life; he was also, by limiting himself to one of the two elements that existed within himself, seeking to end the conflict, in his mind and being, between the teachings of Christianity and those of the Hellenes. In his poetry Merezhkovskiy wrote only about the seemingly boundless extremes of the ancients. These extremes, however, were but symbols representing the Hellenic love of live and of bodily beauty and the freedom permitted by the Olympian gods. In contrast to the apparent wildness of his poems, Merezhkovskiy revealed in the essays that are included in one of his earliest collections, *Eternal Companions (Vechnye sputniki)*, the calmer aspects of the culture and the religion of the ancients which attracted him equally as much.

This author, whom many rebuked for lack of measure, primarily because of his "singing of extremes" in his later poems,[1] was especially impressed by what he considered to be the secret of Hellenic charm—the inherent measure of values of the ancients. They knew when and how to stop without penetrating too deeply, contenting themselves with the great but not the infinite.[2] An example of this sense of measure was the ancients' attitude toward death, an attitude that Merezhkovskiy adopted and preached himself. They understood that all pleasures were temporary and fleeting; therefore, one should enjoy life to the full and cling to one's pleasures as long as possible. There was no fear in the face of death: although it inspired in the ancient Greeks a graceful yet superficial melancholy, death was regarded as a liberation, a freeing of man from all troubles. Such an attitude toward death Merezhkovskiy had also advocated in his poetic works.

The Greeks also approached love naturally, recognizing the "holiness" of love between the sexes, as opposed to the Christian concept of brotherly love. Moreover, they observed the principle, the definition of which Merezhkovskiy attributed to Montaigne, that "each is obliged to love himself."[3] To love oneself with a true and noble love brings with it the advantages of permanent benefit and happiness. Merezhkovskiy, an individualist and aristocrat, would most certainly subscribe to such a sentiment.

Above all, for Merezhkovskiy the ancients represented a synthesis. They united into one harmony all that contemporary mankind was separating: heaven and earth; nature and people; good and evil. Yet the one single revelation of the Hellenes that attracted Merezhkovskiy most strongly was the love of beauty and nature, which he and they held in common. Merezhkovskiy's description of his first visit to the Acropolis offers ample testimony of the impact that Hellenic beauty had on him:

And when the doors shut, it seemed to me that all my past,

the whole past of mankind, all twenty unhealthy, turbulent, and doleful centuries, remained there, behind me, beyond the sacred fence; and nothing disturbed any longer the harmony and eternal peace that reigned here. At last there had come into life that for which it was worth living![4]

Harmony is the key word; and it was through this harmony of the Acropolis that Merezhkovskiy first understood the true meaning of beauty. He realized for the first time what the harmony of beauty consists of, for "the beauty of the Parthenon and the Propylaeum is only the continuation of the beauty of the sea, the sky, and the severe outlines of Hymettus and Pentelikon."[5] Beauty is the synthesis of human creation and nature, one accentuating the other. In the Greeks' comprehension of this, Merezhkovskiy detected the spirit of a free, great nation.

The most significant revelations of the ancients were that the creation of the artist was the highest deed and that the action of the hero was the highest level of beauty. This led Merezhkovskiy to conclude that the hero was the poet of action, and the poet the hero of contemplation.[6] He praised the synthesis of the ancients, contrasting it to the seemingly irreconcilable bifurcation that he found to exist in contemporary humanity. His desire to overcome this bifurcation caused him to exclaim: "Is there no salvation for us, and are the contradictions of our mind and heart insoluble? Are people not fated to repeat what has already been here, and will a new Parthenon never be created by a new Hellene, a godlike man on earth?"[7]

Yet Merezhkovskiy was also attracted to Christianity. He realized that Christian brotherly love was as essential as pagan love. The reason for his casting Christianity aside, at least temporarily, is also apparent here. He viewed the advent of Christianity as a coming of barbarism and death, for it denied all that Hellenism stood for: a love of nature and beauty, and the freedom of man. Merezhkovskiy's main objection to Christianity, therefore, was that it denied life, and for him hatred of life and the denial of its reality were the highest possible crimes.[8]

Merezhkovskiy observed a basic contradiction within Christianity. Christian love should have exerted a profound influence on the world; yet Christianity denied its own Christian love in its barbaric, inhuman, and inquisitorial approach to the things of the world. To disentangle himself from the meshes of this contradiction, he divided Christianity into two parts: mediaeval Catholicism (later he was to term it "historic Christianity")—which by 1891 he could regard calmly, for he considered it to be a dead foe[9]—and Galileanism, in which he found the true essence of the Christian idea. In Merezhkovskiy's view, "this idea is contained in the illusiveness of all the material world, in the spontaneous intercourse of the human soul with God, in the renunciation of our 'I' for a complete merging with the source of universal love, that is, with Christ."[10]

These were the attractions that Merezhkovskiy found in both Christianity and paganism. He was aware of his duality in this respect, and he sought to end it. First, he formulated the idea that both, though at opposite extremes, were holy, each in its own way. Next, he stated that, separated and isolated from one another, neither was complete; and this completion, oneness, was essential. Finally, he had to demonstrate that paganism had not died out as a powerful element in humanity.

There is no doubt that Merezhkovskiy believed in the continued existence of paganism in the contemporary world. While he conceded that classicism had ceased to exist as a historic moment, he stressed that it existed as a psychological one. Hence he stated:

> The controversy of Christian and ancient morals cannot be considered finished to this very day. The classical view of earthly happiness as the extreme bound of human aspiration is resumed in positivism, in utilitarian morals. The same protest, which the first Christians raised against the ancient world, is repeated in the demands of the adversaries of positive morals, in their desire to find a basis for duty in other than the same aspiration for temporal happiness.[11]

He pointed out, moreover, that man was under the influence of both these elements:

> Man's nature is dual: his will can stop at nothing, can surrender itself wholly neither to vice nor to virtue, neither to complete freedom nor to complete self-renunciation, neither to earthly happiness nor to divine happiness. It yearns for calm, and eternally it fluctuates, because we are children of two worlds.[12]

The ancient world offered a moral system in which earthly happiness appeared as the ultimate aim, whereas Christianity presented a spiritual happiness. This was their essential difference, for both were a flight to nature; but Christianity was a uniting of oneself with God in nature, and paganism was a uniting in oneself, in one's ego. Merezhkovskiy made his deduction even clearer. He defined Christianity (indeed, any religion of pity and chastity, of which Christianity is but one) as the eternal striving of the human spirit toward self-denial and to a merging with God, thus freeing oneself in God from the bounds of one's consciousness. On the other hand, he regarded paganism as the striving of the human personality toward boundless development, toward completion, and toward the idolization of one's ego; consequently, it is a movement away from the heavenly to the earthly, the struggle of man against god.[13]

This problem, the one that beset Merezhkovskiy himself—his proud, aristocratic individualism and his desire for a love for others, for self-denial in the name of God—he therefore ascribed to the whole world. Furthermore, he declared them to be irreconcilable extremes: "These two irreconcilable or unreconciled principles, two universal currents—one toward God, the other away from God—are eternally in conflict and cannot vanquish each other."[14] This was the tragedy of humanity: to live between the death of the ancient and the birth of the new gods. It was Merezhkovskiy's own tragedy to be caught in the struggle between two such elemental forces; it could only lead to bifurcation and to man's conflict between his convictions and beliefs, which attach him to the present, and the customs and temperament that bind him to the past. Such was the result of the contest between the two equally powerful but irreconcilable forces.

To add weight to his argument, Merezhkovskiy drew on the past to show that even then humanity was aware of the need to solve the enigma and to overcome and reconcile the contradiction presented to it by paganism and Christianity. The attempt to fuse Christianity and Hellenism in the fourth and fifth centuries ended in failure, just as it did during the Renaissance, when the result was the Inquisition of the second half of the sixteenth century and the cold academicism of the seventeenth. The only solution to the problem was in a synthesis of the two extremes of knowledge and faith, of paganism and Christianity. Although attempts to reconcile them had failed in the past, true syntheses also had appeared in men of great genius, such as Sophocles, Plato, Pushkin, and principally in Leonardo da Vinci.[15] There was no higher point in mankind's history than when these elements merged unconsciously: "The most valuable fruits of the efforts and struggles of mankind, the indications of its ascent to the heights of creation, are those rare moments when the two worlds attain but an unconscious and incomplete reconciliation, but an unsteady equilibrium."[16]

These are the views and concepts that delineate the background upon which Merezhkovskiy projected his trilogy of historical novels, *Christ and Antichrist (Khristos i Antikhrist)*. The best known and most universally acclaimed of his compositions, *Christ and Antichrist* marks the apogee of his literary endeavor. It not only surpasses the remainder of his belles-lettres in artistic merit, it also occupies a central position among his religio-philosophical works and in his own personal religious search. The trilogy's purpose was to show the clash of Christianity and paganism in the past, to reveal why attempts at reconciliation were failures, and ultimately to provide an arena wherein Merezhkovskiy could thresh out the problem for himself and then present his panacea for it.

In order to reveal his philosophical concept of the conflict between man's ego and God, Merezhkovskiy selected three outstanding periods of history in which he felt this struggle to be most pronounced and most clearly defined: the reign of Julian the Apostate, the Renaissance, and the reign of Peter the Great. In spite of whatever failings he had as a novelist, Merezhkovskiy proved himself capable of presenting an able, even brilliant, picture of the three historic moments with which he was dealing. The fact that the trilogy entailed a period of twelve years from the time of its conception in 1892 until its completion in 1904 testifies that the preparations that Merezhkovskiy made before commencing the writing of this vast enterprise were indeed most elaborate. He traveled throughout the countries that provided the settings of his novels in order to procure firsthand knowledge of them: he visited Greece; he spent a great deal of time in Italy, studying Renaissance art and manuscripts; he lived with the Old Believers of the Volga region. His study bore fruitful results, for it was due to his deep knowledge of the periods, even down to minor details of costume and decoration, that he was able to reproduce the very spirit of each epoch. Although there are masses of archaeological details in his novels, one cannot agree with many of his contemporary critics who considered that their abundance spoiled the work and detracted from its main purpose. It is in just such external appearances that Merezhkovskiy stood out as a historical novelist.

One must concur, however, that he was somewhat overlavish in producing a bewildering mass of secondary personages, many of whom appear once and then are swallowed up into obscurity. Yet, from Merezhkovskiy's point of view and in accordance with the purpose of the trilogy, these secondary characters are necessary. They are there to show how widespread were the ideas and the conflict of Christianity and paganism in those eras. Merezhkovskiy presupposed that all mankind was affected by this question, which was so close to his heart. That conglomerate—the masses, the crowd—was used by him to this end. Throughout the trilogy he emphasized the externals of this duality: in *Julian the Apostate*, for example, the swearing of oaths in the names of Dindymene and Hercules and, in the same breath, in the names of Christ and Moses; the mistaking of statues of the pagan demigods Castor and Pollux for statues of the Christian saints Cosmas and Damian; the rushing from church to the circus; the coming of a Christian woman to the priest of Aphrodite to petition for assistance in a love affair. To cover the broadest field in his effort to reveal the universality of this duality, it was essential for Merezhkovskiy to present as extensive a number of personages as possible, hence the proliferation of minor figures in the novels.

In full accord with his Nietzschean concept of the superman, Merezhkovskiy chose three dynamic personalities as the central figures of the three novels: Julian, Leonardo da Vinci, and Peter the Great. There have been complaints that he completely misrepresented the historical persons with whom he was dealing, ascribing to them qualities that were not theirs, minimizing or neglecting entirely certain aspects of their careers that should have been taken into consideration, and overemphasizing in them the qualities that he wished to find: those that indicated the struggle between their ego and God. Yet one must recall that Merezhkovskiy was not interested in presenting biographies of historical personages, that they are characters in fictional works. Furthermore, it is doubtful that he intended his heroes to appear as ordinary human beings; they are set apart, they are different, they are supermen, albeit they possess certain traits that prevent them from being completely superhuman. Julian, Leonardo, and Peter have in common certain characteristics which Merezhkovskiy emphasized. They are beyond good and evil; within themselves they contain a duality—elements of Christianity and paganism; and they are, in varying degrees, syntheses of these same elements. Furthermore, each, in his own way, searches for the solution to his duality. Perhaps it would be more precise to say that in them Merezhkovskiy approached the problem of the solution of duality in various ways.

It is in this duality that the entire grief of the world rests. Beside it everything else is as nothing:

These are the eternal torments of childbirth. Before them all other torments are nothing. People think that they suffer from poverty; in reality, they suffer only from the thought that perhaps He does not exist. This is the sole grief of the world. Some dare to say: "He does not exist," and some know what strength one must have to say: "He exists."[17]

Man fell away from God in an effort to be like God, to be God; but he could not be, for he was unable to fall all the way, to separate himself from God completely:

And there, along the staircase of birth and death, the souls of all beings ascend and descend, to Him and from Him. They try to leave the Father and cannot. Each soul wants to be God itself, but in vain: it grieves for the Father's bosom; it has no peace on earth; it yearns to return to the Indivisible.[18]

Thus Merezhkovskiy represented the struggle in man of the two elements, of his ego against God. It is significant that Merezhkovskiy stressed the fact that man was unable to separate himself from God completely, for he was firmly convinced at this time that if one could assert one's ego—that is, be a pagan, a Mangod completely—then one could attain freedom and be like God, just as surely as if one were to renounce everything (friends, parents, the world, and oneself) and so merge with God and become one with God. These were paths leading to equal truths and to equal freedoms, although they were direct opposites of one another. One must choose between them, bear the burden of the two truths, but follow one's chosen path to the end. Merezhkovskiy had attempted to do so in his poetry by singing of Bacchic extremes, but he realized that it was impossible, and he presented his proof of this conclusion in the figure of Julian the Apostate, for this is Julian's tragedy.

Less a synthesis than Merezhkovskiy's other heroes, Julian is primarily an example of the author's idea of the duality in man that is occasioned by the equal truths of paganism and Christianity. This is the motivating force in the life of Julian, just as it was in Merezhkovskiy's life. It forces him to seek an end to the contradictions that plague him and to search for a single truth. It is what causes him to select paganism and attempt to renounce Christ. Julian's error is not in his choice, but in his not having the strength to succeed. Merezhkovskiy presented his contentions that Hellenic paganism and Christianity are equal truths, equally holy, and that they lead to equal freedoms in a conversation between Julian and Maximus of Ephesus, who avers:

"If you believe in Him, take the cross, follow Him as He has commanded. Be meek, be virginal, be a silent lamb in the hands of your executioners; flee into the desert; give up to Him your flesh and spirit; suffer; believe. This is one of two paths: great martyr-Galileans will attain the same freedom as Prometheus and Lucifer."

"I will not."

"Then choose the other path: be strong and free; do not pity; do not love; do not forgive; rise up and conquer all; do not believe but know. And the world will be yours, and you will be like the Titan and the Angel of Dawn."[19]

Although Julian attempts to follow the second course, he is unsuccessful, for he is unable to bear the weight of the two truths. What he really desires, subconsciously, is a synthesis of the two, for he is seeking, as Merezhkovskiy was seeking, one truth and one God. A synthesis of the two truths is essential; it is also the greatest deed that man can achieve. Maximus of Ephesus tells Julian: "Unite, if you can, the truth of the Titan with the truth of the Galilean, and you will be greater than all those born of woman on the earth."[20] This is the momentous task that Merezhkovskiy set for himself, the task to which Julian is unequal, just as he is unequal to remaining true to one truth only. While he proclaims the reign of the Olympians, his very rule is tempered by reflections of Christ's teachings: mercy, in the sparing of his enemies; charity, in the setting up of almshouses for the poor; and the avoidance of needless bloodshed, by putting an end to the cruel games of the circus. He cannot even destroy the force of Christ in him by resorting to extremes, such as the massacre of Christian fanatics and the rape of his Christian wife in the presence of an icon of Christ, for he experiences only self-disgust. Throughout his life his combat with Christ is never successful, and inevitably, on his deathbed he renounces his gods, admitting: "How I loved You, Good Shepherd, You alone."[21]

Merezhkovskiy attributed Christ's victory to Julian's inability to destroy all trace of Christianity in himself and also to Julian's being behind his time. Julian loves the past and the Mangod who lived in freedom and who, like Socrates, "died like a god."[22] He realizes too late that such men no longer exist, when he cries: "Where are these godlike old men, stern husbands, proud lads, pure wives in white fluttering garments?"[23] A return to past ages is impracticable, although Julian refuses to believe it. Thus he is doomed to perish.

A parallel figure to Julian is that of Constantius. This is Julian in reverse, a Christian who attempts to destroy the Olympian gods, while supporting Christianity. Yet he, too, is unable to stamp out all traces of the second truth: he believes in auguries; his methods are the cruelties of the pagans—the sports in the arena, murder, and persecution, even of his fellow Christians. There is no Christian humility or mercy in him; moreover, he never doubts his worth before God; and in this he is more pagan than Christian. Like Julian, he perishes from the bifurcation within him; and like Julian, who renounces his gods before his death, Constantius also renounces God before he dies. Finally, like Julian, he is branded Antichrist. The seeming contradiction that arises from the applying of this term to a pagan and also to a Christian, especially since Merezhkovskiy has repeatedly referred to the equal holiness of Hellenism and Christianity, is dispelled by Merezhkovskiy's division of each into two halves, the holy and the evil.

The holiness of Greek paganism lies in the concept of the Mangod, in joy and happiness on earth, in knowledge, in childlike innocence in the presence of the beauty of the human body, and, above all, in beauty itself. "We revere not lifeless stone, copper, or wood, but the spirit, the living spirit of beauty in our idols, which are examples of the purest divine charm."[24] These words, applied by Julian to himself and his fellow believers in the Olympians, apply equally to Merezhkovskiy; he, too, worshiped the "living spirit of beauty" behind the external appearances of Hellenic paganism. B. Griftsov was right when he said that the scene in which Julian worships before the statue of Aphrodite, proclaiming: "Aphrodite! Aphrodite! I will love you forever!"[25] was also the expression of Merezhkovskiy's worshiping of pagan beauty as represented by this goddess.[26]

What Julian cannot comprehend, and what Merezhkovskiy had only recently come to understand, is the evil side of Hellenism. This is that the pagan gods are the opposite to what Julian hopes to find in them. Instead of being merciful and benevolent, they are cruel and bloodthirsty, enjoying the torments of their victims. The statement, "Without blood there is no merriment. The smell of Rome is the smell of blood,"[27] indicates that Merezhkovskiy was no longer suffering from the delusion that the pagans' absolute freedom and joy of life are without fault. His description of the remnants of the epicureans—sated with feasting and sexual excesses, old and ailing before their time, and seeking cures at the spa of Baiae—leaves no doubt that he had ceased to accept all of the pagan excesses:

> Neither the fresh salt water of the sea's waves nor the seething sulphurous streams of the springs of Baiae offered any healing to the flaccid, chill bodies of these young people, bald, toothless at twenty, aged by the debauchery of their forefathers, surfeited with literature, wisdom, women, ancient feats, and new vices, witty and impotent, in whose veins was the insipid blood of belated generations.[28]

Nor does paganism put an end to human vices and crimes, for there is the same deception, thievery, murder, and persecution on the part of the worshipers of the Olympians, after Julian has reestablished the preeminence of the gods, as there was formerly among the Christians.

Still, Merezhkovskiy made it clear that this unholy aspect of paganism is no worse, indeed is not as bad, as the Christianity current at the time. This historic Christianity is symbolized in the image of Christ fashioned in mosaic in the Arian church: "a threatening dark, emaciated face in a golden aureole and a diadem like the diadem of a Byzantine emperor, almost senile, with a long thin nose and austerely compressed lips."[29] This conception of Christ is reflected in the very life of the Christians. Love, mercy, and charity are not practiced by them; in their places are intolerance, cruelty, and persecution, directed not only against the heathens but also against those who interpret Christianity differently. Every extreme is permitted in God's name and to the glory of God: murder, even fratricide, and, among certain sects, rape and suicide. One of the most reprehensible expressions of Christianity, in Merezhkovskiy's estimation, is the attitude towards the human body. It leads to filth, the repulsiveness of which Merezhkovskiy made strongly felt by comparing a hermit who refuses to wash, since it means removing his garments and seeing his body, to the shining beauty and innocence of the statue of Aphrodite; it also induces self-chastisement in an effort to mortify the unclean flesh, for the sight of the body is "a temptation for the Christian."[30] One cannot but sympathize with Merezhkovskiy's views when, in the words of the poet Publius, he contrasts the Christian attitude to the former Hellenic outlook:

"Oh, how modest and ugly we are now! We fear our gloomy and pitiful nudity; we hide it because we feel unclean. But in the past! All this once was so, you know, Julian! Spartan girls went out into the palaestra naked, proud, before the entire nation. And no one was afraid of temptation. The pure looked upon the pure. They were like children, like gods."[31]

It is obvious that the Christianity that is delineated throughout the novel is in every respect contrary to Christ's teachings. Hence, it is no less antichristian than the most extreme paganism, and far more so than the Hellenism to which Merezhkovskiy himself was attracted. Furthermore, it readily becomes apparent that he considered much of what is deemed pagan to be part of true Christianity and, if one is to make use of the evidence in *Julian the Apostate*, that historic Christianity falls within the realm of Antichrist. Merezhkovskiy did not regard this to be a fault inherent in Christianity itself, but the result of man's darkening the spirit of Christ's teachings, to which the Hellenic sages came close:

"Did not the sages of Hellas come close to what He said? Those who torment their flesh and their soul in the wilderness are far from the gentle Son of Mary. He loved children and freedom and the gaiety of feasts and white lilies. He loved life, Julian. Only we have left Him; we have become confused and clouded in our spirit."[32]

Merezhkovskiy expressed this opinion through the words of Arsinoë, a seeker after truth. Like Julian, Arsinoë searches for freedom and for an escape from the contradiction of Christianity and paganism. Her first attempt is a delving into Hellenic paganism, and Merezhkovskiy at first presents her as a symbol of all that is good in pagan Greece. She is the incarnation of grace and beauty, of joy and happiness on earth, of childlike innocence in the presence of the human body. She tells her Christian sister, Myrrha: "One must be light, completely naked, Myrrha—just as I am now—and deep, deep in the sky, and feel that this is forever, that there will be nothing more, there cannot be, than the sky and the sun around the light, naked body!"[33] Arsinoë also reflects Merezhkovskiy's conviction that knowledge and art are properties of Greek paganism, for she is keenly interested in physics and mathematics and is a competent sculptress. Moreover, like Julian, she is eager for power, for the assertion of her ego, for the return of the Mangod to earth. To this end she is willing to ally herself to Julian and his cause.

Merezhkovskiy attributed his own conversion and his thirst for Christ to the death of his mother. A parallel incident, the death of her sister, alters Arsinoë's outlook. She comes to realize that paganism cannot present complete freedom, though it has much to offer, and it is she who reveals to Julian that the Olympian gods are dead and that pagan freedom and art are no more. As in Merezhkovskiy, so in Arsinoë the change is not complete. There is no miraculous, sudden shift of belief from one extreme to another. Arsinoë's words "I will and shall believe!"[34] are indicative of Merezhkovskiy's early delvings into the mystery of Christianity. He and Arsinoë do not believe fully, but they desire to believe and are firmly convinced that they will believe in Christ. Therefore, Merezhkovskiy has Arsinoë search for absolute freedom in Christianity among the anchorites in the desert. This is historic Christianity; in order to attain freedom in it Arsinoë must tame her intelligence, which is considered a property of the devil, and must master herself. The torment, which she must inflict upon herself, cannot induce her to believe; it even deprives her of the ability to love: "I wished to love myself and others, as He commanded. But I cannot: I hate both myself and others."[35] Freedom is not to be found here, just as it is nonexistent in paganism. But Arsinoë learns through her experience with the anchorites that one cannot retire from the world, that she, and man in general, must live in the world, "to live and die what God has made me."[36] This is one of Merezhkovskiy's most trenchant statements against the historic Christianity that demanded a renunciation of the world, for man was created to live in the world and therefore cannot renounce it. To this he added the argument that Christ loved life and the things of life. Faith (Christ) and life (paganism) are inseparable. One without the other is incomplete.

This is the synthesis that Merezhkovskiy hoped to establish between paganism and Christianity. In *Julian the Apostate*, however, a synthesis does not occur; there are only hints of it. Near the beginning of the novel it is present in an early representation of Christ the Good Shepherd, significantly hidden away in a dark corner of the Arian church where Julian worshiped as a child:

Small, tender nereids, panthers, and merry tritons were sculpted there; and beside them Moses, Jonah and the whale, Orpheus calming beasts of prey with his lyre, olive branches, a dove, and fish—naïve symbols of a childlike faith; in the midst of them is the Good Shepherd carrying a sheep on His shoulders, a lost sheep which was found again, the soul of a sinner. He was joyful and simple, this barefoot youth, with a beardless, humble, and meek face, like the faces of poor settlers; His smile was one of quiet merriment.[37]

Later it is couched in the words of the dying Myrrha when she tells Arsinoë that all—sinners and righteous alike—will be saved by Christ's love, that everything, even Bacchic singing, is holy.[38] Then it is to be seen in the sculpture by Arsinoë of an Olympian god, in which she combines the inexorability and awesomeness of Mithra-Dionysos with the mercy and meekness of Christ.[39] Lastly, it is apparent in the symbolic merging of a hymn to Pan and the chanting by monks of a hymn to God.[40]

Merezhkovskiy did not present the synthesis as having taken place, for *Julian the Apostate* is merely the first act in the drama of humanity. The principal actors have been introduced: the supermen, the seekers, the pagans, and the Christians. The action has been set in motion. As the curtain falls on the triumph of historic Christianity, the author prepares the way for the second act, *Leonardo da Vinci*, by prophesying that the conflict will begin anew when the Olympians have been resurrected in the Renaissance.

The resurrection of the Olympian deities is symbolized in the discovery of the statue of Venus and its removal from the tomblike vault in which it has been preserved through the centuries.

> The goddess rose slowly.
> With the same bright smile as in the past, when she rose from the foam of the sea's waves, she emerged from the darkness of the earth, from her millennial grave.
> "Glory to thee, golden-limbed mother, Aphrodite,
> Joy of gods and men!"
> Merula greeted her.
> All the stars grew dim, except the star of Venus, which sparkled like a diamond in the radiance of the dawn. And the head of the goddess rose above the edge of the grave to meet it.[41]

With the resurrection of the gods there came a resurrection of knowledge, for Merezhkovskiy persisted in regarding knowledge as a pagan attribute. The Middle Ages, in which the Church was the sole holiness—a period in which ignorance, superstition, and, in general, the overlooking of the things of this world prevailed—was brought to an end by the Renaissance, although the Church struggled to maintain its preeminence. Merezhkovskiy attributed the darkness of the Middle Ages to the Church, to historic Christianity. He was convinced that the Church had hindered the growth of knowledge by condemning the study of natural sciences, since it considered such a study to be a delving into the "black arts"; by retarding medicine, in particular anatomy, because of a sense of shame before the naked body; and in fostering a belief in demons, witchcraft, sorcery, and a battery of necromancers and similar "servants of the devil." Yet the Church itself harbored such a belief in black magic that it considered anyone who professed disbelief to be in league with the devil; "that is why it is said: to be a sorcerer is heresy, but not to believe in sorcery is doubly heretical."[42]

Merezhkovskiy presented a magnificent symbolic picture of the end of the Middle Ages in the section of the novel entitled "Witches' Sabbath." The early part of the scene, which takes place in darkness illuminated only by occasional fires, sums up the ignorant and superstitious mediaeval interpretation, hence that of the Church, of the things of the flesh. It is a scene of corruption, of obscenity, of unnatural sexual relations between foul creatures. But when the light once more shines forth, when the sun of Dionysos rises into the heavens after the Goat of the Night is transformed into the handsome god, the ugly creatures of mediaeval imagination become the delightful denizens of antiquity, maenads and satyrs, taking part in a Bacchic celebration. The things of the flesh are revealed again as Merezhkovskiy considered them to be: innocent and holy. Thus Merezhkovskiy established once more the existence of the two extremes and proceeded to show the resultant clash.

However, Merezhkovskiy had progressed in his thinking. While he continued to regard Christianity and paganism as holy, each in its own way, he now rejected his earlier contention that a solution might be found in either extreme. Only the synthesis of the two would resolve the world's dilemma. The one-sided pagan and the one-sided historic Christian were equally at fault.

Fra Benedetto, Savonarola, and Fra Giorgio da Casale continue into the Renaissance the historic Christianity of the Middle Ages. In Fra Benedetto, the artist-monk, is to be seen the hindering of the development of art by the Church. Only religious themes are acceptable, and even then the ever-present fear of temptation leads to a deliberate neglect of the human body. Fra Benedetto's lack of knowledge of art is evident in the advice that he gives to his pupils:

In explaining his sole rule of anatomy, that one must consider the length of the male body to be that of eight and two-thirds faces, Fra Benedetto added with the same scornful expression, as though speaking about dragon's blood, "as for the female body, it is better to leave it aside, for it has nothing proportionate in it."[43]

Fra Benedetto is harmless compared with Savonarola, who is intent on destroying everything that he himself considers heretical. The result is a senseless destruction of priceless works of art and manuscripts, the negation of knowledge, and the horrors of the Inquisition. It is but a small step to Fra Giorgio, the chief inquisitor, who is entrusted with the tortures and crimes perpetrated in the name of God, supposedly out of a sense of love and mercy for the victims. "But," queried Merezhkovskiy through his character Giovanni, "who was more terrible, who more insane—the judges or the accused?"[44]

No less culpable of bigotry are those who support only pagan antiquity, who regard it alone to be the epitome of perfection, and who deny anything that does not proceed from it. Such is Merula, the neopagan, who worships classical sculpture and literature to such a degree that he considers Leonardo da Vinci to be lacking in learning because the latter cannot read Latin or Greek. Merula is convinced that the ancients achieved everything that could or would be achieved on the earth and that one can only emulate them. Leonardo's experiments in physics and the natural sciences are of no consequence to Merula, who states: "To fit intricate little wheels into machines, to look at birds flying in the sky, grasses growing in a field—this is not science, but an amusement, a game for children!"[45]

A second negative attitude to be found in the neopagan is revealed in Marc' Antonio della Torre. Marc' Antonio is the advocate of reason and is fanatically opposed to the ignorance and superstition of the Church. His studies, instead of revealing to him the ultimate mystery, as Merezhkovskiy believed that they should, cause him confusion and almost fear before this knowledge. While Merezhkovskiy praised him for being a priest of science and pitied him for being its victim because of his antichristian approach, the author ascribed the coming of academicism with its rejection of miracles, faith, and mysteries to such a sole belief in reason. Merezhkovskiy considered this result to be as vile as its opposite, the Inquisition of the Church.

On the whole, these supporters of only one of the two extremes are rare in the vast panorama of the Renaissance as Merezhkovskiy has described it. As in his previous novel, he depicted the almost universal mixture of Christianity and paganism in everyone—from the members of the masses, through the aristocracy of the day, to the most exalted members of the hierarchy of the Church, even to the Borgia pope Alexander VI, who, while pious enough, indulged in depraved pastimes, substituted portraits of his mistress for those of the Madonna, and had a jewel bearing an image of Venus embedded in the cross, so that during Mass he could kiss both the cross and the naked goddess.

Amid the neopagans, historic Christians, and the multitude who represent the imperfect mixing of the two extremes, stands the imposing figure of Leonardo da Vinci. Merezhkovskiy would have him seen as the long-awaited synthesis. Yet although he employed his favorite device, sudden and often dramatic contrast, Leonardo appears not as an ideal synthesis, but as a man of many facets, some of which may be grouped under the heading of pagan and the rest under that of Christian attributes. Moreover, Merezhkovskiy's psychological study of Leonardo is based on the presentation of externals—to be more precise, a juxtaposition of them. Leonardo is compared to Michelangelo, Raphael, Machiavelli, and a host of other characters, just as Julian had had his counterpart in Constantius and Peter would have his in Alexis. There is a contrasting even of Leonardo's own artistic creations: the painting of the Last Supper, as opposed to the statue of Sforza; the artist's depicting the horrors of war, while at the same time designing machines of war. Indeed, Leonardo emerges as a complex individual. However, he appears to be a mass of contradictions, rather than a synthesis of them, as Merezhkovskiy desired. He is proud, yet humble; merciful and kind, while also cruel. He watches impassively the destruction not only of the works of classical art and knowledge, but also of his own compositions. At the same time he is capable of deep emotion in the presence of beauty and also in the presence of great ugliness.

Even in the physical description of Leonardo, Merezhkovskiy stressed an ambivalence. It is, however, a characteristic that later was to become an important factor in his religious philosophy. This is the merging of the male and female in one individual. While he did not elaborate on it in this instance, since he had not yet definitively formulated the concept, Merezhkovskiy pointed out that in some respects Leonardo contained elements of both sexes: while he possessed a mighty physique, he had a high-pitched voice; although his hands were so strong that he could bend iron, in appearance they were like a woman's hands, soft and fine, with long fingers.[46]

Yet none of this detracts from the superhuman aspect of Leonardo, for Merezhkovskiy was still under the influence of Nietzsche's superman. Leonardo is beyond good and evil: he is willing to serve any master, be he Pope, duke, or king, his own people or their enemy, as he does when he draws a plan of his native city, Florence, while he is in the service of those who are waging war against it. In Merezhkovskiy's estimation, if not in that of others, such an act does not brand Leonardo a traitor; on the contrary, he feels that it is proof that the artist is too great a man to be concerned or to comply with such trifles as the concept of good and evil. His actions cannot be judged by the standards of ordinary mortals. Yet Merezhkovskiy weakened his supposition by having Leonardo bewail the effect of his activities and ideas on his faithful servant, Zoroastro, who is physically crippled while attempting to fly in Leonardo's flying machine; on his pupil, Cesare da Sesto, who is spiritually crippled by his association with Leonardo; and finally on Giovanni Beltraffio, who is torn between Christianity and paganism. Leonardo blames himself for these tragedies when, in the scene in which he soothes Zoroastro after his mishap, he parodies the words of the Gospel: "Because of me, he too because of me! I tempted one of the least among them; I bewitched him, as I did Giovanni!"[47]

Merezhkovskiy introduced this episode to detract purposely from the figure of Leonardo the superman. It was not Merezhkovskiy's intention to have Leonardo appear as a superman pure and simple, for such a person would be wholly pagan, and Merezhkovskiy wanted his reader to see in Leonardo an example of the uniting of both paganism and Christianity. This is why at one moment he portrayed his hero as a superman, and at the next had him doubt the righteousness of his actions and regret the effect that he has had on the little people of the world. By means of such contrast Merezhkovskiy hoped to reveal Leonardo as a synthesis.

Above all, Merezhkovskiy relied on the opinions of the other characters in his novel to prove that Leonardo is this synthesis. By having the artist rejected by both Christians and pagans alike, he aspired to show that he is in reality a union of the two extremes. The pagans disown him because he refuses to accept the creation of the ancients as perfect, for to him only nature can be the source of beauty and perfection. The Christians reject him because he reveals himself too much a pagan and a practitioner of the black arts, while at the same time they brand him a heretic for his lack of belief in necromancy and witches.

Perhaps it is because Merezhkovskiy has failed to reveal Leonardo as a synthesis, hence failed as a thinker, that he gained in stature as an artist, for his portrait of Leonardo is far less schematic and is therefore more convincing than are his portrayals of the other major figures in the trilogy. He was, however, more successful in presenting his ideals when dealing with Leonardo's search for the ultimate truth. For da Vinci–Merezhkovskiy everything in nature reveals God. This is the truth that lies at the bottom of the abyss of nature, the truth that Marc' Antonio della Torre cannot admit, because it is contrary to reason. Leonardo's belief leads to God, for he is able to accept this truth. Merezhkovskiy was convinced that knowledge points the way to God. Instead of detracting from faith and love, knowledge must increase them. One must know in order to love; Merezhkovskiy had Leonardo express it thus:

> "To study the phenomena of nature is a task pleasing to the Lord. It is just the same as praying. By coming to comprehend the natural laws, we praise the first Inventor, the Artist of the universe, and we learn to love Him, for great love for God springs from great knowledge. He who knows little, loves little. If you love the Creator for the transitory favors that you expect from Him and not for His eternal mercy and strength, you are like a dog that wags its tail and licks its master's hand in the hope of a tidbit. Think how much more strongly the dog would love its master if it understood his soul and mind. Remember, my children: love is the daughter of knowledge; love is the more ardent, the more exact is knowledge. And in the Evangels it is said: be as wise as the serpent and as simple as the dove. . . . Together, one without the other is impossible; complete knowledge and complete love are one and the same thing."[48]

Merezhkovskiy's attitude toward knowledge had changed since he first declared it to be a pagan attribute. Now he realized that the neopagan attitude toward knowledge was as negative as that adopted by the Church. Merezhkovskiy now conceived knowledge to be a middle road between the two, parallel to faith, augmenting and emphasizing it, and leading to a deeper cognizance of God.

Merezhkovskiy admitted that such a path was not an easy one to follow. To this end he introduced the character of Giovanni

Beltraffio, the real victim not only of the clash between Christianity and paganism, but also of the synthesis of the two. Throughout the novel, Merezhkovskiy reveals the increasing anguish that assails Leonardo's young pupil. Raised as a true son of the Church, Giovanni is attracted to everything considered antichristian—to knowledge and to beauty—which is symbolized for him in the person of the "White She-Devil," the marble statue of Venus. Merezhkovskiy was at his best when portraying the vacillations of the young man, for this personage is undoubtedly a reflection of Merezhkovskiy's own period of inner struggle. Unlike Merezhkovskiy, Giovanni, who comes to realize the need for a synthesis, cannot accept such a solution, so he perishes.

It is Monna Cassandra, whose activities in *Leonardo da Vinci* follow the same course as those of Arsinoë in the previous novel, who acts as the author's spokesman on the synthesis. Having passed through paganism and then historic Christianity, she comprehends that one extreme is not enough, that Christianity and paganism must merge: "The gods will be resurrected only when the Bright Ones unite with the Dark, the heaven above with the heaven below, and when that which was two will be One."[49] Through Cassandra, Merezhkovskiy expounded his theory of not only linking but uniting Dionysos and Christ. Dionysos, he claimed, intoxicated the world with his blood and wine, just as Christ did. Merezhkovskiy presumably believed that by noting such chance similarities between two such diverse religions, he was adding authority to his arguments in favor of a union of Christianity and paganism, which was crystallized into the symbol of Dionysos-Christ in the words of Monna Cassandra to Giovanni, when she invites him to drink to the last Reconciler: " 'Do not be afraid,' she said, 'there is no forbidden witchcraft here. This wine is pure and holy: it is from vines growing on the hills of Nazareth. It is the purest blood of Dionysos the Galilean.' "[50]

In the image of Dionysos-Christ, Merezhkovskiy was convinced that the heaven above and the heaven below, Christianity and paganism, would be reconciled. The reconciliation would come about in the future, for Merezhkovskiy was certain that it had not occurred in the past, at least not consciously. It is Cassandra who sheds light on the imperfect synthesis that is Leonardo. He represents an unconscious synthesis, hence his never-ending search for the ultimate truth: "He only strives and does not attain, only seeks and does not find, only knows but does not acknowledge. He is a forerunner of him

who will follow and who is greater than he."[51] Leonardo appeared
too early to effect Merezhkovskiy's much-desired synthesis, in contrast
to Julian's having come too late to reestablish the rule of the Olympians. Merezhkovskiy attempted to make his reader believe, often
falsely, that just as Julian's works came to nothing, so Leonardo's
creations suffered the same fate, simply because he was ahead of his
time.

Merezhkovskiy developed further the concept of the future conscious synthesis in the concluding work of the trilogy, *Antichrist:
Peter and Alexis (Antikhrist: Petr i Aleksey)*. Once again he had
selected a period in which he felt that the conflict between Christianity and paganism was most clearly revealed—in the reign of Peter
the Great, the era of the Russian Renaissance and of the struggle between "old" and "new" Russia.

Although it is the most important of the three novels, *Peter and
Alexis* is not a worthy successor to its predecessors. It is considerably
weaker than they, for it is far more confused and mixed up, as if it
were the author himself, instead of his heroes, who was stumbling
blindly in the dark, seeking salvation, and who was wavering uncer-
tainly between the choices open to him. Merezhkovskiy took pains
to link *Peter and Alexis* to *Julian the Apostate* and *Leonardo da
Vinci* by rather obvious means: by referring to Leonardo and Julian
in the course of the third novel and, in particular, by introducing
into it the symbol of paganism, the statue of Venus—the very statue
that Julian had worshiped in the temple near Macellum and that
Giovanni Beltraffio had looked upon with fear as it was raised from
its tomb near Florence. Yet *Peter and Alexis* barely fits into the
framework of the trilogy. While Merezhkovskiy's ideas had altered
during the course of the first two novels, his basic motif had remained easily visible; but in the third, the all-important theme becomes so entangled in a web of other themes that it is often difficult
to follow.

The entire novel resolves into a variety of conflicts which cloud
the issue of the primary struggle of humanity, as Merezhkovskiy saw
it, that of Christ versus Antichrist. Whereas earlier he had kept this
conflict in the foreground in his concept of the Olympians and the
Church, here it is deeply hidden in the guise of many things: Russia
and Europe, Peter and Alexis, old Muscovite Russia and the new St.
Petersburg Russia, the schismatics and the revised Orthodoxy—all of
which oppose one another and struggle with one another throughout

the novel. Yet in all of them Merezhkovskiy saw a religious implication, which is the mainspring of their action and interaction.

Such is the case with the major conflict in the novel, that of Peter the Great and his son, Alexis. In this instance, Merezhkovskiy sided with neither of them, or he took sides with both of them, as the case may be. As a result, he achieved his purposes of ascribing elements of right and wrong to both of them and of winning sympathy equally for the father, who is responsible for the death of his son, and for the son, who is overcome by his father.

It is Merezhkovskiy's contention that Peter and Alexis are like the obverse and reverse of a coin. They are exceedingly different, yet they are part of one another, a complement to each other. Merezhkovskiy pointed out the external, superficial likeness by remarking from time to time on the brief moments when the son resembles the father, usually when Alexis is in the throes of a bout of drunken, violent anger. The most significant mention of the likeness of tsar and tsarevich appears toward the beginning of the novel, in the diary of Fräulein Arnheim, for here there is an indication of an inner resemblance, as well as a forewarning of the final outcome of the clash between father and son.

> It is strange! When I looked at them both in the mirror today, as though in some magic "mirror of divination," it seemed to me that in these two very different faces there was one trait of resemblance—the shadow of some presaged sadness, as if both of them are sacrifices and great suffering is in store for both.[52]

This element of sacrifice and suffering in the relationship between Peter and Alexis is one that Merezhkovskiy developed more fully later in the novel.

Otherwise, father and son are infinitely different. Peter is the closest approximation to a complete superman of the three heroes of the trilogy. He is a man of might and power; yet, like Leonardo da Vinci, he is subject to his own weaknesses and bifurcation, which at times reduce him to a man of flesh and blood. He is a mixture of extreme cruelty and of rare kindness; of intrepid bravery in the face of great dangers, such as the St. Petersburg flood, and of fear of negligible creatures, such as spiders and snakes. Merezhkovskiy introduced such minor characteristics of Peter's mentality in order to add to his presentation of Peter's duality, for he considered Peter to be dual in his very essence: "At times it seems that in him the contradictions of the two elements dear to him—fire and water—have merged into one strange, wonderful creature; I do not know whether it is good or evil, divine or satanic, but it is superhuman."[53] Merezhkovskiy constantly holds this enigma before the reader, partly by alternating the presentation of Peter's good and evil deeds, but mainly by reporting the opinions of others as to whether Peter is god or devil. To the Old Believers, he is most assuredly the latter, for they consider him to be, if not Antichrist himself, then at the very least the forerunner of the Beast. To others who admire his deeds, Peter appears to be a pagan god, a Titan or Mars. To all, he seems inhuman or superhuman. It is thus that Merezhkovskiy regarded him, for he admired Peter's efforts to forge a new Russia and to create a new race of men.

Peter tries to accomplish these tasks by uniting East and West, Russia and Europe, through Russia's adoption and imitation of what he understands to be great in Europe. What Peter reveres in the West is its pagan aspect: its art, education, and military techniques. These he seeks to impose on Russia: new buildings and gardens are based on European designs (his Summer Garden in St. Petersburg is a copy of that of Versailles); and he sends Russians abroad to study European methods. While Merezhkovskiy admired Peter for his valiant attempt to make his country great, he certainly did not approve of Peter's one-sided assimiliation of Europe, and he was unhappy with the result. Inspired by his own religious convictions, Merezhkovskiy thought

> that the Europe that Peter introduced into Russia—arithmetic, navigation, fortification—is by no means all of Europe and is not even the main thing in it; that the real Europe has a higher truth, which the tsar does not know. And without this truth, only with all the sciences, instead of the old Muscovite barbarism there will be just a new Petersburg flunkyism.[54]

In short, Peter has ignored the spiritual significance of Europe.

It is on a religious plane that Peter's duality is most clearly, yet enigmatically, revealed. Ostensibly Peter is a member of the Orthodox Church, the revised Orthodoxy which he has subordinated to himself, that is to the state. However, his attitude toward the Church is one of mockery: his setting up of the "Most Drunken Conclave," with its prince-pope, its pagan symbols of Bacchus and Venus, and its drunken, debauched meetings, indicates that Peter certainly is not a Christian. Moreover, he seemingly attempts to destroy the faith of

Christians in their beliefs, as in the episode where he proves a miraculous weeping icon to be a fraud. His setting up of the statue of Venus in St. Petersburg and the forcing of his entourage to bow before it and to revere it appear, superficially, to represent the reestablishment of the pagan deities on earth. Yet Merezhkovskiy has Peter declare that he cannot comprehend how the Greeks, who knew so much, could call their soulless idols gods. While his fellow Russians might give credence to the existence of such gods and such other fantastic creatures as mermaids and satyrs, Peter himself no more believes in their existence than he believes in the possibility of miracles.

Peter is an advocate of science. Often his actions in this sphere take on a horrifying aspect, as when he orders the corpses of stillborn infants to be pickled for future study. But Peter is like Leonardo, for in the laws of nature and in science he sees God.

Peter's God is not Christ, nor is He a resident of Olympus. His God is pagan only insofar as the God of the Old Testament, Jehovah, is pagan; for this is Peter's God. He is a God of wrath and of revenge; there is none of Christ's humility or mercy in Him, just as there is none in Peter. When Peter is praying before his favorite icon, it is not Christ he sees, but Jehovah; and in his prayers he bypasses Christ in order to address himself directly to the Father.[55] Paganism now takes on the significance of any religion that is pre-Christian.

Alexis is in almost every way the antithesis of Peter, from his physical appearance to his religious convictions. He is weak, vacillating, and frightened—a contemplator rather than a man of action. Even though he knows that he should abandon his slothfulness and assist his supporters against his father, he cannot; his one desire is to be permitted to retire from the world and become a monk. Like his father, Alexis suffers from a bifurcation in his very essence. He is a Christian, in the sense of Merezhkovskiy's historic Christianity, and an upholder of the old Russia, the Russia prior to Peter's reforms; and as such, he is regarded by the schismatics to be the savior of both Russia and Christianity.[56] Yet he is also attracted to Europe and to paganism. Merezhkovskiy again makes use of a woman as a symbol for the latter, in this instance Evfrosin'ya, Alexis's mistress. The reference to her as Venus, Aphrodite, and other creatures of Greek mythology are but a preparation for the scene that climaxes and crystallizes Alexis's worship of paganism and leaves no doubt that in Evfrosin'ya Alexis reveres not the woman herself, but what she symbolizes—Greek paganism.

In the quadrangle of the doors, which opened onto the blue sea, her body appeared, as though it emerged, from the sparkling blue of the sea, golden-white, like the foam of the waves. In one hand she held a piece of fruit; the other she lowered, covering her nakedness with a chaste gesture, like the Foam-born. And behind her played and seethed the blue sea, like a goblet of ambrosia; and its noise was like the eternal laughter of the gods.

It was the same serf girl Afros'ka, who one spring evening in the Vyazemskiys' house on Malaya Okhta, bent low and with skirt tucked up, was washing the floor with a mop. This was the wench Afros'ka and the goddess Aphrodite in one.

"Venus, Venus, the White She-Demon!" the tsarevich thought in superstitious terror, ready to spring up and flee. But from the sinful yet innocent body, as from an opened flower, there was wafted towards him a familiar, entrancing, and frightening scent; and without knowing what he was doing, he bowed still lower before her, kissed her feet, looked into her eyes, and whispered like a supplicant:

"My Sovereign! My Sovereign!"

And the wan flame of the icon lamp flickered before the holy and mournful image.[57]

In this episode Merezhkovskiy established the incomplete merging of flesh and spirit, of Christianity and paganism in Alexis.

Alexis's love of Russia is based on the religious element in it. Like Merezhkovskiy, he recognizes the barbarity and coarseness of the Russian people; but he proclaims Russia a God-bearing nation, and he supports the messianic mission of his people. He explains this to his wife's German companion:

"You are wise, strong, honorable, famous. You have everything. But Christ is missing. And what need is He to you? You save yourselves. But we are stupid, poor, naked, drunken, stinking, worse than barbarians, worse than cattle, and we always perish. But Christ our Father is with us and will be for ever and ever. We will be saved through Him, our Light."[58]

Again like Merezhkovskiy, Alexis ultimately arrives at the conviction that Europe, which he comes to love as much as his native Russia, is also holy; and he begins to doubt the truth of his own words.

The tsarevich recalled that from childhood it had been repeated to him over and over that in the whole world only Russia was a holy land, and all other nations were unclean. He recalled, too, what he himself had once said to Fräulein Arnheim at the dovecote in Rozhdestveno: "Christ is only with us." Did he really mean that? he thought now. What if Christ is also with them and not only with Russia, and all Europe is also a holy land? The earth there is completely covered with the blood of martyrs. Can it really be an unclean land?[59]

Alexis echoes Merezhkovskiy in concluding that Peter the Great may have been right in trying to unite Europe and Russia, but that he had failed to see all or even the best of Europe. Thus, like Merezhkovskiy, both Peter and Alexis are the meeting places of extremes, a thoroughly Russian trait, according to Merezhkovskiy: "To unite such extremes is a special Russian talent."[60]

A mixture of extremes within themselves, Peter and Alexis are the antitheses of one another. Hence, their inevitable struggle and their ultimate tragedy. On a human level, it would be more understandable if father and son hated one another; but Merezhkovskiy carefully stresses the love that each bears for the other, a love that cannot prevent the death of one of them, but that makes the victory of one over the other more poignant and tragic. Merezhkovskiy was convinced that there could be no compromise: "It was as if each had his own truth, and these two truths were forever opposed, forever irreconcilable. One had to destroy the other. But, no matter who was victorious, the victor would be guilty and the vanquished right."[61] The truths are Peter's paganism and Alexis's Christianity. In presenting the essence of their clash in this manner, Merezhkovskiy implied that neither was wholly right or wholly wrong. While the contest, in a historical appraisal at least, was a political one—in his attempt to create a new Russia, Peter had to destroy Alexis's support of the old, the Muscovite, Russia—Merezhkovskiy emphasized its religious aspect. For him, Peter's sacrificing Alexis for the good of the state was like God's sacrificing Christ for the salvation of the world. Even Peter, a worshiper of Jehovah, realizes the enormity of what he must do:

God so loved the world that for its sake He did not spare His Son, His Only Son; and the Father's anger is appeased by the eternally shed Blood of the Lamb, the Blood of the Son.

At this point he felt a very near, very necessary mystery, but one so terrible that he dared not think of it. His thought failed, as in madness.

Did God want him to punish his son or not? Would he be forgiven, or would he be punished for this blood? And what if the punishment were to fall not only on him but on his children, grandchildren, and great-grandchildren—on all Russia?

He fell face down on the floor, and for a long time he lay thus, prostrate and motionless as a corpse.

At last he again raised his eyes to the icon, but now, with a desperate frantic prayer, he passed by the Son and addressed the Father:

"May this blood fall on me, on me alone! Punish me, o God; but have mercy on Russia!"[62]

Peter feels justified in his decision and is willing to accept his guilt. Merezhkovskiy also supported this justification with the claim that "the son will redeem him before the Eternal Judgment and explain to him what he could not comprehend here: the meaning of Son and Father."[63] Peter has chosen God the Father and has excluded Christ, His Son. Alexis has followed Christ to the exclusion of God the Father. Neither truth alone is satisfactory.

Once again it is for the seeker after truth to discover and comment on Merezhkovskiy's synthesis. Never before has the seeker assumed such importance as in the final novel of the trilogy, for the multiplicity of themes and conflicts bedims the issue of Merezhkovskiy's main religious thesis. If it were not for Tikhon, it is likely that the question of the search for faith would be lost altogether. Yet this aspect of Tikhon's presence in the novel is of minor consequence in comparison to his peerless discovery. Not only does he recognize the need for a synthesis, as do the seekers in the preceding novels; he actually reveals the form it will take.

Unlike Arsinoë and Cassandra, Tikhon is at first a Christian. He has been brought up in the old faith, for which his father had died at the hands of Peter. Then, while under the guardianship of one Pakhomich, the boy becomes impressed with the teaching of Grigoriy of Talitsa, one of the first to brand Peter as Antichrist, and Korniliy, a preacher of self-immolation and of the Coming of the End, a presentiment that Tikhon shares with them. These are Tikhon's contacts with the East. Soon, however, he is to come into contact with the West; like the rest of the Russian youths, on the tsar's orders he is forced to attend school in order to study foreign sciences. For the first time he faces the problem of East and West, faith and science, and he is confused by it. On the one side there stands Pakhomich, the representative of old Russia, who denounces science as being contrary to God and refuses to believe that the earth moves around the sun; on the other, there are the writings of Spinoza, the advocate of reason. In the middle is Tikhon's teacher, the German pastor Glück, who attempts to reconcile God and science, a task that is difficult even for him. The dilemma that besets Tikhon is temporarily solved for him after he overhears a discussion on the similarities between Newton's *Commentaries* and those of the schismatics on the Apocalypse. Here, Merezhkovskiy believed, the extreme West and the extreme East met:

> But this is what is most curious: at the very time when Sir Isaac Newton was composing his Commentaries at the other end of the world, here in our country, in Muscovy, wild fanatics, who are called schismatics, also composed their commentaries on the Apocalypse and came almost to the same conclusions as Newton. Expecting the end of the world from day to day, some lie in coffins and perform funeral services for themselves, and some burn themselves to death. For this they are hounded and persecuted; but I would speak about these unfortunates in the words of the philosopher Leibnitz: "I do not like tragic events, and I would wish that all could live well in the world; as for the delusions of those who calmly await the end of the world, it seems to me that they are completely innocent." This is, as I say, what is most curious: in these apocalyptical ravings the extreme West meets with the extreme East, and the greatest enlightenment with the greatest ignorance, so that very likely it could really inspire the thought that the end of the world is at hand and that we will all soon go to the devil![64]

This convinces Tikhon that only one of two alternatives is open to him. He must choose either knowledge without faith or faith without knowledge; he must turn either to the West or to the East. He selects the latter and joins the schismatics; though he does not believe in all their concepts, he at least shares with them the presentiment of the end. Thus he turns his back on the world, hoping to find the answer to his problem in faith alone.

However, Tikhon is soon to reach Merezhkovskiy's conclusion that one cannot renounce the world, for Merezhkovskiy endowed Tikhon with the same love of life as he himself possessed. Least of all can Tikhon find the right path among the Old Believers, who are unable themselves to agree on what course they should follow and what they should believe. Tikhon is disgusted when dissension over minor points of dogma leads their priests to anger and to blows: "It seemed to him that these were not men quarreling about God, but beasts fighting; and that the silence of his beautiful mother wilderness was forever profaned by these blasphemous arguments."[65] Nor does Tikhon condone self-immolation, though he succumbs to the fanaticism of Korniliy and submits to it. Yet even before he is subjected to the horrors of burning and to the sexual excesses that are permitted and advocated by the schismatic priest, Tikhon understands that only "mother earth," life itself, can save him from the fiery ravings of the Red Death and its false beliefs. When he has been saved from the flames, it is to the earth that he turns for comfort.

> When Tikhon was left alone, he turned away from the sky, which still blazed with the bloody glow of the flames, and fell prostrate on the earth.
> The dampness of the earth soothed the pain of his burns; and it seemed to him that the earth had heeded his prayer, had saved him from the fiery heaven of the Red Death, and that once again he was emerging from the womb of the earth, like a baby being born and the dead resurrected. And he embraced and kissed it as a living being, and he wept and prayed:
> Wondrous Mother of God,
> Earth, earth, damp Mother![66]

In this episode, obviously modeled on the scene in Dostoevskiy's *Brothers Karamazov (Brat'ya Karamazovy)* where Alesha kisses the earth, Merezhkovskiy had Tikhon begin to follow the right path. Moreover, he now had Tikhon reject the old Church as well as the new Church of Peter's making, just as Merezhkovskiy rejected them: "He understood that the old church was no better than the new, and he decided to return to the world, to seek for the true church until he found it."[67] The true Church, in Merezhkovskiy's estimation, was to be found in the world, in life; it was not a separate entity.

From the Red Death, Tikhon ventures through the White Death, a heretical sect which believes that Christ becomes incarnate in some pure person—in this case a runaway Cossack—whenever the world is in danger of being destroyed.[68] Merezhkovskiy introduced this section into the novel in order to show that a worship of the earth and earthly things alone is false and is, in a sense, a continuation of Tikhon's kissing of the earth; it is a warning lest the significance of that act be carried to an extreme. Although this sect purports to be Christian, it is actually a pagan, Dionysian rite, accompanied by frenzied dancing which engenders the same intoxication as at Bacchic celebrations. The dance also leads to sexual excesses, which are condoned, for the sect believes that there is no sin, even when carnal intercourse takes place between brother and sister, provided that they live in "true Christian love."[69] Moreover, in a ritual that parodies the Eucharist, a human sacrifice is made and cannibalism is practiced. Tikhon, however, is spared this ultimate horror, and he escapes from the toils of the White Death.

Then, to reaffirm his stand on the Church of Peter's creation, with the sovereign as its head, a Church based on the false path of reason without Christ, Merezhkovskiy places Tikhon once more in the company of its followers and has him reject it. It is no less murderous than the madness of the Red Death and the White Death. In Merezhkovskiy's opinion, the result could only be the same in Russia as it was in Europe: the separation of Christ and faith from reason and the world: "He [Tikhon] felt that these people had set out on a path that could not be followed to its end, and that sooner or later they would reach the same point in Russia that had already been reached in Europe: either with Christ against reason, or with reason against Christ."[70] Thus Merezhkovskiy formulated his primary concept of Christ and Antichrist in different terms than heretofore. It now remained for him to reveal in what he considered the solution to lie.

As a prelude to this solution, Merezhkovskiy presented two representatives of Christianity divorced from the world. The first, Father Ilarion, is of that ilk of historic Christians who consider the flesh unholy: he chastises his body, fasts strictly, and never washes, for to expose or to touch the body is a sin. Moreover, he believes that few people will attain salvation.[71] Contrasted to him is Father Sergey, who is opposed to unreasonable abstinence and who believes, as Merezhkovskiy did, that "every creation of God is good, and nothing is rejected."[72] While Sergey and his beliefs are essentially right, in Merezhkovskiy's estimation, he is of little help to Tikhon, for he is only a contemplator and not a man of action; he has chosen God without the world. Yet it is near the wilderness cell of the two monks that the truth is revealed to Tikhon.

There is no rational, logical explanation. Indeed, despite the continuous searching that fills the novel, Merezhkovskiy did little to prepare the reader for the conclusion of his work. In the final brief episode, John the Son of Thunder appears to Tikhon, who is symbolically lost in the wilderness. The revelation is sudden, unexpected: only in a universal Church, the Church of John, which is based on the prophecies of the Apocalypse, will the problem of the duality occasioned by the truths of Christianity and paganism be resolved. Tikhon is struck dumb during the moment of insight; yet he is joyful. He is unable to inform mankind of his new-found knowledge; but he knows that in the future, when it is God's will, the truth will be made manifest.

Merezhkovskiy concluded his trilogy with this simple declaration of his faith. He had passed from thesis, through antithesis, to synthesis; from the First Testament, through the Second Testament, to the Third Testament; from paganism, through historic Christianity, to the posthistoric Church of the Second Coming of Christ. Merezhkovskiy did not expand his concept further in *Peter and Alexis*. The tasks of presenting a full account of his newly evolved religion, of modifying it, of applying it to the contemporary world, and of convincing mankind of the need to adopt it were to be his life's work.

6

The Second Coming

In the final volume of his trilogy Merezhkovskiy revealed his latest religious concept: that only in the religion of the Second Coming of Christ would the bifurcation of man be ended. Although he attempted to present *Peter and Alexis* as a continuation of the struggle of Christ and Antichrist in the world, Merezhkovskiy's whole religious conception had altered since the time when he had begun the trilogy, some ten years earlier. This undoubtedly accounts for the third novel's appearing to be of a different order from the preceding two works. Merezhkovskiy was conscious of this difference himself, and he wrote about it a few years later.

> When I began the trilogy *Christ and Antichrist*, it seemed to me that two truths existed—Christianity, the truth of heaven, and paganism, the truth of the earth—and that the absolute religious truth lay in the future union of these two truths. But as I was finishing it, I already knew that the union of Christ and Antichrist was a blasphemous lie; I knew that both truths—of heaven and earth—had already been united in Jesus Christ, the Only Begotten Son of God, the one who professes ecumenical Christianity; that in Him alone is not only the perfect, but also the eternally self-perfecting, the eternally growing, truth, and that there will be no other than He. But I now also know that I had to follow this lie to its end, in order to see the truth. *From divarication to synthesis*; such is my path.[1]

While it was in *Peter and Alexis* that Merezhkovskiy gave a literary presentation of his latest concept, he had actually revealed it in much more detail a few years earlier in *L. Tolstoy and Dostoevskiy*.

As all his works of literary criticism, *L. Tolstoy and Dostoevskiy* is an example of Merezhkovskiy's subjective criticism, in which he makes use of a writer and his compositions as a vehicle to put forward his own ideas. This does not prevent the critic from demonstrating perspicacious and penetrating insights into the object of his study: indeed, Merezhkovskiy's extensive scrutiny of Tolstoy and Dostoevskiy remains a significant contribution to our knowledge of them. Nevertheless, what is most important is that Merezhkovskiy has selected the two greatest Russian writers for his purpose, not solely because of their position in Russian literature, although this was undoubtedly of importance in ensuring him a widespread audience, but primarily because they were the best choices possible for the presentation of his religious beliefs. He recognized in Tolstoy and Dostoevskiy the same elemental duality that was present in himself: the ambivalence of the spirit and the flesh. Furthermore, each in his own way was aware of the conflict and strove to overcome it, although hesitating to take the final step. In this respect Dostoevskiy and Tolstoy were similar; yet, at the same time, they were opposites. In Dostoevskiy, "the seer of the spirit" *(taynovidets dukha)*, Merezhkovskiy observed the preponderance of the spirit over the flesh; and in Tolstoy, "the seer of the flesh" *(taynovidets ploti)*,[2] he observed the preponderance of the flesh over the spirit. For Merezhkovskiy, Tolstoy's contemplation of the flesh represented the thesis, and Dostoevskiy's contemplation of the spirit represented the antithesis; a synthesis was therefore necessary. This synthesis is what Merezhkovskiy presented in delineating his new religion in its entirety. For this reason alone, *L. Tolstoy and Dostoevskiy* is the most important of Merezhkovskiy's compositions. The new religion remained with him throughout his life, although as the years passed, he both expanded it somewhat and rejected certain aspects of it which he praised at the time of writing this work.

The most astonishing points included in Merezhkovskiy's ideas at this period were his acceptance of both Orthodoxy and autocracy, and his belief in their religious role. They were also among the first appendages to his new Christianity that he was to excise and condemn, even before writing *Peter and Alexis*. Merezhkovskiy's acceptance of Orthodoxy and autocracy hinged on his views concerning East and West, Russia and Europe.

Merezhkovskiy was a lover of both Europe and Russia, and for this reason he could not support either the Slavophiles or the Westernizers in Russia. His attempt to reconcile the two led him to the conclusion that "to be a Russian means to be a European in the highest degree, to be universal."[3] This belief was largely responsible for his admiration of Peter the Great, for he contended that Peter was at one and the same time the most Russian and the most European of all Russian heroes. It was indubitably this Peter whom he attempted to reproduce in his novel *Peter and Alexis.* As his novels testify, Merezhkovskiy considered both Russia and Europe to be holy, but in opposite ways. The West was the realm of the Mangod and paganism. The East was the kingdom of the Godman and the Third Rome—to this extent he supported the Slavophile Messianism of Russia. Merezhkovskiy felt the conflict of the two, and he insisted that they be united: "We cannot renounce one of them; we must either perish or unite both brinks of the abyss in ourselves."[4]

He was convinced that the Western Church—that is, Roman Catholicism, or the Church of Peter—had embarked on the wrong path. In it was the essence of paganism, the spirit of the "holy flesh," for it comprehended the secret of the incarnation of the flesh being born.[5] The very historical development of the Catholic Church followed this path, for in Europe the Church attempted to make itself the state; that is, it moved from the heavenly to the earthly kingdom, from the spirit to the flesh.[6]

This view of the Catholic Church also contributed to Merezhkovskiy's temporary acceptance of autocracy and Orthodoxy, which had been closely allied since Peter the Great's reforms. Indeed, he justified these very reforms as having saved Orthodoxy from the same fate as Western Catholicism. He saw in the patriarchate the seeds of papacy; and he was convinced that, had the patriarchate continued to exist, the Orthodox Church would have followed the course of Catholicism. Merezhkovskiy could hardly condone Peter's subjection of the Church to the state on a historically religious level; therefore, he claimed it to be on a superhistoric plane, a weapon of the Supreme Will. He even went so far as to proclaim that Peter's control of the administration of the Church (though not of its canonical duties) in addition to his being the head of the state would lead to a theocracy.[7] As a result, Russia had set out on the true path, that of the state's becoming the Church, the transformation from an earthly kingdom to the heavenly one, and to the rule of the Godman. Of course, this had not been carried out in the past, and to achieve it called for the uniting of the Eastern and Western churches into one Universal Church—the Church of John, the Church of the Second Coming—in which the resurrection of the flesh would take place. The basis for this Universal Church of the future was to be Russian Orthodoxy:

> When the Second Coming begins to come to pass (and it has already imperceptibly begun to come to pass), when the force of repulsion, of negation, of the mortification of the flesh is replaced by the force of attraction, of affirmation, of the resurrection of the flesh, then the *future* Western-Eastern Church will at last find its universal-historic name and activity: it will appear, as the Church of John, beside the Churches of Peter and Paul; then the deviation of Peter will end, and Peter will be united with John, and John will reconcile Peter and Paul; Orthodoxy, the freedom of Christ, will reconcile in love Catholicism and Protestantism, faith and reason. The lightning of revelation will strike the rock of Peter, the rock of tradition, and a spring of living water will flow from the stone. And in this final union of the Churches of the three Supreme Apostles—Peter, Paul, and John—into one ecumenical and apostolic, now truly universal Church of Ste. Sophia, the Wisdom of God, whose head and pontiff is Christ Himself, the ultimate destiny of the Christian world will come to pass.[8]

The external similarity between Merezhkovskiy's concept of the Universal Church and that formulated by Vladimir Solov'ev is immediately apparent. In both cases it was to be based on the union of Catholicism, Protestantism, and Orthodoxy. There is, however, an essential difference. Solov'ev, who had become disillusioned by what he termed the state control of Russian Orthodoxy, advocated an equal union of the three Churches under the aegis of the pope, as the first among equals. Merezhkovskiy, on the other hand, did not envisage a union of the three Churches as equals; Orthodoxy was not only to show the way to this Universal Church, but was also to be supreme in it. Yet Merezhkovskiy's support of Orthodoxy and autocracy, while sincere at this time, could be little more than momentary, for Orthodoxy, like Catholicism and Protestantism, was a part of that historic Christianity which his basic concept of Christianity opposed. It is not surprising, therefore, that he was to refute this argument himself a short time later.

Merezhkovskiy's opposition to any accepted form of Christianity derived from the fact that he was unwilling, even unable, to submit himself to the generally acknowledged interpretation of Christ's teachings. His was not merely the superficial discarding of minor dogmas, but the elemental struggle of his whole nature and being both towards God and away from God. The very essence of Christianity as visible in the Church was so divorced from his aristocratic nature that it not only offered no solution to him, it even repelled him. Yet his desire and his need for God were so great that he attempted to reconcile both sides of his being by creating his own religion through his personal interpretation of Christ and his teachings. Merezhkovskiy did not pause to consider whether his new interpretation was false. Instead he contended that historic Christianity had not interpreted Christ's words correctly, nor had it accepted His teachings.

Merezhkovskiy oppugned what he termed the Semitic or Judaic elements in historic Christianity: the tendency to regard the flesh as unholy. Even those who in the past had attempted to avoid these elements had been unable to do so:

> In Christianity what struck them—captivated them as horror captivates and attracted them as an abyss attracts—was precisely the aspect of it that was most alien and contrary to their own nature, the exclusively Semitic aspect: virtue as a mortification of the flesh, as a renunciation of the world, as a seclusion in a dreadful spiritual wilderness, on the summit of those columns on which stylites grew numb; the conception of their own bodies as something inexpiably sinful, bestial, brutish; the conception of the whole animal, elemental nature, from which they had just emerged and which they still loved too much, as a product of the devil.[9]

The spirit of Judaism grew in the Middle Ages until it overcame the fruits of Graeco-Roman knowledge; as proof of its continued existence in contemporary humanity, Merezhkovskiy cited man's shame before the naked body.

Historic Christianity was wrong in accepting only the spiritual holiness of Christ's teaching and in denying the flesh and considering it to be unclean and sinful; such a religion could only lead to Buddhistic nothingness, to Nirvana.[10] Moreover, the God of historic Christianity was not acceptable to Merezhkovskiy; this was not a God of love, before Whom one humbled oneself out of love, but a God of wrath, before Whom man bowed down out of fear and mistrust: "Such a God deprives man of any human dignity, reduces him to the level of an animal, puts the human soul and body in the most degrading position."[11] This statement is extremely important for the understanding of Merezhkovskiy's religious search. He wanted a religion that would permit him to retain his sense of self-worth, his pagan inclinations; Christianity—historic Christianity—was not such a religion. Therefore, he both renounced and denounced it.

Merezhkovskiy had long been advocating the necessity of uniting Christian holiness and pagan holiness in order to attain the ultimate true religion. While his opinions on what were pagan and Christian had changed somewhat by this time (1897–1899), he continued to uphold what he had formerly called pagan. He formulated the idea that in the ultimate, unconscious depths of paganism there was the beginning of the future change to Christianity. This was to be seen in the religion of Dionysos and in Hellenism in its highest form—in Plato and Socrates—which Merezhkovskiy regarded to be pagan Christianity and which inevitably led to Christianity.[12] He wrote in 1903:

> Religious paganism is none other than unclarified, unconscious Christianity, the incompleted path to Christ, the revelation of the Father which precedes the revelation of the Son, the Old Testament as the expectation of the New; religious paganism in its utmost, highest points is "Christianity before Christ."[13]

Merezhkovskiy did not delve more deeply into this startling discovery at the time of writing *L. Tolstoy and Dostoevskiy*, but he was to develop it fully much later.

Paganism had attracted Merezhkovskiy because it proclaimed the holiness of man, which he now reduced to the concept of the holiness of the animal, or the beast, in man. He considered that true pagan religiosity lay in the boundless depths of the mystery of this godly animality, and he was prepared to defend his contention: "I say godly in order to express that, from a religious point of view, the animal in man is just as holy and divine as the spiritual, for flesh and spirit are antithetical only in their semblance, only in appearance; but in their final otherworldly essence they are one."[14] Thus he declared the very basis of his new Christianity: paganism and Christianity—or, as he now called them, "holy flesh" and "holy spirit"—are not equal truths; they are one truth. In its failure to comprehend that these are contradictory poles of Christian holiness, historic Christianity was at fault. In asserting only the holiness of the spirit, historic Christianity completely falsified Christ's teaching, for Merezhkovskiy was convinced that Christ affirmed the equality, the equal holiness, of the spirit and the flesh. From this point he went on:

> If this is so, then the spirit is a different "flesh," transfigured, superior, but nonetheless "flesh," even more "flesh" than ever; the spirit is flesh of the flesh; it is the most solid, imperishable, real, and at the same time most mystical in the flesh—by means of which it grows strong and stands firm. *The spirit is not only the denial of the lowest but also the affirmation of the highest state of the flesh*; the spirit is the uninterrupted movement, the aspiration of the flesh from the lowest state to the highest— "from light to light," to the ultimate white light of Transfiguration, of Resurrection, in which all the separate colors of the rainbow blend into one. The spirit is not incorporeal holiness, but *Holy Flesh*.[15]

Christ showed the way to the holy spirit and the holy flesh in the three main moments of existence: the beginning, or birth; the continuation, through the mystery of Communion, the sacrament of Flesh and Blood; and the end, the mystery of the Resurrection of the Flesh. Although historic Christianity did not reject them, it did not follow them, but merely transformed them into dogmas in inactive sacraments, so that the truth of the holy flesh remained unrevealed. Yet Merezhkovskiy admitted the historic necessity of Christianity's employing asceticism against paganism in the past, for this was its strongest weapon against Graeco-Roman paganism.[16] In the present, Christianity was at a point in cosmic space between the First and the Second Coming of Christ. The time had come for the poles—holy flesh and holy spirit—to attract one another again, so that death and mortification, which are inherent in false Christianity, would cease to exist and would be replaced by the life and resurrection of true Christianity. This was to be accomplished in Merezhkovskiy's Church of the future, "The Church of the Holy Flesh and the Holy Spirit."[17]

Merezhkovskiy had therefore revised his earlier opinion that the holy flesh and the holy spirit are two truths at opposite extremes. Now he regarded them as but two poles of one and the same truth: they are not paganism and Christianity, but both are parts of Christianity. Contrary to his former belief, he claimed that flesh and spirit, or paganism and Christianity, had indeed been united in the past in the person of Christ: "The Godman and the Mangod have no longer been two but one, since the moment when it was said: 'I and my Father are one.' "[18] Merezhkovskiy's main argument in favor of this revelation is in Christ's giving man to eat of His Flesh and to drink of His blood, for this meant that

> the sacrament of our God is not the sacrament only of the spirit and the word, but also of the flesh and the blood, for our Word became Flesh. "Whoso eateth not my flesh and drinketh not my blood, hath not eternal life." Therefore, not without the flesh, but through the flesh to that which lies beyond the flesh.[19]

Christ's appearance did not make paganism a second truth, a second half of the world, contradicting and negating Christianity; rather, Christ's teachings were a joining of the two halves of the world, for what appeared to be Christian and antichristian were not two but one.[20] In this manner Merezhkovskiy obtained his long-desired synthesis of the two elements that were within himself, without having to sacrifice his pagan egotism and aristocratism to Christian humility.

Merezhkovskiy was not prepared to give up everything and follow Christ. He was aware of this himself; so in order to overcome his resulting sense of guilt, he argued that one need not take this commandment literally. It was his opinion that Christ meant it to be only a last resort, if man could not free himself from his possessions by any other means. Christ was flesh as well as spirit, and this commandment "is beyond human strength, this is a revolt against one's own flesh and blood."[21]

In yet another instance, Merezhkovskiy's egotism and aristocratism led him to a completely reversed interpretation of Christ. Much earlier he had admitted his inability to love others, and throughout his works he revealed his self-love, his egotism. The latter he could not stamp out in himself, or perhaps he did not wish to do so. Instead he reasoned that to love oneself in God's name is as holy as to love others in the name of God.

> If I love people not for their own sake, but for the sake of God and in God, I am holy; if I love myself not for my own sake, but for the sake of God and in God, *I am just as holy*. Both courses are equally holy or equally unholy; but they are not completely holy, for the ultimate holiness lies in unifying, symbolic contemplation and the justification of both courses in the knowledge that love for oneself and love for others is one and the same love for God.[22]

Such a concept sprang from his belief that Christ was a synthesis not only of the Godman but also of the Mangod, for the latter is the zenith of the affirmation of the individual. For that reason, Merezhkovskiy contended that "Christ's teaching is not only the greatest self-denial, but also the greatest self-affirmation; not only eternal Golgotha, or crucifixion, but also eternal Bethlehem, or birth—the Renaissance of the personality."[23]

Closely allied to this loving of oneself was Merezhkovskiy's concept of a love of the earth and earthly things, which he also did not want to surrender. He saw in the Lord's Prayer a phrase that convinced him of the holiness of the earth—perhaps it would be more correct to call it one that could be applied to his desire to see the earth as holy. This was the sentence "Thy will be done, on earth as it is in heaven." It was not difficult for Merezhkovskiy to mold this to his ideas and to declare:

> We must love the earth *to the end,* to the ultimate edge of the earth—*to heaven*; we must love heaven *to the end,* to the ultimate edge of heaven—*to the earth*; and then we shall comprehend that these are not two but one love, that heaven descends to earth and embraces the earth, as a lover embraces his beloved (two halves, two *sexes* of the world), and the earth will surrender itself to heaven, will open itself to heaven.[24]

It was historic Christianity which again separated earth and heaven, the flesh and the spirit. The reason for its failure to accept Christ was not because historic Christianity could not understand Christ's love, but because it could not bear Christ's freedom: the uniting of the flesh and the spirit. In other words, historic Christianity accepted only the divine aspect of Christ, completely overlooking the human aspect.

In declaring that the flesh is a part of Christian holiness, Merezhkovskiy considered himself to be on the right path for the solution of man's most disturbing enigma, the problem of sex. This problem is so great that on it "depends the entire future of Christianity, its entire second, unrevealed *half.*"[25] One must agree with Merezhkovskiy that this has been one of the most puzzling of all problems raised by Christianity: how to reconcile sex with Christianity. As Merezhkovskiy so often charged, historic Christianity accepted only the spiritual side of Christ; consequently it reduced sex to the level of the bestial and shameful. Yet even historic Christianity had to do something about it, so it permitted sex in the guise of lawful marriage. It had to condone sex in some way, for sex cannot be destroyed as long as the flesh lives. It was Merezhkovskiy's contention that historic Christianity misinterpreted Christ's words on marriage and sex. He himself fastened on the passage Matthew 19:3–12, and in particular on the words of the Lord "They are no more twain, but one flesh," using them as the keystone of his argument against the accepted interpretation. He reasoned:

> And in this word about the mystery of sex, as in all His words, there is an unfathomable, yet completely clear, transparent profundity; and in this word, as in all His words, the two opposite shores of the indivisible profundity are revealed with precision: the shore of spiritual holiness, or chastity, and the shore of carnal holiness, or the holy union of the sexes, and consequently even holy sensuality; for why be hypocritical? Without ultimate sensuality in the conditions of human nature it is impossible to attain that definitive, irrevocable cohesion of the sexes which ruptures the most vital paternal and maternal bonds ("For this cause shall a man leave father and mother"), about which the Lord said: "They are no more twain, but one *flesh*," not one *soul*, but one *flesh*; at first one flesh, and later one soul. The sacrament of marriage is chiefly and before all else a sacrament of the flesh; in this instance holiness is not directed from the spirit to the flesh, but, on the contrary, from the flesh to the spirit. The uniting of souls is possible even outside marriage; but the completely holy union of flesh with flesh cannot exist outside the sacrament of marriage.[26]

Christ did not renounce or condemn the mystery of sex; He accepted it as the basis of existence, even blessing it. As long as one accepts it as such, it is holy; otherwise it seems evil. The reason that sex was regarded as evil in contemporary society, Merezhkovskiy claimed, was that, in an effort to be more Christian than Christ, humanity overlooked its holiness and godliness. "We 'did not receive' His word about holy chastity or about holy sensuality; instead of chastity, there is castration; instead of holy sensuality, or holy marriage, there is legal marriage."[27]

The recognition of two manifestations of marriage, the holy and the lawful, was of course an outgrowth of Merezhkovskiy's belief in the holiness of the body and his conviction that holy marriage is primarily of the flesh and not of the spirit. For Merezhkovskiy, lawful marriage might be no more than legal fornication. In this case he was referring to a marriage without love, one in which sex is not the prime concern—a marriage of convenience or of like souls. Regardless of the motive, if the body—the flesh or sex—was not the main consideration of the union, then the marriage was unholy and adulterous. He attributed the guilt for such marriages to all strata of society, which was steeped in the tradition of black, monastic Christianity. As a result there occurred "the murder and suicide of sex."[28]

On the other hand, holy marriage might occur outside wedlock, provided that it was the uniting of flesh with flesh, the sexual love which he regarded as the basis of all holy marriage. Sex was holy, because God was the creator of sex; but the Church rejected it and condemned it if it did not fall within the bounds of lawful marriage. Merezhkovskiy went no further at this time. Indeed, he had taken a considerable step away from the norm, a revolutionary step, and perhaps he felt that he should bide his time before going more deeply into this controversial aspect of his new religion. However, he did continue to affirm his credence in the importance of sex: "Precisely here, on the radiant point of sex, as in their own optical focus, all the contradictory rays of the heaven above and the heaven below—of the two halves of the world, of the two half-worlds—intersect and cross."[29]

Merezhkovskiy was alluding to the mysteries of birth and death, the two certainties of human life which, he believed, were united into one by Christ's teachings on sex. These are the two eternities, the two abysses that he had discussed in his novel *Leonardo da Vinci*. Birth is the lower abyss, the introduction into life on earth, into the flesh; death, the upper abyss, is the entering into the life of the spirit. Merezhkovskiy had long ago stated that one should not fear death, although at that time he was attracted by the example of the Hellenes' lack of fear before man's ultimate end. While he still esteemed the pagan sentiment that death deepened the meaning of life, he now realized that Christ gave an even more valid reason for not fearing death. Death is not the end; there is a life after death, for Christ lived, died, and then returned from the dead.

Yet men still feared death, for mankind had moved away from Christ: "During the digression that European humanity has just experienced, it was as if Christ had died on the cross and the miracle of resurrection must take place anew: now, as at that earlier time, this miracle will occur in the human heart before it does in the grave."[30] The miracle had to occur again in human hearts; this, too, was a significant part of Merezhkovskiy's latest religious convictions. He recognized all too clearly why it was difficult to believe in this miracle of resurrection. Reason and perception reveal to man that the laws of nature are necessary and unalterable; and this, obviously, means that the body must decay and never be seen again. Merezhkovskiy was keenly aware of the evident contradiction posed by the decaying of the flesh and the promise of the resurrection of the flesh. It seems that he himself was subject to many misgivings and much suffering from this ambivalence; in consequence, his writings on resurrection appear to be not only an attempt to convince others that physical resurrection is possible, but a means of convincing himself and of overcoming the clash between reason and miracle within himself. Reason forced him to find an explanation and a justification for his belief in the miracle of resurrection. To be sure, he could not do so on a rational plane; yet he wanted reason to be a part of this justification. For this purpose he formulated the concepts of the world's having innumerable possible states and of a "mystic reason," the roots of which he claimed were found in human reason and experience. In the light of this mystic reason he discovered a vindication for his belief in the resurrection of the flesh:

> The revelation of the same mystic reason and experience testifies to us, as one of the realities of the future state of the world, that *"the Word was made flesh"* and that in this incarnate Word, Father and Son—the Spirit and the Flesh—are one, and consequently the carnal personality in its definitive, most worldly meaning is equivalent to the spiritual personality; the immortality of the spiritual personality, demanded by our mystic reason and experience, demands in its turn the immortality of the carnal personality. But surely this means: "Verily, verily, I say unto you, the hour is coming, and now is, when the dead shall hear the voice of the Son of God"—and will rise from their graves. The miracle of resurrection seems unbelievable, like the most unbelievable fairy tale. But is it more credible that, as a result of the contact of the male seed with the female, scattered particles of inanimate material begin to whirl in vortices of movement, combining and uniting around a single stationary point, around a new "monad," which never before existed in the world, some sort of ineradicable nucleus which is the new spiritual-carnal personality of the one being born? The mystery of birth, or incarnation, is no more and no less than the mystery of resurrection; *the fact that we have been born is as incredible as the fact that we shall be resurrected*: the second incredibility differs from the first only in the fact that, as a consequence of its novelty, we are less accustomed to it.[31]

For skeptics, Christ's resurrected body, instead of being "spiritual flesh,"[32] was merely a dead body, subject to general physical, natural, and historic laws. Yet for those who did not believe that Christ's appearance was bounded by these laws, Christ indeed had risen from the dead. Faith did not proceed from miracle, "but miracle from faith";[33] and nothing could destroy this new, this true and final, miracle.

Historic Christianity, in separating the spirit from the flesh and in raising the spiritual half of the world over the carnal, accepted only the resurrection of the spirit and not the resurrection of the flesh. Consequently, not only does the flesh die, but also the spirit dies, so that of the living flesh there remains only the decaying spirit. Christ's miracles were reversed in historic Christianity. In lieu of water being turned into wine and wine into blood, and in lieu of stone being turned into bread and bread into flesh, Merezhkovskiy observed that wine turned into water and tears and bread turned into stone—the stone of dogma. Only in returning to these miracles in their original form could salvation and resurrection be attained:

> It is necessary that the first of Christ's miracles occur again, the miracle of Cana of Galilee, the transubstantiation of the bitter, tearful water of old Christianity into "the wine of the new, into the wine of new joy," in order that the last miracle of Christ come to pass, the miracle of the second resurrection, the Second Coming.[34]

Thus, Merezhkovskiy revealed the reason for his religion of the Second Coming, for only in it would the resurrection of the flesh take place; and for Merezhkovskiy the resurrection of the flesh was all-important.

What is readily apparent is the affinity between many of Merezhkovskiy's views and those of Soren Kierkegaard, despite the fact that the latter was primarily concerned with ethical problems, while Merezhkovskiy was not. Although Kierkegaard's works had not appeared in Russian translation, it is possible that Merezhkovskiy became conversant with them, or with commentaries on them, during the course of his research for *Peter and Alexis*, most notably in connection with the character and ideas of Pastor Glück. It is equally possible that Merezhkovskiy developed analogous views quite independently and that he was unaware that they had been expressed earlier by the Danish Lutheran theologian. The conclusion to be drawn in the latter instance is that these ideas emerged from the universal *Zeitgeist* of the last half of the nineteenth century.

It is not solely that similarities occur in the broad attack by the two writers on historic Christianity, but that in this attack Merezhkovskiy echoed much that Kierkegaard had stated earlier. The very basis for Merezhkovskiy's rejection of Roman Catholicism is identical with that of Kierkegaard's: that it sought to turn Christianity, which is otherworldly, into a temporal kingdom of this world.[35] Monasticism, the renunciation of the world and of the flesh, leads to the guilt of pride, selfishness, and a special kind of worldliness. Man, for Kierkegaard as for Merezhkovskiy, cannot escape from the finitude of the world and must forever live in it, cherish it, and cling to his loved ones; but he must love God more.[36] Further, despite the fact that for a time Merezhkovskiy placed the state religion of his nation, Russian Orthodoxy, outside the bounds of his vehement rejection of organized Christianity, he was soon to repudiate it for essentially the same reasons that Kierkegaard had denounced the state church of Lutheran Denmark. In seeking to enjoy aid and comfort from the state, which in turn attempts to use Christianity to produce good and obedient citizens, the Church becomes no less worldly than the Church of Rome, thereby revealing that it is not truly Christian.[37]

The central feature of Kierkegaard's philosophy, as of Merezhkovskiy's, is the individual. Every religious man is an individual;[38] indeed, it is the individual alone, with his personal relationship to God, who is truly human and who, together with similar individuals, composes a fitting human society. Kierkegaard's emphasis is on the solitary man-God-man relationship, without the Church as intermediary. He does not insist that man should renounce family and possessions, or that he should love his neighbor more than himself. Very similar to Merezhkovskiy's view of self-love is Kierkegaard's belief that to love oneself is to make the love of God one's goal;[39] this in turn will lead to the love of one's fellow men.[40]

Even Merezhkovskiy's stress on the duality of man is reminiscent of Kierkegaard's. For the latter, man is a combination of the temporal and the eternal.[41] Hence, Kierkegaard accepted sensuality and sexuality, arguing that bodily life is good in itself, but that, being temporal, it should be subordinate to the eternal goals of the spirit.[42] Furthermore, he allowed the beauty of the pagan erotic within Christianity, insofar as it could be combined in marriage.[43] While Merezhkovskiy may have equivocated as to what constitutes Christian marriage, in this, too, Kierkegaard's thought is visible.

For both Kierkegaard and Merezhkovskiy, only the spiritual rebirth of the individual could heal modern man; and this rebirth could be effected only by a return to the true Christ, to God's being born afresh in the hearts of men.[44] There is, for Kierkegaard, a distinct difference between the historical element of Christianity—that God became man on earth—and the history of Christianity. The Christian must try to return to Christ, to become Christ's contemporary, to ignore the confusions and errors of historic Christendom.[45] Christendom is actually destroying Christianity by its evasion of the spiritual life of Christianity and the assumption that everyone is Christian as a matter of course. Christ has been poeticized, for men have been unwilling to accept Him as He is in reality, the paradoxical merging of the temporal with the eternal, both man and God in one. Instead, the living Christ has been replaced by an institution that makes Christian life easier and makes faith reasonable and comfortable.[46] Faith should not and does not rest on miracles, though miracles are indicative of divine authority. Kierkegaard was appalled that Christendom had abandoned the doctrine of resurrection, replacing it with the Platonic concept of immortality, which prevents man from being fully concerned with the eternal and his relationship to it.[47] As for Merezhkovskiy, so for Kierkegaard, resurrection is central to Christianity.

Parallels between Merezhkovskiy's religious thought and Kierkegaard's do not end with these few examples. Differences of belief are also extensive, but the fundamental one is the goal of their striving. Merezhkovskiy's aim was the establishment of the Kingdom of God on earth. For Kierkegaard, this could never be a possibility: existence must be a tension and a striving for the eternal.[48] Christianity is therefore an expectation, not a fulfillment; indeed, finite man could not exist in or fully enjoy the eternal. God remains ever transcendent, though he breaks into time in order to make possible a redirecting of man's life.[49]

Merezhkovskiy, however, was convinced that religion was a superhistoric path. He was no less firmly convinced that history had run its course and that "when history ends, religion begins"[50]—his own apocalyptical Christianity. Merezhkovskiy asked himself, and his readers, whether universal-historic development had as its goal the eternal continuation of humanity in time and culture, or whether its aim was a higher form of existence, that is, the end of the world. He was aware that such a question was alien to all aspects of the life of contemporary humanity, nonetheless he stressed its importance:

> This question seems mystical, abstract, far from the real and active social, political, and moral life of contemporary humanity: indeed, consciously or unconsciously, but inevitably, it enters into it. Just as the thought of the earthly end, of death, cannot fail to influence not only the abstract and the contemplative but also the real life of each individual man, so this same thought cannot fail sooner or later to influence the real, active cultural-historic life of all humanity.[51]

The influence of this question on the life of humanity was inevitable, for Merezhkovskiy believed that his second premise was correct, that the ultimate result of all universal-historic development would be the end of humanity and the world: the Second Coming.

Merezhkovskiy also thought that never before in the history of the world had the human spirit sensed so acutely how close was, if not the End, then the Beginning of the End, as in his day. Never before had the world been as ready for religion—consequently the end of the world, since religion would only begin when history was at an end—as at that time. He envisaged that there were three courses open to modern European humanity: a definitive healing of the "illness" called God; a loss of this "illness" in a fall into decadence, into the madness of Nietzsche and the victory of the Mangod over the Godman; and finally, the right choice, "the religion of the last great synthesis, of the great Symbol, the religion of the Second Coming, no longer veiled and secret like the First, but manifest in might and glory—the religion of the End."[52]

Throughout *L. Tolstoy and Dostoevskiy* Merezhkovskiy revealed his faith in the messianic role of Russia. Europe would not come to the realization of the correct path itself. The weighty task of leading the world to Christ was to be left to Russia and, in particular, to the people of the new religious cognizance, those who had the presentiment of the End. Merezhkovskiy claimed for himself and those who adhered to his new religion of the End a unique position:

> We believe in the end, we see the end, we desire the end, for we ourselves are the end, or at least the beginning of the end. In our eyes is an expression that has never before been in human eyes; in our hearts is a feeling that no one has experienced for nineteen centuries . . . we see what no one sees; we are the first

to see the Sun of the great day; earlier than all others we say to Him:

"Come, o Lord!"[53]

Merezhkovskiy was, in fact, claiming for himself alone an exalted status; for although he spoke in the plural, his new religious convictions were shared only by the person closest to him, Zinaida Gippius, and even she did not wholly accept his beliefs. The task of impressing the only true religion on his contemporaries was left to Merezhkovskiy alone, and for the next twenty years he attempted to carry out his self-appointed mission.

On the whole, Merezhkovskiy remained faithful to what he promulgated in *L. Tolstoy and Dostoevskiy* regarding resurrection, sex, and historic Christianity. However, during the first two decades of the twentieth century, four new premises entered his religious program.

The first of these innovations was his plan of the evolution of religion, which he likened to the three stages of dialectical development:

> To the triplicity of mystical cognition corresponds the triplicity of metaphysical cognition at three moments, which are brought about by the law of dialectical development and in which is revealed the deepest essence of life accessible to human reason: the first, the lower, synthesis, the unconscious unity of life and consciousness—I am I—divides into thesis and antithesis, subject and object, I and not-I, an internal and external world, in order to be completed by a final higher synthesis, by a final conscious union, which is required by the metaphysical and is brought about by mystical cognition. From the first unity through bifurcation to the final union, from one in one, through two in one, to one in three—such are the three moments of dialectical development.[54]

The three stages of the religious development of humanity corresponded to his concept of the three Testaments—of God the Father, God the Son, and God the Holy Ghost—and they were centered on the problem of the flesh and the spirit.

The first stage, that of God the Creator as the absolute being and the only God, was exemplified by Judaism. Merezhkovskiy had abandoned his earlier conviction that Judaism was a religion denying the flesh and had accepted V. V. Rozanov's view that Judaism, no less than most pagan religions, was a religion of birth, consequently a religion of the flesh.[55] Moreover, he considered that the one God of Israel was the one God towards whom all paganism with its multiplicity of gods strove. Human sacrifice symbolized for him the unity of God the One in One. He ascribed human sacrifice to all ancient religions (later he excluded Greek and Roman paganism), and while it did not take place in Israel, the possibility of it was apparent in God's commanding Abraham to sacrifice Isaac. Above all, Merezhkovskiy observed it in the Hebrew rite of circumcision:

> A relic of these human sacrifices, in which the deepest metaphysics of all objective religions was manifest in former times, is preserved in circumcision—the sacrament of the First Testament, of the first unity of the Creator with the creature, of the Spirit with the flesh.
>
> The ultimate symbolization of objectivity for human consciousness is the tangible outer substance, since the flesh of man himself—his flesh, as well as cosmic flesh—is matter. This is why the first stage of religious evolution is primarily *a religion of the flesh.*[56]

God the Father, who presented the reality of the flesh, offered the first thesis. The second stage, which revealed the Son as the second hypostasis, separated the first lower unity into two higher elements: the spirit and the flesh. This was the religion of the Two in One, in which by Christ's resurrection all men received absolute life in God's being.

Merezhkovskiy ceased to be as bitterly opposed to historic Christianity as he had formerly been, now that he acknowledged it as a necessary stage in the evolution of religion. He himself did not accept Christianity as the final religion; he still complained that it failed to surmount the contradiction of its two elements, flesh and spirit, and that it resulted not in a synthesis but in the absorption of the thesis by the antithesis, that is the flesh by the spirit. This was what caused the duality that plagued humanity:

> The religious problem of the spirit and the flesh, of the polarity of the abysses, of duality, does not spring from the ontological dualism of human nature, but from the greatest mystery for us of God's division into two Countenances and the relation of this divarication to the plural world that emanates from God.[57]

Nonetheless, he at least conceded that Christianity was necessary in order to attain the religion of the Trinity. Indeed, his own religion derived essentially from Christianity, for his Coming Christ would have been impossible if it were not for the Christ who had already come; therefore, the Church of the Second Coming, apocalyptical Christianity, would accept the Church of the First Coming, or historic Christianity, for there was truth in the latter, though not the whole truth.

He was also adamant in his opinion that brotherly love was not the basis of Christianity:

> Indeed, Christianity is not at all based on love for one's neighbor, as is usually thought—this love is present in the law of Moses and also in all ancient teachers of wisdom from Socrates to Marcus Aurelius, from Confucius to Bodhisattva—not on the righteous life and crucifixion of Christ, but on the real possibility, which has been proven by experience, of physical resurrection.[58]

Consequently, this resurrection of the flesh was the first and most important point of Merezhkovskiy's new world order, which was the third and final stage of the religious evolution of humanity. This was the kingdom of the Holy Ghost, in which the thesis and the antithesis, the flesh and the spirit, would be synthesized, and in which the Three in One would be realized:

> At the present time the religious consciousness of mankind has risen to this stage. Christianity is coming to an end, because it has fulfilled itself to the end, just as "the law and the prophets" were finished with the advent of Christ. Christ *did not violate but fulfilled* the law. And the Holy Ghost *will not violate but will fulfill* Christianity.[59]

Thus Merezhkovskiy continued to aver that the end was at hand.

Resurrection of the body was always of cardinal importance in the religion of Merezhkovskiy. The problem of the victory of life over death continued to be a source of anxiety to him, and he constantly returned to it. Death represented for him the destruction of the individual—an unacceptable fact to this epitome of individuality; for "if death exists, then there is nothing but death; if death exists, then all is nothing."[60] Christ, the absolute individual, vanquished death; this was a belief that Merezhkovskiy had held for a long time. To strengthen it, he added his newly formulated conviction in the power of love over death, for his God was a God of love. Love was the main action of life, for it was the affirmation of existence: "Not to exist is not to love; only the one who does not love may accept death as nonexistence. The one who loves, loves the living person of the beloved. Love is the will to the immortality of the personality."[61] The importance of love for Merezhkovskiy cannot be overlooked. He himself had loved deeply only once. The object of his love, his mother, had long since died; yet he had to believe in her continued existence, and he sought it through his love for her.

> For the one who loves there is no death, because love is the absolute affirmation of life. Absolute negation is destroyed by absolute affirmation; death is destroyed by love. Love is life; he who loves is alive; and isasmuch as he loves, inasmuch is he alive, is he immortal—"is he risen from the dead." Love is not a superficial virtue, not the strength of the soul, but the soul itself. Love is unable not to love; the soul cannot avoid living in love, not only the future life beyond the grave, but also the present life of this world, which is not the abstract "immortality of the soul," but a real resurrection of the flesh and the spirit in the perfect unity of the personality. Love is not the road from this world to the other, but the absolute revelation of the other world in this—the perfect union of the two worlds. Love is not the knowledge of God; love is God.[62]

In this way Merezhkovskiy indicated not only the power of love but also its holiness and its necessity for the immortality of the individual.

It was in connection with sex, or fleshly love, that he at last proclaimed a conclusion that had long been germinating in his mind, since the time when he had commented on the female qualities of his hero, Leonardo da Vinci. He decided that the individual, the complete individual, must contain both male and female elements, since sex was a division, a splitting into two halves. Here, too, Merezhkovskiy's habitual desire to achieve a synthesis is apparent:

> Not only according to Christian metaphysics, but also according to common sense, the personality, *individuum*, is *indivisible*, is whole; sex is a half, a bisection (two sexes), a division, a fraction of the personality. The perfect human being, the perfect personality, is not a man, *only* a man (male), and not a woman, *only* a woman (female), but something more . . . in every man there is the feminine, and in every woman the masculine. The union of male and female—not in the sexual act, outside the personality, but within it—is the basis of personality.[63]

Merezhkovskiy expressed this opinion in 1913. He was to take it up again in an expanded form as one of the bases for his later religious convictions. It is interesting to note that Merezhkovskiy considered sex for the purpose of propagation of the species to be the death of individuality. He felt that sexual love of this nature was basically lust and not, as it should be, a love for the spiritual "glorified" flesh.[64] The complete union of the sexes could only occur in a more exalted love, which Merezhkovskiy termed *vlyublennost'* in order to distinguish it from ordinary love *(lyubov')*.

From this point, *vlyublennost'*, sprang Merezhkovskiy's concept of eternal womanhood. Once again he came close to Vladimir Solov'ev, but there is a considerable difference both in the method by which each adopted this symbol and in the contents of it. Solov'ev derived his eternal woman from three visions that he is reputed to have had of Ste. Sophia, the divine glory of the cosmos, whom he presented as the salvation of the world. Merezhkovskiy himself pointed out the essential trait of Solov'ev's eternal woman: it was heavenly— too heavenly and too Christian in comparison with his own.[65]

Merezhkovskiy's eternal woman was not the result of a vision, but, like the whole of his work, was the product of a more rational contemplation and was a symbol of the uniting of heaven and earth. One might trace the origins of his eternal woman back to Venus-Aphrodite, whose statue played such an important role in his trilogy, *Christ and Antichrist*. This was a purely earthly woman, and he needed a heavenly one as well, so that earth and heaven could be synthesized in one heavenly-earthly woman, the symbol of his Church of the Second Coming. He was not content with the eternal woman either as Venus or as divine beauty; eternal womanhood was synonymous with eternal motherhood, and in this lies the main difference between Merezhkovskiy and Solov'ev. Here, also, may be seen once again the influence of Merezhkovskiy's undying love for his mother, who apparently represented for him the ideal of womanhood: motherhood. This, together with the important position ascribed to Mary, the Mother of God, both in the Orthodox and in the Roman Catholic faiths, also influenced his judgment. He found a link between the Mother, who petitions Christ in the interest of mortals, and the Holy Ghost:

> At the last judgment the Mother intercedes with the Son for the convicted. But the Spirit, which *intercedes for us with unuttered sighs,* is this not also Eternal Motherhood? The first appearance of Eternal Womanhood is the Mother of God in Christianity; the last, in the Apocalypse—*the woman clothed*

with the sun—is the revelation of the Holy Spirit, the Holy Flesh, the Church as the Kingdom, the Godman in God-humanity.[66]

The Eternal Mother, who therefore appeared in the beginning and the end, led him to conclude that "Eternal Motherhood and Eternal Womanhood, that which existed before birth and that which will exist after death, become one."[67]

Merezhkovskiy then examined the popular concept of the Mother of God. He found that this was inextricably bound up with the concept of the Mother Earth, which he himself had upheld for some time. Earthly and heavenly were thus joined, and therefore God the Father and God the Son could be reconciled by the Holy Ghost—that is, the Eternal Woman-Mother—just as Merezhkovskiy and his father had been reconciled on numerous occasions by the intervention of his mother:

> Christianity separated the past eternity of the Father from the future eternity of the Son, the earthly truth from the heavenly truth. Will they not be united by what comes after Christianity, the revelation of the Spirit—Eternal Womanhood, Eternal Motherhood? Will not the Mother reconcile the Father and the Son?[68]

Only this revelation of the Third Testament offered the solution to the enigma of the earth and heaven, that is, the flesh and the spirit, in the Holy Ghost as the eternal woman, who contained both love-motherhood *(vlyublennost'-materinstvo)* and love-virginity *(vlyublennost'-devstvennost')*, the uniting of the earthly and the godly in one Virgin-Mother.[69]

These were the contemplative elements that were evolved simultaneously with Merezhkovskiy's more active sociopolitical ideals during the first twenty years of this century. Together with his belief in universal humanity, they were to form the basis for his writings as an exile in France after the Revolution of 1917.

7

The Application: Social and Political Ideals

The period from the end of the nineteenth century to the Revolution of 1917 was an era in which God-seeking reached an unprecedented peak in Russia.[1] Merezhkovskiy was therefore not alone in striving to reconcile Christianity with man's reason and his increasing scientific knowledge of the world. However, it was symptomatic of the times that in religious-philosophical thought, no less than in the Modernist movement as a whole, diversification of individual systems was paramount. Merezhkovskiy's new religious cognizance was but one of the many, and he consequently found himself in constant conflict with his fellow seekers.

During the last two years of the nineteenth century Gippius and Merezhkovskiy joined S. P. Dyagilev's group, which later centered around the journal *Mir Iskusstva* (World of Art). Here they became acquainted with V. V. Rozanov, D. V. Filosofov, A. N. Benois, L. Bakst, and others.[2] Together with them, Merezhkovskiy and Gippius became active collaborators of *Mir Iskusstva* after its establishment in 1899; and it was in this periodical, which he termed "the refuge of all the 'persecuted and outcasts,'"[3] that Merezhkovskiy finally was able to publish *L. Tolstoy and Dostoevskiy*.

Among the members of Dyagilev's entourage Merezhkovskiy found a few who were interested in religious problems. Thus it was that a small group, which included Merezhkovskiy, Gippius, Rozanov, and Filosofov, began to hold private meetings for the purpose of discussing religion. This did not constitute a break with *Mir Iskusstva*, although it certainly weakened their contacts with that journal. It was not until 1901 that Zinaida Gippius suggested that they should turn their private gatherings into a public society dedicated to the open discussion of religious problems.[4] Merezhkovskiy eagerly responded to this idea and soon gathered a number of supporters around him. A delegation composed of Merezhkovskiy, Rozanov, Filosofov, V. S. Mirolyubov, and V. A. Ternavtsev approached K. P. Pobedonostsev, the procurator general of the Holy Synod, to seek permission to form the Religious-Philosophical Society in St. Petersburg.[5] Official sanction was granted, and the clergy agreed to participate in the proposed society.

The first meeting was held on 29 November 1901 in the hall of the Geographical Society. Bishop Sergiy, rector of the Ecclesiastical Academy, was installed as president; the office of vice-president was also held by a high church official.[6] Members of the clergy—among whom were professors of the Ecclesiastical Academy—as well as representatives of the intelligentsia evinced a keen interest in the proceedings. The Religious-Philosophical Society was indeed a unique organization. Not only did it provide one of the first meeting grounds for the intelligentsia and the clergy; it also permitted, at a time of intense reaction, the expression of views and ideas that would have been forbidden at any other public gathering. It soon earned for itself the reputation of being the sole refuge of free speech in Russia.[7]

No journal, not even *Mir Iskusstva*, was willing to publish the reports of the Religious-Philosophical Society. Moreover, Merezhkovskiy and Gippius were now in the position of having no close ties with any of the existing periodicals. The suggestion of their recent acquaintance P. P. Pertsov that they should found their own periodical was all that was needed to set them to work at establishing it.[8] Neither Pertsov nor Merezhkovskiy had sufficient funds to embark on such an enterprise, but Merezhkovskiy eventually received support from Suvorin. In January 1903 the first issue of *Novyy Put'* (The New Path) appeared in print. It was a journal dedicated to the propagation of religious ideas; it was the organ of the Religious-Philosophical Society; and it provided Merezhkovskiy with an outlet for his works, although the precarious financial position of the journal obliged him to publish in it without receiving an honorarium.

Pertsov accepted the editorship of *Novyy Put'*, and Gippius and Merezhkovskiy took active parts in directing it. However, as Merezhkovskiy became more and more occupied with study for his proposed novel *Peter and Alexis*, he gradually left management of *Novyy Put'* in the hands of others. Nevertheless, he continued to be one of the most constant contributors to the journal. Several of the contributors to *Mir Iskusstva*, including Rozanov, came over to *Novyy Put'*. Younger writers also appeared in its ranks, among them Blok, K. D. Bal'mont, S. N. Sergeev-Tsenskiy, and M. P. Artsybashev. Whether alarmed by the loss of so many contributors, the competition provided by the new periodical, or the deplorable financial state of *Mir Iskusstva*, Dyagilev suggested a merging of the two journals, but his proposal was rejected.[9]

Novyy Put' and Merezhkovskiy suffered a setback in April 1903, only a few months after the founding of the journal, when the Synod suppressed the Religious-Philosophical Society. Even the support of Metropolitan Antoniy could not reverse the decision of the authorities; nor was Merezhkovskiy's personal appeal to Pobedonostsev of any avail. Nevertheless, *Novyy Put'* continued to be published, and Merezhkovskiy did not break off relations with representatives of the clergy; others continued to contribute to *Novyy Put'*, but no longer openly.[10] Moreover, reports of the meetings of the Religious-Philosophical Society, which appeared many months after the meetings themselves, were contained in *Novyy Put'* until the issue of February 1904, when it announced that "due to circumstances beyond the control of the editorial board, the printing of the reports of the Religious-Philosophical Society are suspended."[11] The initial raison d'être of the journal was thus destroyed.

Furthermore, *Novyy Put'* had only recently emerged from a serious crisis. Pertsov had tendered his resignation as editor after the closing of the Religious-Philosophical Society, and the task of finding a new editor of sufficient reputation who was willing to lend his name to the journal had proved to be an impossible one. In these circumstances, Merezhkovskiy was able to prevail upon Pertsov to remain as editor for another six months. The contributors, who received no payment for their articles and poems, were mainly young writers whose names were not yet sufficiently well known to attract a large audience. (The number of subscribers, including one in Australia, which were listed in the December issue for 1903, was only 2,558). To overcome this difficulty, Merezhkovskiy decided to place his recently completed novel, *Peter and Alexis*, in the forthcoming issues, in spite of losing the substantial payment that he would have received from another periodical. In addition, he obtained permission to print as yet unpublished notes from Dostoevskiy's diary; these appeared in January and February 1904.

The spring and summer of 1904 differed little from those of preceding years. Merezhkovskiy and Gippius made another of their almost annual trips abroad. The only incident of note was Merezhkovskiy's visit to Tolstoy at Yasnaya Polyana, after which he considered that his treatment of Tolstoy in *L. Tolstoy and Dostoevskiy* had been unfair. While he still opposed Tolstoy's religious views, Merezhkovskiy now felt that he understood Tolstoy and his tragedy.[12]

Dmitriy Filosofov, who had rejected Merezhkovskiy's friendship when *Novyy Put'* was established, had now left Dyagilev's group. The friendship between Filosofov and Merezhkovskiy, and especially between Filosofov and Zinaida Gippius, grew until he became more intimate with the Merezhkovskiys than did any other of their acquaintances. For the next fifteen years Merezhkovskiy, Gippius, and Filosofov formed an inseparable trio. Close associations also developed at this time with Aleksandr Blok and with the two members of the newly created Moscow Symbolist journal *Vesy* (The Balance), Valeriy Bryusov and Andrey Belyy. The latter, who was often in St. Petersburg, was a frequent visitor to the Merezhkovskiys' salon.[13]

By the summer of 1904 *Novyy Put'* was again in financial difficulties. Filosofov, who had taken over the editorship on Pertsov's resignation, advocated a drastic change in the policy of the journal, in order to bring it into line with existing conditions. It was no longer to be merely a religious journal, since members of the clergy had ceased to support it in any case, but was to be dedicated to social and political questions. This entailed attracting writers on social and political problems to participate, for *Novyy Put'* had no such contributors. A group of idealists (formerly Marxists) accepted an offer to join the ranks of the co-workers of *Novyy Put'*. With the issue of October 1904, S. N. Bulgakov, N. A. Berdyaev, G. N. Shtil'man, and V. V. Vodovozov took charge of the social and political department of *Novyy Put'*; the field of literature and literary criticism was left to Merezhkovskiy's group. Within a short space of time the atmosphere of the journal had changed, for Bulgakov and his associates were assuming ever-increasing control. By the end of the year they had taken over the journal completely. The last issue of *Novyy Put'* was published in December 1904, and in January 1905 the first issue of the new journal, which bore the name *Voprosy Zhizni* (Questions of Life), appeared.

The loss of *Novyy Put'* gave Merezhkovskiy the opportunity to carry out a plan that he had long had in mind: to spend two or three years in Paris. His intention was to investigate Catholicism, Modernism, and European political life, to which he had become deeply attracted. His response to the Revolution of 1905 also made it advisable for him to leave Russia for a time. The two-and-a-half-year sojourn in Paris, from March 1906 until July 1908, was a busy one. Numerous trips to the Riviera, Brittany, Normandy, and Germany did not disturb Merezhkovskiy's interests in Paris; they were only periods of respite.[14]

There was a considerable Russian colony in the French capital. Some members of it were wealthy patrons of the arts, but the majority were penniless workers, soldiers, and sailors who had fled from Russia after the abortive uprising. There were also numerous political exiles, for whose benefit some soirees were given, but who were ignored for the most part.

Merezhkovskiy, Gippius, and Filosofov mingled extensively with the exiles, particularly with those of a revolutionary tendency. Many of their Paris acquaintances had been known to them in Russia. They found Minskiy; Bal'mont, who had left Russia in fear of arrest after the publication of his poem "The Dagger" *(Kinzhal)*; Mme. A. M. Anichkova, who wrote under the pseudonym "Ivan Strannik"; Vera Figner, the well-known terrorist; and Count Prozor, who undertook to translate *L. Tolstoy and Dostoevskiy* into French. Among the Russian émigrés they became especially intimate with I. Bunakov, a Social Revolutionary, and the terrorist Boris V. Savinkov, with whom they had frequent serious discussions.[15] On his return to Russia, Merezhkovskiy managed to have Savinkov's reminiscences published under the title *The Pale Horse (Kon' blednyy)* and the pseudonym "V. Ropshin." Towards the end of Merezhkovskiy's stay in Paris, Berdyaev and Belyy appeared on the scene.

Merezhkovskiy did not move solely in Russian circles. He was primarily in France to explore Catholicism, so he was soon mixing with members of the Catholic clergy, among them the rector of the Paris Seminary, Abbé Portal.[16] Entrance into the Modernist movement was more difficult. Of the members of the latter he came to know Father Laberthonnière and Henri Bergson. With both groups he discussed religious problems and ideas.

Despite his wide circle of acquaintances, the resulting busy social life, and the numerous lectures he gave, Merezhkovskiy did not cease his writing. His affiliations with Russian journals and newspapers, never strong at the best of times, were not weakened by his absence from Russia; on the contrary, they became slightly stronger. Not only did he write many articles, the majority of which were later incorporated in the collection *Not Peace, But a Sword (Ne mir, no mech)*, but he envisaged, in collaboration with Gippius and Filosofov, a collection of articles on Russia, autocracy, and revolution, which was to be published in Paris under the title *Le Tsar et la révolution*. It was in Paris, too, that he wrote the first part of his second trilogy, the drama *Paul I (Pavel I)*, which was being translated into French even before it was published in Russian.

The death of Merezhkovskiy's father in March 1908 broke off the protracted stay abroad; and in April, Merezhkovskiy, Gippius, and Filosofov returned to St. Petersburg.[17] The atmosphere in Russia was much different from what had existed before their departure. Everywhere, especially in Moscow, there was an air of bustle, which Merezhkovskiy could not, or refused to, understand. They found, too, an officially authorized Religious-Philosophical Society in St. Petersburg. Founded by Berdyaev, it had deteriorated and had almost died out after his departure for Paris. Merezhkovskiy and his two followers joined it immediately, intending to revive it and put it on the same footing as its predecessor. However, the present society was one-sided, for representatives of the church did not participate. It became nothing more than an arena in which the intelligentsia could air their quarrels.[18]

Merezhkovskiy now became closely associated with the journal *Russkaya Mysl'* and had *Paul I* published in it. The drama was promptly seized by the authorities when it appeared in a separate edition shortly thereafter. For a brief period Merezhkovskiy held the position of literary editor of *Russkaya Mysl'*; but an altercation with the Moscow editors P. B. Struve and Bulgakov over an article by Blok, which Merezhkovskiy wished to publish, led to his resignation.[19]

Merezhkovskiy's many activities, among them the writing of countless articles and the preparations for a long-contemplated novel, had an adverse effect on his health. During the winter of 1908–1909 he suffered a severe heart attack, the first of many. Rest was the only treatment; in the spring, with Gippius and Filosofov, he went to Lugano, and then to Paris for further discussions with Savinkov and Bunakov, in whom he still hoped to instill his apocalyptical Christianity.[20]

The following years were difficult ones for Merezhkovskiy. As usual, he spent much of his time abroad, particularly on the Riviera, where he worked especially well. These were to be periods of rest, in an attempt to alleviate his heart condition. Despite the ailment, Merezhkovskiy could not put aside his work. In addition to his constantly appearing articles, he completed the novel *Alexander I (Aleksandr I)*; and before that had been written in its final draft, he began to make preparations for its sequel, *December the Fourteenth (Chetyrnadtsatoe dekabrya)*. In connection with the latter, he planned a trip to the Ukraine in order to familiarize himself with the locale of the Southern Society of the Decembrist movement. This intention was not carried out, because of the unrest prevalent in Kiev after the assassination of Peter Stolypin in September 1911.[21]

Merezhkovskiy's friendship with Savinkov and other revolutionary exiles, whom he met and associated with on almost every trip abroad, did not pass unnoticed by the Russian authorities. One of Savinkov's acquaintances was arrested for having visited him; and Merezhkovskiy himself, abroad at the time, was advised that unfavorable rumors concerning him were going about in St. Petersburg. Later, in the spring of 1912 when he crossed the Russian border at Verzhbolovo, police officials seized all his papers, including a large portion of *Alexander I*, which was still in manuscript form.[22] That year he also learned that, after four years of waiting, he and M. V. Pirozhkov, the publisher, were at last to be prosecuted for lese majesty in his drama *Paul I*.[23] The case was begun on 18 September, and it lasted several days. Both Pirozhkov, whose position was the more serious, and Merezhkovskiy were acquitted of the charge, and the ban on *Paul I* was lifted. Yet even after this, Merezhkovskiy did not break off his friendship with Savinkov and Bunakov, for he spent considerable time with them on his visits to the Riviera and Paris in 1913 and 1914. When Merezhkovskiy, Gippius, and Filosofov returned to Russia in the spring of 1914, they had little thought that six years of war and revolution would pass before they again would see Merezhkovskiy's "douce France."[24]

During Merezhkovskiy's long and full career as a writer, no period was more prolific than the one that fell between the early years of the twentieth century and the Revolution of 1917. It was a period in which he ceased to be a purely religious writer, for despite the variety of media and the seemingly diversified themes that he had indulged in previously, there was, in essence, one common factor to his early literary activity: the search for a true religion. Once he believed that he had found it in the prophecies of the Apocalypse, he turned his attention to the contemporary scene, to the existing social and political institutions and conditions—those of the world at large, as well as those of Russia.

Creative literature was relegated to a secondary position. Whereas formerly Merezhkovskiy had made use of poetry and the novel to transmit his latest thoughts, now his novels and dramas merely repeated, rather than introduced, ideas that were more forcefully expressed elsewhere. Furthermore, the integration of the ideas into the works is less successfully accomplished, so that from a literary standpoint his new novels are of a lower caliber than the novels of his earlier trilogy. In *Julian the Apostate* and *Leonardo da Vinci* he had maintained a unity of purpose; in *Peter and Alexis* he began to be enmeshed in a series of themes, but had managed with difficulty to retain the thread of his main thought. In *Alexander I* and *December the Fourteenth*, Merezhkovskiy limited the scope of the action and the time that elapses to those of the era of the Decembrist movement. Yet he also sought to symbolize the entire revolutionary movement in Russia—that of 1905 no less than that of 1825. Moreover, he wished to include all his current ideas into one work; for *December the Fourteenth* is less a sequel than a conclusion to *Alexander I*. His tendency toward diffusion therefore intensified and produced an excess of the flaws that were apparent, but that were not yet overly objectionable, in his earlier novels. Both the diversity of his tendentiousness and the determination to make everything conform to, and demonstrate, his preconceptions culminated in all too easily identifiable historical inaccuracies, anachronisms, and one-sided, if not actually distorted, portrayals of historical personages.[25]

Similarly, two of his five plays, *There Will Be Joy* (*Budet radost'*, 1916) and *The Romantics* (*Romantiki*, 1917), suffer seriously from an excess of philosophizing on the part of the characters and from a proliferation of quotations, a frequently objectionable trait in his belles-lettres as a whole and one that is deadly for drama, as V. G. Malakhieva-Mirovich quite rightly points out in her review of *There Will Be Joy*.[26] Only *The Poppy Flower* (*Makov tsvet*, 1908), which V. Kranikhfel'd considered to be the most significant literary work to arise from and to reflect the Revolution of 1905,[27] *Paul I*, and *Tsarevich Alexis* (*Tsarevich Aleksey*, 1920) rise above the ideological content and stand as creditable dramatic compositions. *The Poppy*

Flower, coauthored by Merezhkovskiy, Gippius, and Filosofov, treats the Revolution of 1905 as it affects one family, which is symbolic of the whole of Russia. It may owe its success to the beneficent influence of Gippius. *Paul I* and *Tsarevich Alexis*, a dramatization of sections of the novel *Peter and Alexis*, have justifiably been termed the best historical tragedies in Russian since Pushkin's *Boris Godunov*.[28] Such praise is not as extravagant as it may at first seem, for the historical drama proved to be a relatively unpopular form with Russian dramatists. Only the trilogy of A. K. Tolstoy bears mention; but in intensity of conflict, character delineation, and general stageworthiness, Merezhkovskiy's two dramas are decidedly superior. Nevertheless, Merezhkovskiy's social, political, and religious ideas remain dominant; and the plays, like all his creative works of the period, had as their purpose the dissemination of his sociopolitical and religious ideas to a broader segment of the public than that which was turning its attention to his essays, which from 1904 onward were to be the most important vehicle for the expression of his thought.

Merezhkovskiy's interest in the social and political spheres was not the common one of his day. His desire was not for social and political betterment per se; the one important factor that influenced his conclusions and his whole program of reform was his religion. Merezhkovskiy's apocalyptical Christianity, based as it was on the concepts of the approaching end of the world, the Second Coming of Christ, and the establishment of the Kingdom of God on earth, was not an abstraction for him. Not only did he believe that this coming kingdom was at hand; he also ardently aspired to assist in its establishment. Consequently, it was necessary to prepare the world for its advent; and this entailed the dissemination of his ideas, the enlightenment of all society, the revelation of what was wrong with the world, and suggestions as to how these faults could be corrected. This is precisely what Merezhkovskiy set out to accomplish with the sole means at his disposal, his literary endeavors.

Just as his religious beliefs had been subject to considerable alteration in the course of his search for the ideal religion, so Merezhkovskiy's social and political convictions and ideals underwent constant revision until he found what he considered to be the only solution to the ills of mankind. In this sphere, as in his religious searching, he did not hesitate to refute what he had once declared to be his ideal. Many of his detractors seized upon this trait in his development and deplored his inconstancy. Even Bryusov, who had at one time defended Merezhkovskiy against those who claimed that his preaching was at best a momentary attraction to new words, took up this cry, writing in 1914:

> In recent years Merezhkovskiy has renounced his former idols, including Tyutchev. *Ad maiorem gloriam Dei*, Merezhkovskiy now hastens to consume in his merciless autos-da-fé "everything he had worshiped." It is not likely that anything but smoke can rise out of these inquisitional conflagrations.[29]

Bryusov had been more lenient and also more just in his earlier appraisal of this seeming inconstancy in Merezhkovskiy's works. Merezhkovskiy's changing of opinion was never a retrograde movement; on the contrary, it was a definite progression. He never returned to a concept that he had once discarded; moreover, his very refutation of ideals that he had held dear at one time or another was not the vacillation of a shallow intellect, but the result of deep thought. If, in the light of his religious beliefs, which were also expanded in this period, Merezhkovskiy concluded that he had made a false appraisal, he had the courage to admit his error and to renounce his former ideal.

It would be false to imply that all Merezhkovskiy's ideas were in a constant state of flux. This was far from the case. In addition to the basic tenets of his religion, which remained unaltered throughout the rest of his life, certain of his convictions in the sociopolitical sphere also remained static. Once he had adopted a negative attitude to an existing political, social, or religious institution, he virtually never altered his opinion of it. Yet his work was not purely negative. Like his one-time teacher Nietzsche, he wanted to destroy the old in an effort to establish the new. The new order he longed to see—theocracy, the Kingdom of God on earth—demanded the almost complete elimination of contemporary society and all that derived from it. He did not realize this at once, to be sure; but as his thought progressed, more and more social and political phenomena fell under the sharp thrusts of his pen.

The most constant of Merezhkovskiy's social convictions was his view of the bourgeoisie and what it represented. The first indications of his antipathy for bourgeois culture and society were revealed in his early poetry. Prompted by his Nietzschean individualism and aristocratism, he had wholeheartedly supported Nietzsche's rebellion against middle-class morality in an attempt to escape from the mediocrity and banality that he observed in contemporary society. Although he later renounced the "childhood disease" of Nietzscheism,[30] he did not part with the concepts of individualism and aristocratism, but incorporated them in his new Christianity; and it was from this religion that he drew his basic arguments against bourgeois society.

Merezhkovskiy's apocalyptical religion was based on extremes. If extremes are holy, of God, then, Merezhkovskiy's logic insisted, evil and the devil lie between these extremes. God is eternal—the end and the beginning of existence—and the devil is the negation of God—the negation of the eternal, the denial of the beginning and the end; therefore, "the devil—the nominal middle of the real, the denial of all depths and summits—is eternal flatness, eternal banality."[31] Merezhkovskiy saw this devil everywhere about him, for the devil's face was the face of the crowd, "almost our own faces during those moments when we dare not be ourselves and agree to be 'the same as all.' "[32] It was visible in all aspects of contemporary culture. It was to be seen, above all, in the attitude of the bourgeoisie toward a paradise on earth. Merezhkovskiy did not object to an earthly paradise; but he was opposed to what the middle classes believed to be important in it: "So-called *comfort*, that is, the highest cultural flower of the contemporary industrial-capitalist and bourgeois system, comfort, which all forces of nature subjected to science (sound, light, electricity), all inventions, all art serve: this is the ultimate crown of earthly paradise."[33] The concern for property, capital, and comfort was a human, as opposed to a godly, truth. It was the very essence of the positivist nineteenth century, which was for Merezhkovskiy the most mediocre of all centuries. Since the extremes—the beginning and the end of the world—were not known to this essence of European culture, then only the mean or the average was accessible to knowledge and experiment; only this was real, for "the sole and definitive criterion for the evaluation of everything is durability, solidity, the 'positivity' of this sensual experience, that is, of the ordinary, 'healthy,' *average* human sensuality."[34]

Merezhkovskiy deplored the mediocre happiness and the calm content of the positivists, who selected only what they needed from universal culture. Whatever was too elevated or too deep for them they rejected or reduced to the level of trivia. Even love of mankind and love of self were lowered to a safe level. Most despicable of all was the achievement of a comfortable serving of both God and Mammon. Regardless of such claims, the real motive for Merezhkovskiy's current attack on bourgeois positivism was that it not only refused to recognize his major premise, that the end of the world would occur in the near future, but denied such a possibility by its very essence—its belief in unending progress:

> The unconscious essence of any form of positivism as a doctrine of the meaning of life, from Confucius to Comte, is the denial of the end, the affirmation of the perpetual continuation of the human race, of perpetual progress: we are fine; it will be better for our children and still better for our grandchildren and great-grandchildren; and so on, without end. Not humanity in God, but God in humanity. Humanity itself is God, and there is no other God. There is no personal immortality, but only immortality in humanity. Each generation "earns its living," "acquires" for future generations; the endless acquisition, the accumulation of *dead* capital: that is the unconscious and absolute essence of progress. Hence the "worship of ancestors" in Chinese positivism, the worship of descendents in European positivism; hence marriage, childbearing, "the family as a religion." "Wife and children"—this is the eternal justification of all the absurdities of the bourgeois system, the eternal objection to a religion that says: "And a man's foes shall be they of his own household"; this is the "solid foundation" on which are broken all winged "chimeras," all Christian prophecies about the end of the world.[35]

It is understandable, from the point of view of Merezhkovskiy's religious desires, that he should oppose the idea of the continuation of the family and the striving to prepare a better world for one's descendents. With the end of the world imminent, as Merezhkovskiy ardently believed, such practices would appear not only reprehensible, but foolish. Yet one cannot prevent oneself from feeling that this is only one side of Merezhkovskiy's animosity toward the concept of family and descendents. Could it not be to some extent an expression on his part of a bitterness at not having children of his own and a revelation of jealousy for those who did have offspring to carry on the family in the future? Whether this is the case or not, Merezhkovskiy was convinced that such a bourgeois existence was a "mediocre kingdom" of countless positivists, or of the future universal "Chinese" which had terrified Vladimir Solov'ev.

Merezhkovskiy took up Solov'ev's symbol of the "Yellow Peril" and examined European bourgeois, positivist culture in its light. He was certain that Europe was moving toward this dreaded Pan-Mongolism, which he deemed the last bound of bourgeois positivism. Merezhkovskiy conceived of positivism as an unconscious religion, which had grown from scientific and philosophical method and which was attempting to alter all earlier religions to its own ends. It was the affirmation of this world and the denial of any supersensual world; it was the assertion of the continuation of the world as it was—a world of mediocrity and of the absolute petite bourgeoisie. Positivism in Europe had not yet reached its fulfilment, as it had in the Orient, where it had become a religion without God, hence a religion of man. He warned Europe that the price of such a religion was high: "In renouncing God and an absolute Divine Personality, man inevitably renounces his own human personality. In denying his divine hunger and divine primogeniture for the sake of a mess of pottage for modest repletion, man inevitably falls into absolute Philistinism."[36] Here we find yet another reason for Merezhkovskiy's opposition to positivism and Philistinism (in Merezhkovskiy's terminology the latter also contains the significance of the preponderance of the petite bourgeoisie). In it he saw the destruction of the individual, and he was never prepared to surrender his own individualism to any philosophical or religious doctrine.

He feared that China would be spiritually victorious over Europe, just as Japan had emerged the victor from the Russo-Japanese War; and undoubtedly this very war was what induced Merezhkovskiy to turn his attention to Pan-Mongolism, or what at least clarified the meaning of Solov'ev's concept. Merezhkovskiy rued the means employed by Christian Europe in its dealings with Asia, where Christian principles were replaced by letters of credit, shells, and war—the very fruits of Philistinism. "Foreign policy is only a cynical baring of internal policy. 'Wherefore by their fruits shall ye know them.' The fruit of internal, spiritual Philistinism is external, international brutality: militarism, chauvinism."[37] Yet he credited Europe's not having reached complete Sinicization to elements of Christianity that still existed within it: "Christianity—this old Semitic yeast in Aryan blood—is the very thing that does not allow it to settle definitively, hinders the ultimate 'crystallization,' the Sinicization of Europe."[38] Unlike Solov'ev, who was certain that Pan-Mongolism inevitably must occur as a prelude to the end of the world, Merezhkovskiy (nonetheless fearing that Europe might well succumb to this religion of positivism) indicated that such a catastrophe could be averted if a spiritual change were to take place in Europe: presumably the acceptance of his own religious ideals. Otherwise, a "mediocre kingdom" would be established throughout the world, ruled by absolute Philistinism; in Merezhkovskiy's opinion, "Philistinism which attains its limits and which rules is Hamism."[39]

Ham (the Flunky)[40] and Hamism (flunkyism, the reign of the Flunky) became the symbols for Merezhkovskiy of the antithesis of his own desire for the coming of the Kingdom of God to earth, the reign of the Godman. Actually, they are just the replacement of the terms Mangod and his kingdom, which Merezhkovskiy had employed so frequently in previous years. In essence, Ham is also another name for Antichrist, whose coming Merezhkovskiy feared. Merezhkovskiy saw the lack of freedom in a social order based on the bourgeoisie, and consequently on Hamism, which he considered to be the worst of all slaveries, for it was the kingdom of the devil.[41] The Coming Ham would limit individual, personal freedom; and Merezhkovskiy, ever rebellious against any restraint whatsoever, would naturally conclude that Hamism was his personal enemy.

Although Merezhkovskiy's antagonism to the bourgeoisie was superficially akin to the Socialist mistrust of this class, and although he added his spiritual support to the Socialists for a short period, he did not share their opinions on the virtues of the proletariat. He recognized the economic differences between the proletariat and the bourgeoisie, of course, but he was convinced that these two social classes shared the same metaphysics and the same religion: "the metaphysics of temperate healthy thought, the religion of temperate bourgeois satiety."[42] Nevertheless, this did not prevent him from associating with the Socialists. Yet his cold appraisal of Socialist doctrine and also his evaluation of anarchism at this time contained not only the reasons for his temporary support, but also the seeds of his later rejection of them. On the eve of the Revolution of 1905 Merezhkovskiy declared:

> The strength and weakness of socialism as a religion lie in the fact that it predetermines future social creation, and by so doing, it involuntarily includes in itself the spirit of eternal mediocrity, of Philistinism, and the inevitable metaphysical consequence of positivism as a religion, on which socialism itself is built. The strength and weakness of anarchism lie in the fact that it predetermines no social creation, that it does not bind itself with any responsibility for the future before the past, and that from the historical shoal of Philistinism it sails out onto a sea of

unknown historic depths, where it is faced either with final wreck or with the discovery of a new heaven and a new earth.[43]

Merezhkovskiy invariably supported what he considered to be a movement towards God, and he zealously attacked anything that denied God. Such was his divided attitude toward anarchism. Despite his own rebellious individualism and anarchic extremes, he opposed these same characteristics in others if they failed to satisfy his religious beliefs. Therefore, it was on religious grounds that he rebuked anarchists, exemplified for him by Gor'kiy's tramps and by Dostoevskiy's underground men.[44] Merezhkovskiy was not interested in the external, socioeconomic similarities of these apparently different breeds of anarchists, but in their inner, psychological "trampism" *(bosyachestvo)*, which he considered to be the ultimate of nihilism. While Merezhkovskiy himself may be cited as an example of this same anarchy and while a large portion of what he states about the tramp and the underground man may be applied to himself, there was a difference between them. The basis of the tramp's and the underground man's anarchy is individualism, and their desire is to destroy all existing order; but Merezhkovskiy's anarchy had a religious purpose, which was lacking in the tramp and the underground man. In Merezhkovskiy's opinion, their anarchy was a flight "from reason to madness, from world order to 'destruction and chaos.' "[45]

In subjecting "trampism" to a religious appraisal, Merezhkovskiy found its basic essence to be antichristian, largely because of the animosity of the tramp to the people, or the peasantry, whom he maintained to be unconsciously religious. He evaluated "trampism" as a religion of humanity without God, but with the possibility of developing into a new Antichristianity, into the religion of the Mangod. In an effort to discredit such an antichristian philosophy, which is proclaimed by Satin in Gor'kiy's *Lower Depths (Na dne)*, Merezhkovskiy drew the following startling proposition:

> Conscious Christianity is the religion of God Who Became Man; conscious trampism, or Antichristianity, is the religion of man who wishes to become God. The latter is, of course, a delusion. Indeed, the starting point of trampism is: "only man exists"; there is no God; God is nothing; consequently, "man is God" means that man is nothing. Sham idolization leads to the destruction of man.[46]

In this evaluation of the extreme affirmation of the individual without God, Merezhkovskiy, in fact, was sounding the death knell of his own convictions on individualism, which he had held prior to his discovery of a religious justification for them. Moreover, in his rejecting of extreme individualism without God as being antichristian, he joined it to his concept of Philistinism, which is also Hamism, or Antichristianity. Both were parts of one whole and were equally detested by Merezhkovskiy.

"Trampism" was but the third, the future, revelation of the Coming Ham, the world ruler of darkness. Two other visages of this abhorred bourgeois, which Merezhkovskiy termed the past and present revelations, were also visible in Russia. These were Orthodoxy and autocracy, which only a few years before he had hailed as instruments of the Divine Will and which he had proclaimed to be the very basis of his desired theocratic state.

It is not surprising that Merezhkovskiy should have altered his views on autocracy and Orthodoxy but a short time after making such statements in their favor. What is startling is that he had justified them at all, for by so doing, he contradicted his own basic beliefs in the falseness of historic Christianity and in the evil of the rule of the Mangod. Roman Catholicism and Protestantism were part of historic Christianity; yet Orthodoxy, which is certainly as historic as Western Christian religions, was exempted. Merezhkovskiy had denounced the concept of the Supreme Pontiff of Christ as both a spiritual and a temporal ruler in the papacy; yet paradoxically he upheld the same concept in Russian autocracy, for he was convinced that the tsar was not only the head of the state but also the head of the Russian Orthodox Church, therefore he was Christ's representative on earth. Such contradictions could not exist for long in Merezhkovskiy's religious contemplation. By accepting Orthodoxy and autocracy he was submitting himself both to religious and to political restraints; and Merezhkovskiy, a rebel and anarchist, could brook no limitation of his personal freedom and individualism. His rejection of Orthodoxy and autocracy was inevitable.

He began to cool toward Orthodoxy even before he revealed his doubts about autocracy. In 1903, at the time of his first major attack on bourgeois society, he began to wonder if the Orthodox Church was not going the way of the Western Church toward the monasticism and the mortification of the flesh of historic Christianity. He began to consider all Christianity, not just Western Christianity, as a part of the eternal mediocrity that he could not abide; and he asked: " 'It is tedious in this world!' Is this not the symbol of all contemporary, mediocre, neither cold nor hot but only warm, neither black nor white but only grey, neither dancing nor weeping but only 'yawning,' Christianity?"[47] Such a lukewarm Christianity, to which Kierkegaard had also objected, could not proffer the solution to his most fervent desire: "that life would be in Christ, and Christ in life."[48] Hence, Merezhkovskiy was bound to discard Orthodoxy.

It was not until some two years later, in 1905, that he became vehement in his denunciation of Orthodoxy and autocracy. His aversion for the latter developed simultaneously with his objections to the former, for he persisted in his belief that Russian absolutism and Orthodoxy were inextricably linked. Without a doubt he was already imbued with antitsarist sentiments, when on 22 January 1905 the shooting on an unarmed delegation of workers and their families further aroused his indignation and culminated in the final proof for him that autocracy was another phase of Antichristianity in Russia.[49] It also evoked his only overt act during the period of the revolution; together with Zinaida Gippius, Dmitriy Filosofov, Andrey Belyy, and many others, Merezhkovskiy assisted in staging an impromptu demonstration of protest.[50]

Orthodoxy, he declared now, like other forms of historic Christianity, was purely spiritual. Since it denied pagan Western universal culture, which was an integral part of the new Russia—the Russia from Peter the Great's time on—the Church "moved away from the new Russia."[51] Merezhkovskiy no longer claimed that only Western Catholicism, but that all historic Christianity, including Orthodoxy, suffered from the same fate after the fall of the Roman Empire. Then the Church split into that of the world and that of monasticism. In the latter, God ceased to be a living God and became a God denying all flesh and blood; thus it admitted Buddhistic metaphysics, or absolute nothingness, rather than true Christianity, which asserted life. Therefore, Merezhkovskiy insisted: "Indeed, this very monastic inclination, the concept of Christianity as a retiring from the world, was the main reason that Christ really left the world and the world left Christ."[52]

He hastened to refute the statements that he made in *L. Tolstoy and Dostoevskiy* regarding the religious origin of state power, calling his former convictions "not only a political, historical, and philosophical but also a deeply religious delusion."[53] No longer did he assert that a Christian state could exist. He now ridiculed the idea, declaring that in any state there was the more or less conscious religion of the Mangod. Merezhkovskiy considered not only the concept of the state, but also that of the monarch to be religious and not simply political in nature. In particular he wanted to convince others, just as he himself was certain, that the Russian tsar and Russian autocracy were a religion of the devil, for he insisted from this time onwards that any human power was from the devil and not from God, as he had formerly averred. He attempted to prove that the Russian autocrat was a direct descendant of the Roman Caesar, the ruler in the sense of an earthly god, a Mangod, such as had existed in the pre-Christian era. Therefore, autocracy was not only moving in the direction of the kingdom of Antichrist, but "autocracy is from Antichrist."[54] After the Gapon affair, Merezhkovskiy became more than ever convinced of the evils of autocracy, and of the Russian version in particular: "The ancient pagan mask of Mangodhood was replaced by the new Christian mask of Godmanhood; but the face remained the same—the face of the Beast. And nowhere in the world has the kingdom of the Beast been as fierce, godless, and blasphemous as precisely here, in Russian autocracy."[55]

Independent of one another, Orthodoxy and autocracy were sufficiently evil; but united, they were infinitely worse. So reasoned Merezhkovskiy, who had but recently deemed this very union to be the essence of their holiness. Instead he declared his hatred for any form of religion used as a pawn of politics, a common practice throughout European Christian civilization:

> The history of European statehood in general, and of Russian, in particular, established an overly tight, almost indissoluble link between religious, especially "Christian," ideas, on the one hand, and the coarsest forms of social injustice and political oppression, on the other. Religion and reaction became almost indistinguishable synonyms.[56]

Religion became reaction, because any state, other than that of Merezhkovskiy's theocratic conception, had to be reaction; for a state meant the limitation of personal freedom, hence was slavery.

Merezhkovskiy seized upon the following passage of legislation of Peter the Great's era—"In the administration of the Church the autocratic power acts through the medium of the Holy Synod established by it"[57]—to prove his contention that the Orthodox Church in Russia was not autonomous, but was ruled directly by the sovereign. Such, of course, was not the case; but Merezhkovskiy can hardly be considered fair in his judgment of anything or anyone to whom he took a dislike; in this instance, however, he was undoubtedly sincere in his belief that, by becoming the supreme judge of the Holy Synod, the autocrat vested himself in the greatest spiritual power: that of Christ himself.[58] The Russian Church was therefore in the same position as the Roman Catholic Church: it became a "papal autocracy," with the autocrat, like the pope, exposed to the danger of standing in Christ's place. Merezhkovskiy voiced a strong condemnation of any human's usurping this role, when in 1907 he wrote for his European audience:

> Any substitution of human flesh or of a human face—pope or Caesar—for the true Flesh of Christ or for the veritable Image of Christ is a blasphemy, is absolute Antichristianity. Who can take the place of Christ and serve as a substitute for Him, if it is not the Antichrist? In this sense, any vicar of Christ, any pontiff and autocrat, is "Christ's impostor"—the Antichrist.[59]

Merezhkovskiy did not limit his remarks to such a general condemnation of autocracy; he did not hesitate to state the final conclusion of his train of thought: "The Russian tsar is the Antichrist."[60]

Merezhkovskiy also considered all other rulers of Europe to be minions of Antichrist. Thus he denied the very concept of the ruler and, together with it, the concept of the state. He had discarded his belief in the possibility of a theocratic state based on existing state forms. In a complete reversal of his own ideas he reasoned:

> In the first case, "state" is understood to be the Kingdom of God, or *theocracy*—that is, the boundlessly free sociality of love, renouncing any external enforced power—and, consequently, is like none of the historic state forms that have existed up to the present time; in the second case, "state" is understood to be external enforced power, or the kingdom of this world, the kingdom of the devil—demonocracy.[61]

The inevitable conclusion of such a definition of the state is that a religious state, or theocracy, must be one in which there is no constraint whatsoever. Religious anarchy became the only possible Kingdom of God on earth. In such a theocratic state Merezhkovskiy could attain his ideal: his individualism and his freedom would be subject to no fetters. Yet it must be established that since his anarchy was to be "the reign of God,"[62] he was not an anarchist whose program was to replace order and power by lack of order and lack of power; his anarchy was a religious rebellion against the concept of the state as a religion. Lest he be misunderstood, he pointed this out himself:

> I am not an anarchist in the political sense. I realize that anarchy may be a more evil constraint than any government. But I do not have to be a political anarchist in order to recognize the state as only a temporary and relative means and not an eternal and absolute aim, as a watch fire of the earth and not a "guiding star" in the heavens, in order not to make the state ideal an idol, and in order not to preach a *religion of state organization.*[63]

Merezhkovskiy's God was a God of absolute freedom, and his Christ was the highest affirmation of the individual. At the same time He was a God of love; therefore, love as freedom was to be the basis of his religious anarchy.

The means of achieving this religious anarchy, this theocracy, appeared to be at hand in the sociopolitical revolutionary movement of 1905. In many superficial respects the aims of the revolutionary intellectuals coincided with Merezhkovskiy's own aims. Both he and they opposed the Russian state as it existed at the time, though for different reasons. Both desired social improvement, although there was a great disparity between Merezhkovskiy's religious purposes and the materialistic desires of the Socialists. Berdyaev was right when he stated that Merezhkovskiy's comprehension of the revolutionary movement and of events in Russia was entirely false.[64] Indeed, it would seem that Merezhkovskiy deluded himself purposely. Perhaps he was blinded by his religious zeal; or perhaps he hoped to convert all the revolutionary intellectuals, even the atheists, to his beliefs and aims. Whatever the cause, the result was that he not only allied himself with the revolutionaries, but he also expended much effort in the justification of the attitudes and convictions of his new-found friends. It is as if the necessity to convince himself of the innate religiosity of the intellectuals (often apparent to Merezhkovskiy alone) impelled him to write the many articles devoted to a defense of, and almost an apologia for, the Russian intelligentsia.

One of Merezhkovskiy's basic convictions regarding the Russian intelligentsia was their uniqueness in contemporary European culture. While the Russian intellectual and the European intellectual were counterparts, the Russian intellectual was superior because he was more religious. Addressing the European intelligentsia, Merezhkovskiy wrote:

You love the golden mean—we love extremes; you are sober—we always become intoxicated; you are just—we are without law; you know how "to save your soul"—we always seek to lose ours. You possess the *City of the present*—we are seekers of the *City of the future.* At last, beyond the greatest liberty that you may have, you recognize the power of the state; we, in the depths of our slavery, have never ceased to be rebels and anarchists in secret. For you, politics is a science; for us, it is a religion. Reasoning and feeling have often pushed us to absolute negation —to nihilism; but our most occult will makes us mystics.[65]

This belief in the fundamental religious quality of the Russian intelligentsia was Merezhkovskiy's reason for supporting their policies, no matter how contrary they were in reality to his own aspirations.

His involved arguments in proof of the intelligentsia's unconscious religious depths often compelled him to resort to very startling asseverations. He was well acquainted with the fact that many of the intellectuals were charged with atheism, and while he could not in all honesty disclaim the truth of this accusation, he set out not only to justify atheism but also to reveal its religious values.

The conscious atheism of the revolutionary intelligentsia was the natural result of the union of religion with reaction, Orthodoxy with autocracy. The intelligentsia wanted political freedom; therefore, they had to oppose the religion that supported the form of government that they detested. Instead of turning to a positive religious truth, such as Merezhkovskiy advocated, they turned to a negative religious truth—atheism. Russian atheism was just the reverse of Russian mysticism; hence it, too, was a religion. It was a form of theomachy, and this struggle of man with God was one of the paths to God. This idea and also his contention that one need not admit belief in God in order to believe were used by Merezhkovskiy to substantiate his claim that the intelligentsia were essentially religious.

Faith and the consciousness of faith are not the same. Not all who think they believe, believe; and not all who think they do not believe, do not believe. The Russian intelligentsia do not yet have religious consciousness, a creed; but they already have a great and ever-growing religious thirst. *"Blessed are they which do hunger and thirst, for they shall be filled."*

Many contrary, not only positive but also negative, paths to God exist. The theomachy of Jacob, the grumbling of Job, the lack of faith of Thomas—all these are true paths to God.[66]

Even to one who might subscribe to these negative arguments, Merezhkovskiy's assertion that by swearing in the name of God and Christ the atheists showed how close Christ was to them must seem a mere clutching at straws; at best it may be accepted as his weakest argument. Although such a claim may appear ridiculous, it was an essential part of Merezhkovskiy's platform, for it led to another of his startling conclusions: that the intelligentsia "are not yet with Christ, but Christ is already with them."[67]

Merezhkovskiy did not fail to bring his views on historic Christianity to the support of this statement. Christianity in its accepted forms was not the true teaching of Christ; only in the religion of the Second Coming was the true teaching of Christ evident. Therefore he argued: "Christ is with him who is no longer within Christianity; Christ is no longer with him who is within Christianity. Not in name but in essence, not in word but in deed, Christ is opposed to Christianity, and Christianity is opposed to Christ."[68] Thus he hoped not only to reveal the religious right of the intelligentsia, but at the same time to put the onus for a false belief on the supporters of historic Christianity.

Having satisfied himself about the religious worth of the intellectuals, Merezhkovskiy explained in what their godlessness lay. It was only in their *intellectus*, their way of thinking. Although their minds might go astray, in their hearts and consciences they were almost always on the right path; and it was to this that Merezhkovskiy attributed their strength, even to the Marxists who seemed to sacrifice Russia to Marx-Moloch when speaking of the iron law of necessity: "In their hearts is stormy youth, but in their thoughts is humble old age."[69] Moreover, Merezhkovskiy, a religious anarchist who wanted the destruction of the state for religious purposes, believed (or wanted to believe) that all those who were opposed to this same state for political and social reasons had to be religious, claiming that "there are tasks that are impossible to perform without a living faith in a living God; such is the main task of the Russian intelligentsia— the struggle against dead autocratic statehood for the liberation of Russia."[70] In this way he expressed his conviction in the religious significance of the Russian Revolution of 1905.

Merezhkovskiy was aware that the revolution was not religious enough when it occurred; and he certainly voiced complaints about it, including the comment that it was as absolutist as the autocracy that it was rejecting.[71] At the same time he ascribed its lack of religious ideas to the fact that the Russian revolution was only in its early stages and that it had not yet awakened the last depths of the popular element.[72] Nonetheless, he regarded the revolution as an unconscious religion, arguing that any revolutionary society contained the beginning of ecumenicity, which in turn was the ultimate, pan-human truth. Although he abhorred the concept of the dictatorship of the proletariat, which he thought would inevitably lead to the dictatorship of one person, hence a form of autocracy, he still found a religious element in the universality of purpose of Social Democracy: "The soul of the Russian revolution, Social Democracy, is already universally ecumenical, consequently it is unconsciously religious."[73] Merezhkovskiy was not an advocate of the rule of all, as preached by the Socialists, for this too was a power, and he was no more willing to submit to this form of restraint than to any other. This form of anarchy, which he believed was a further appearance of the Mangod, was consequently another manifestation of Antichrist. He had no doubt that

> it is not enough to deny authority: such a denial is bare abstraction, a deserted place or an all-destroying anarchy, devilish chaos, more devilish than state coercion; it is necessary to show the practically implemented transition from state coercion to religious, free sociality, from the power of man to the power of God.[74]

Merezhkovskiy was convinced that the only means of achieving his concept of theocracy, which he frankly admitted to be anarchy that recognized only the power of a God of love and freedom, was revolution. Reform was unsatisfactory, if not impossible. The granting of a constitution to Russia did not satisfy him, for it did not do away completely with the power of the state, nor did it render autocracy less antichristian. Neither could the Church, even if reformed, offer a solution to the problem that he posed.

> In order for the Church to reply, there would have been needed more than a reform—but a revolution; more than a new interpretation—but a new revelation; not the continuation of the Second Testament, but the beginning of the Third Testament; not a return to the Christ of the First Coming, but a bound toward the Christ of the Second Coming.[75]

Thus Merezhkovskiy declared the need for a revolution both in the sociopolitical and in the religious order of the day. He found elements of both revolutions in Russian history: the sociopolitical uprising of the Decembrists, and the religious rebelliousness of the schismatics and other sects that broke away from the accepted Church; and he expressed his desire and also his deep conviction that these two revolutions would merge into one religious revolution, for "the only real path to the Kingdom—the power of God—is the destruction of all human power, that is, the greatest of all revolutions."[76] More than ever he saw the need in contemporary society for the merging of revolution and religion, which had developed separately and offered a choice of freedom without God, on the one hand, and God without liberty, on the other. With his concepts of Christ the Liberator and Christ's love as complete freedom, Merezhkovskiy wanted the union of religion and revolution in order to attain a tabula rasa; for Orthodoxy (historic Christianity) and autocracy (the state) had to be overcome together before anarchic theocracy could be achieved. For this reason he labeled the accepted order as antichristian and the revolution as true religion, and he proclaimed the inseparability of religion and revolution:

> Religion and revolution are not cause and result, but one and the same phenomenon in two categories: religion is none other than revolution in the Godly category; revolution is none other than religion in the human category. Religion and revolution are not two, but one; religion is also revolution, revolution is also religion.[77]

Having convinced himself that revolution and religion were one, he also tried to convince himself that the Russian intelligentsia were not far from the same conclusion. His argument was that, since revolution was a religion for the intellectuals, it was but a short step for religion to become revolution; when this occurred, true religious revolution would result.[78] Thus he declared that the sociopolitical revolution that took place in 1905 was the forerunner of the final, complete religious revolution, in which new state forms would be forged.

Revolution, like religion, had to be universal; for its goal, the establishment of the Kingdom of God on earth, had to be universal. The ultimate Christian ideal of God-humanity could be attained only through the ideal of pan-humanity, of universal salvation, the salvation of all instead of the salvation of the individual alone. Consequently, no nation could fulfill its supreme Christian predestination in its own culture; universal culture was essential. Once again

Merezhkovskiy resorted to an odd form of negative reasoning to stress the value of his conviction:

> One may say the same thing about every nation that one says about every man: a nation that desires to preserve its soul, its exclusive national truth, loses it; and the one that loses it for the sake of universal truth preserves it. Every nation must renounce itself, its "synthetic personality, its particular god"; it must sacrifice itself for all other nations; it must die as a nation in universal humanity, in order to be resurrected in God-humanity.[79]

Here he not only expressed his distaste for the linking of Church and state in any country, but at the same time he attacked the essence of the concept of Russia as a God-bearing nation and as the Third Rome. This did not prevent his being confident that Russia would lead the way to the true apocalyptical religion and pan-humanity; for the Russians, judging from Merezhkovskiy's words, were the most universal of all peoples, thanks to Peter the Great, who was responsible for the Russians' having two fatherlands: Russia and Europe.

Up to this point in discussing Merezhkovskiy's views on revolution we have seen primarily the negative aspects of his program, including his concept of anarchic theocracy, in which only the power of God was to be recognized. The essence of his positive program may be reduced to two words—religious sociality, or the revelation of the Holy Ghost—for he was convinced that "neither religion without sociality nor sociality without religion, but only *religious sociality*, can save Russia."[80] Merezhkovskiy considered religion and sociality to be two incompatible manifestations in the world: historic Christianity, which recognized only a personal, individual, inner holiness —the holiness of the spirit—was basically opposed to sociality, which proclaimed the uniting of individuals, or human plurality—the holiness of the flesh. The latter, the quintessence of Merezhkovskiy's ideas of pan-humanity and God-humanity, was also an important element in his conception of theocracy as the Third Kingdom, the Kingdom of the Holy Ghost, which could begin only when all statehood came to an end. For this reason he longed for the destruction of Russia as a state through revolution.

Yet just as he rejected religion without sociality, so, too, did he reject sociality without religion. Sociality as a religion in itself, such as the Socialist ideal of collectivism, would sacrifice the individual to the impersonal, collective whole:

The religion of sociality, collectivism, in its mystic end, which is already foreboded though still not conscious in contemporary socialism, sacrifices the individual to the impersonal whole; whether to the old state system or to a new Socialist sociality makes no difference, since in both cases the quarrel between the individual and society, One and All, is resolved *in the last analysis* by external coercive force, by the compulsory influence of the state or society on the individual, of All on One. This is why socialism as a religion does not solve, but only eliminates, the religious problem of the absolute personality.[81]

Thus he repudiated socialism for essentially the same reasons as Kierkegaard did.[82] But he had also denounced anarchy, the affirmation of the individual. Now he added to his accusations the fact that in an anarchistic society all would be sacrificed to one, the opposite of what he witnessed in a Socialist society. Neither socialism nor anarchism, which Merezhkovskiy conceived to be "not two truths and not two lies, but two polarly opposed halves of a single higher truth,"[83] could solve the enigma of one and all; the solution could only be attained by the assertion of oneself and all in God and in God-humanity, in religious sociality:

The antinomy of the Personality and Society, of the metaphysically maximum I and Not-I, Anarchism and Socialism, is resolved only in a synthesis, in the complete union of the God-man with God-humanity, in the boundlessly free and boundlessly loving religious community, in the coming, true, indivisible, universal, and ecumenical Church.[84]

Such a synthesis could only occur in Merezhkovskiy's religion of the Coming Christ and not in Christianity in its historic manifestations. To his earlier objections to historic Christianity he now added complaints that it did not answer to his concept of sociality. It was the antithesis of it in its acceptance only of Christ the Godman and not in Merezhkovskiy's ideal of God-humanity, which could be reached only when the Church was truly universal. Moreover, the existing Church proclaimed the Kingdom of God only in heaven and not on earth. It accepted only God without man, while in Merezhkovskiy's interpretation, Christ showed the way from the Godman (God in man) to God-humanity (God in humanity), in His uniting of a love for God and a love for man. From this, Merezhkovskiy evolved the main dogma of his religious sociality: "One may love God only in man; one may love man only in God; love for Christ, the

Godman, is the ultimate uniting of a love for God with a love for man."[85]

Merezhkovskiy placed his hopes for the establishment of his religious sociality, his theocracy, in the Russian intelligentsia, those chosen few whom he desired to awaken into a cognizance of his socioreligious ideals. He wrote to this effect in 1905:

> First of all, the religious-social consciousness must be awakened in that place where there is already conscious sociality and unconscious religiosity—in the Russian intelligentsia, which not only in name but also in their very essence ought to become the intelligentsia, that is, the *intellectus* incarnate, the reason, the consciousness of Russia. Reason, carried to its very end, arrives at the idea of God. The intelligentsia, carried to their end, will arrive at religion.[86]

Merezhkovskiy's placing his faith in the intelligentsia and the Revolution of 1905 proved to be ill founded. Both failed to achieve the exalted results that he so ardently desired, and it was with great bitterness that he surveyed Russia on his return from abroad in 1908. His first complaint on seeing St. Petersburg again after an absence of three years was that nothing seemed to have changed; everything appeared to be as it had been before.[87] The very liberation movement was silent. It had failed because it had lacked universal sociality. Consequently, it had been a personal, not a social, revolution, in which the individual, and not society, was asserted.[88]

In his disappointment, Merezhkovskiy began to consider all Russia to be in every way, especially politically and religiously, reaction itself. Since this was so and since Russians were themselves only in reaction, there could be no real revolution in Russia, only a conspiracy, or, as he complained: "Our revolution is primarily a strike, a stoppage, a lack of motion in the midst of motion, inaction in the midst of action itself."[89] The reason for its being no more than a strike was that the intelligentsia were unable to perceive the deceptive religious mysticism of absolute monarchy and therefore failed to oppose it from a religious point of view. The Vekhi (Signposts) movement, which developed at this time, and Berdyaev's series of essays collected in 1910 under the title *The Spiritual Crisis of the Intelligentsia (Dukhovnyy krizis intelligentsii)* would appear to indicate that the intelligentsia had lost faith in themselves; yet Merezhkovskiy still retained his belief in them to some extent and hoped that they would revive and prove to be the instrument of liberation that Russia needed. He rejected, of course, the extreme left wing of the intelligentsia, for he had turned completely against Social Democracy because it was a religion that denied the worth of the individual. Indeed, it could lead to the worst of all autocracies, "the autocracy of the new god—the collective,"[90] for it failed to recognize Merezhkovskiy's concept of God-humanity.

It seemed to Merezhkovskiy that on the whole the Russian intelligentsia were inactive after the Revolution of 1905. At first he thought that they were merely unconscious from the blow dealt them by the collapse of the movement for liberation, but he also believed that they would recover and once again commence to fight for freedom. Ultimately, he admitted that religious questions were beyond most people's field of vision and that his attempts to bring a religious significance to the social sphere had failed.[91] Moreover, these attempts would be unfruitful until the intellectuals could humble themselves before the people; and this they could not do until they ceased to believe that God did not exist. As long as they maintained this view, they could only regard the faith of the people as mere superstition:

> God on earth; the earth in God. The power of the earth is the power of God. The people will not accept an unearthly God, just as they will not accept a Godless earth. *Thy will be done, on earth as it is in heaven.* "All the will and all the earth for the people" means: the will of God on God's earth. This is what the intelligentsia do not wish to, or cannot, understand. And without comprehending this, no matter how much one "goes to the people," one will not enter.[92]

Merezhkovskiy further decided that the intelligentsia had grown tired of being themselves, at least what he considered them to be— namely, the conscience of Russian society. Instead, having cast off this role, they were turning into simple inhabitants of Russia, "senseless and carefree creatures, whose complex ideologies have been replaced by shortish, everyday wisdom."[93]

Such were the bounds of Merezhkovskiy's despair in the decade following the Revolution of 1905. Although a constitution had been granted to Russia, although reforms were being instituted, and although literature was flourishing in what has been termed its "Silver Age," Merezhkovskiy, like his revolutionary-minded contemporaries who had aspired to far more, considered the revolution a failure and the most constitutional period of Russian history an era of reaction.

140

Merezhkovskiy had desired action to overthrow the existing forms of state and Church, but action had not materialized. He had placed his faith in the Russian intelligentsia, but his faith had not been justified. The Revolution of 1905 had not become a religious revolution. Merezhkovskiy could only lament that fact, and he could hope, in vain, that the intelligentsia could be awakened in the future and that when another revolution occurred, as he was convinced it must, it would be a religious revolution, which would establish religious sociality, the Kingdom of God on earth.

8

The Third Humanity

When Merezhkovskiy left Paris for St. Petersburg late in the spring of 1914, the talk of an impending war, so prevalent throughout 1913, had almost ceased to exist as a topic of conversation. In Russia it was the same, and since Merezhkovskiy, Zinaida Gippius, and Filosofov retired to the country for the summer shortly after their arrival, the news of the mobilization and of the declaration of war came rather unexpectedly.[1] It necessitated a revision of Merezhkovskiy's attitude toward war.

The earliest suspicions of the advent of a war in Europe had stimulated Merezhkovskiy to contemplate the question of nationalism and to develop more fully than heretofore his views about it. At the outset he mildly condemned it as an evil, which he blamed for the nonacceptance of his concept of pan-humanity. Gradually, however, his pronouncements became more violent and extreme. He began to regard nationalism as a religion, a form of atheism and nihilism, for it led one nation to consider another nation bestial and worthy only to be driven from the face of the earth. Thus, it recognized human hatred and murder. In Merezhkovskiy's opinion, "Every murderer is an apostate, an atheist in the highest degree. A nation is just like a man: in order to see the face of the beast in another nation, it must itself become brutalized, lose its human visage. 'Nationalism' is the call to brutality."[2] The primary fault with nationalism was its limitations. It affirmed a national but not a universal truth, which Merezhkovskiy desired. Moreover, it tended to destroy culture, for Merezhkovskiy conceived culture as universal, or supranational.[3] The

First World War—the first universal war—was the fruit of absolute nationalism, not just the nationalism of Germany, but of Russia as well. He warned that one nationalism could not overcome another; only a true absolute—humanity—could do so, but as yet no one was willing to die for that abstract humanity.[4]

On religious grounds, Merezhkovskiy had always opposed war and the taking of human life. During World War I his ideas underwent a marked change. At first he could not permit himself to support war actively, but he realized that it was not in the best interests of Russia to oppose it. He remained passive, as did Zinaida Gippius and Filosofov, who shared his views. Yet, as the war progressed, Merezhkovskiy began to justify it and to see in it what was not really there. He considered the war to be a struggle between cultural barbarity (the result of German nationalism, which in turn sprang from the reaction of the Prussian monarchy) and true culture, that of the Anglo-French and Slavic nations, which was based on intuition, inner experience, and inner sight.[5] Basically, Merezhkovskiy's support of the war was a religious one, for he believed that the war showed the falseness of existing Christianity more clearly than did any other historic event. German nationalism and militarism were the products of Protestantism's preaching religion as a private affair, the affair of the individual, which led to a religion of the Mangod.[6] Europe, by which Merezhkovskiy really meant France, accepted the teachings of Christ as action, and it applied them to the social field: hence Europe was revolution. Russia accepted Christianity only as contemplation, therefore Russia could only suffer and endure, but not act.[7] Thus Europe and Russia were two halves of one whole and had to be united to oppose Germany; but they had to be united in Christ in order to wage war against religious individualism.[8]

The military alliance of Turkey with Germany provided Merezhkovskiy with additional ammunition for his attacks on his country's enemies. It confirmed his conviction that the beginning of the end of the world had commenced. Islam had always been the foe of the Christian West, and at this time there occurred an alliance of Moslem Turkey and Protestant Central Europe (Merezhkovskiy overlooked the fact that Catholic Austria-Hungary also participated in this alliance). Both Protestantism and Islam were religions of reaction, since they were rational, natural, measured religions of healthy thought.[9] Islam waged war for the sake of war, while in Christianity, war was waged for the sake of peace. In the alliance of

Turkey and Germany, Merezhkovskiy believed that he saw two Islams uniting in one single dogma of war for the sake of war, that is, war as a religion. In Islam such was excusable, for Merezhkovskiy accepted Mohammedanism as a true religion, the religion of the Father; whereas Kaiser Wilhelm's waging of war was not excusable, since Christianity does not wage war for its own sake:

> If in the first Islam the absolute truth is "obedience to the One God," then in the second the absolute lie is obedience to man alone.
> But the lie is not in one of the Christian nations, but in all Christian humanity. Not only Germany, but also all nations to a sufficient degree have taken Christ out of Christianity, have affirmed the "second Islam": obedience not to the One God, but to man or humanity alone; they have affirmed atheistic nationalism and militarism, the most sinful of wars as a Holy War.
> The lie does not come from without, but is within. And if we do not vanquish it from within, if we do not vanquish ourselves, we will vanquish no one. Behind the second Islam is the third, the fourth, the tenth, the numberless, the invincible, the irreparable, the definitive.
> This lie will be vanquished by truth; regenerated Islam by regenerated Christianity.[10]

In this way Merezhkovskiy lent the weight of his apocalyptical religion to his concept of the war. Nothing could defeat war but his new Christianity, with its religious sociality. For this reason he insisted that the war had to be waged to the end, for he remained adamant in his belief that the end of World War I would be the end of all wars, a misconception and a hope that was widely credited both during and immediately following the war. Just as he had believed that revolution would succeed in fulfilling his desires, he now attributed fulfilment of them to the war. It would be the end of the old, the bourgeois, order and the beginning of a new, as yet unknown, order: final peace and final liberation, the establishment of religious sociality.[11] Merezhkovskiy convinced himself that this would take place, but he was to be disappointed for a second time.

At first the war had little effect on Merezhkovskiy's life in St. Petersburg. He continued to participate in the Religious-Philosophical Society; he also worked on his novel and plays, and produced a steady stream of articles. There were also constant visitors at the Merezhkovskiy residence; and throughout the winter of 1915–1916,

A. F. Kerenskiy, an acquaintance of long standing, was one of the most frequent. Merezhkovskiy and Gippius were not adherents to any political party, but they maintained contacts with most of them. The Social-Revolutionary party, to which Kerenskiy and also Savinkov and Bunakov belonged, appeared to them to be the best organized and the one best fitted to Russian conditions.[12]

As the war continued and the situation became more and more grave, the war lost its initial popularity, and discontent with the government increased. Yet, when Merezhkovskiy went to Kislovodsk in the spring of 1916 to rest, after having become fatigued with the rigors of the now Petrograd winter and the amount of work he had done, he found unrest there too, though of a different kind from that existing in the capital. Nonetheless, on returning to Petrograd in the autumn, the oppressive atmosphere was even more unbearable than that of the south, and he hastened back to Kislovodsk in December.[13]

Merezhkovskiy and Gippius were back in Petrograd when the revolution occurred in March 1917. With the majority, Merezhkovskiy accepted the change wholeheartedly. He heralded it with the words "There has been created a historically new country, which never existed before—Free Russia."[14] At last, revolution had achieved what he had long advocated: the abolition of autocracy. He was not to see the fruition of the rest of his program, and he had no opportunity to reproach the new free Russia for not applying his religiosocial ideals. The provisional government was too weak, especially in view of the Soviets of Workers' and Soldiers' Deputies, to take decisive action on any point. The military situation was rapidly deteriorating. Kornilov's attempt to restore military order and to set himself up as a strong man ended in failure, further weakening the already tottering provisional government. Merezhkovskiy was also present in Petrograd for the second revolution of 1917. He witnessed the Bolshevik coup d'état on the night of 7 November from the balcony of his apartment, which overlooked the Tauris Palace.[15] Social Democracy, to which Merezhkovskiy could never submit, was victorious.

Throughout the year 1918, conditions grew worse. Transportation came to a standstill. Food was scarce and fuel almost nonexistent. Electrical power was in short supply and was available only a few hours a day. Black marketeers and enterprising speculators extorted what money and goods they could from all and sundry. Prices for food, such as it was, were exorbitant, and they continued to rise still higher. The number of deaths from cold, starvation, and disease (dysentery became widespread, and epidemics of cholera broke out) increased daily.

Merezhkovskiy's income, a fairly substantial one from the allowance set up by his father's estate, was wiped out by the Bolshevik Revolution. Those whose subsistence came from writing—Merezhkovskiy, Gippius, and Filosofov now among them—were in particularly serious straits. They were unable to earn, for after an initial brief period of liberalism, all but Bolshevik publications ceased; and it was impossible for them to leave the country. Many writers allied themselves with the policies of the new regime, Blok and Belyy being among the first. Merezhkovskiy and Gippius could never reconcile themselves to the new regime. During the months immediately after the revolution they managed to live on the little money that they had been able to save from the disaster; but it was not enough to keep them for long. It was necessary for them to sell their possessions, including Merezhkovskiy's extensive library, little by little in order to avoid starvation.[16] Yet Merezhkovskiy continued to work. He had long envisioned a novel on Egypt, and at this time he not only began to read in preparation for it, but he also began to write it.

The position of writers and of the intelligentsia in general had become extremely serious before Gor'kiy came to their assistance by organizing the state-supported publishing enterprise International Literature, which was to publish foreign works of literature in Russian translations. A large number of scholars and writers were employed as translators, researchers, and editors; and while payment for translating and correcting was low (300 Soviet rubles per page for translation and 100 for correcting), it was an income. In spite of their animosity towards Gor'kiy and the Soviet state, their destitute condition obliged Gippius and Merezhkovskiy to toil long hours for this pittance.[17]

Merezhkovskiy expected the imminent overthrow of the Bolshevik regime. However, by the summer of 1919 the hope placed in intervention by the former allies of Russia or by the White armies ceased to exist. Merezhkovskiy could never renounce his ideals and make peace with the Soviets; rescue from without would never occur; consequently, the idea of flight from Russia grew in his mind. As Merezhkovskiy envisioned it, only one of two terrible alternatives was open to him: slow death—physical or spiritual decay—if he remained in Russia; or self-exile, which was almost suicide—literally, for there was a possibility of being shot in an attempt to cross the frontier, and figuratively, for he would be cut off from his own country.[18] The decision to flee, therefore, was not an easy one to make. He realized that there was nothing for him to do in Russia. In Europe he would find freedom; moreover, he considered that it was necessary, and also his duty, to reveal to Europe what was actually taking place inside Russia and to warn the West of the potential danger to itself. Those Russians who had been living abroad for years had no conception of what was occurring in their homeland, and the recent émigrés did not have a sufficient reputation in Europe to make themselves heard. Merezhkovskiy, on the other hand, was well known in France, and he counted on his considerable reputation there to add weight to the facts, which, he felt, he must impress upon Europe.

At first he applied for permission to leave Russia for reasons of health. His appeal was treated no differently than the appeals of others, including that of Alexander Blok; it was refused.[19] Plans for flight then began to be made during the last six months of 1919. Two proposals had to be abandoned. The first was to take Merezhkovskiy and his companions to Finland during the winter by a hazardous crossing of the frozen Gulf of Finland. This was ultimately rejected as being too dangerous because of the concentration of Red troops in that area and too strenuous for Gippius, Merezhkovskiy, and Filosofov. The second proposed means of escape, through Rezekne, in company with several other acquaintances, also came to nothing.[20]

The third, and final, plan was to cross the Polish frontier. Merezhkovskiy obtained permission to leave Petrograd, ostensibly to lecture to Red Army soldiers in the south of Russia. Indeed, the partially written *The Birth of the Gods: Tutankhamon in Crete (Rozhdenie bogov: Tutankamon na Krite)* was camouflaged in a cover bearing the words "Material for lectures to Red Army units."[21] All the members of Merezhkovskiy's party—Zinaida Gippius, Filosofov, and V. A. Zlobin, a student (subsequently Merezhkovskiy's secretary and heir)[22]—had passes to Gomel', declaring that they were comrades going to lecture on literature and art to the Red Army. They left Petrograd on 24 December 1919, carrying all their money and as many of their possessions as they could without arousing suspicion. Even then, it was necessary to abandon a large part of their baggage because of the overcrowding of the train. Though the jour-

147

ney was to take them to Gomel', the train went no farther than Zhlobin. Here they contacted a certain Yankel', who had been recommended to them in Petrograd. Yankel' rented them a room and arranged to have a contraband-runner lead them to Polish territory. One may well imagine the consternation of the fugitives when their guide did not appear on the appointed day, forcing them to remain at Zhlobin while further arrangements were made. They were more fortunate in their second choice of a guide, a Latvian. The surreptitious passage through the Russian lines took two days and two nights, but finally they reached neutral territory and were admitted through the Polish lines without mishap.[23]

At Bobruisk, their first stopping place, they were just four more Russian refugees. Merezhkovskiy's books served as a passport; his reputation, together with the assistance of a young Russian, Ivan I. Dudyrev, enabled them to avoid many of the bureaucratic formalities and move on to Minsk, where they all gave lectures on bolshevism. Merezhkovskiy, now a Polophile, since Poland was fighting the Russian Communists, also prepared a lecture on Mickiewicz; but the enmity on the part of the Russians in Minsk towards their traditional enemies, the Poles, was so great that the Pushkin Library refused to sponsor the lecture.[24]

From Minsk, Merezhkovskiy and his companions traveled to Vilnius, where more lectures were given. Then, in the middle of February, they went on to Warsaw. Merezhkovskiy's sojourn in Warsaw was a busy one. His name attracted the interest of many representatives of the Polish *szlachta*, in whom he strove to instill anti-Communist, as opposed to anti-Russian, sentiments. He met with Russian émigrés, including members of the Russian Committee, with whose policies he disagreed. He gave lectures, again on communism, and he repeated his lecture on Mickiewicz with great success. Savinkov arrived from Paris shortly afterwards; and he, Merezhkovskiy, Gippius, and Filosofov held many discussions on what should be done. Filosofov tended toward the Russian Committee and Savinkov, both of which Merezhkovskiy opposed. Eventually Filosofov, who was elected president of the Russian Committee, broke with Merezhkovskiy and Gippius—a bitter blow for both Merezhkovskiy and his wife after their fifteen years of intimate friendship with Filosofov.[25]

Up to this point all factions had agreed on one item of policy: that a Russian regiment should be formed within the Polish army. Savinkov approached President Pilsudski with this proposal; and

Merezhkovskiy, who perceived more clearly what difficulties might arise from having two such ancient enemies fighting side by side, also arranged to have an interview with Pilsudski. The result of the meeting was twofold. Merezhkovskiy prevailed upon Pilsudski to issue an edict stating that Poland was not at war with the Russian people but with the Communists, and another calling on Russians to join in the struggle. The way had been prepared for the formation of a Russian regiment. The second outcome of the meeting was a popular brochure written by Merezhkovskiy in 1920 entitled simply "Joseph Pilsudski." Merezhkovskiy believed that he had found in Pilsudski a Hero: "the reflection of God's face in a man's face—in the face of a Hero. For the Hero is still today what he was long ago— the unchanged revelation of the Godhead, the Theophany."[26] Pilsudski, he stated, was chosen by God to save Poland, who was God's "illustrious daughter,"[27] and perhaps the world. Merezhkovskiy's excessive trust and hope in Poland and Pilsudski as victors over communism were soon shattered. The signing of the armistice between Poland and Russia in Minsk on 12 October 1920 put an end to his usefulness in Warsaw. Now, accompanied by his wife, he went to Paris.

Immediately before the war, Zinaida Gippius had had the foresight to purchase a residence in Passy. The intention of the time had been, of course, to obviate the necessity of finding accommodation on each of their frequent and protracted visits to the French capital. This fortuitous event proved to be an invaluable asset to the exiles, for while Merezhkovskiy's and Gippius's finances were low, they at least had a permanent residence at their disposal.

Paris had already become the center of settlement for the majority of Russia's intellectual émigrés. Merezhkovskiy and Gippius immediately joined their ranks and came into contact with many of their former acquaintances as well as with numerous distinguished Russians hitherto unknown to them, the most notable being Ivan Bunin.[28] However, the exiles soon split up into their respective groups as they had formerly existed in Russia, and Merezhkovskiy gradually rallied around him a body of intellectuals who endeavored to carry on the St. Petersburg traditions of religious and literary discussion. Among the many representatives of the "old" generation who met regularly at the Merezhkovskiys' apartment on Sunday afternoons from four o'clock until seven were the novelists Bunin, M. Aldanov (pseudonym of M. A. Landau), and B. K. Zaytsev; the literary critic K. Mochul'skiy; and the religious thinkers Berdyaev, G. Fedotov, and L. Shestov (pseudonym of L. I. Schwartzmann). But more significant, perhaps, was the fact that younger writers, who had begun their literary careers as émigrés, were also attracted to the Merezhkovskiys' "Sundays."[29] On Merezhkovskiy's initiative and with the Sunday group forming the nucleus, a public society named the Green Lamp (Zelenaya Lampa), after the early-nineteenth-century society to which Pushkin had belonged, held its first meeting on 5 February 1927.[30] Although primarily oriented toward ideas of concern to the Merezhkovskiy circle, the Green Lamp remained of interest to the Russian émigré community in Paris throughout the prewar years, occasionally having an audience of several hundred persons.

In addition to his full social life, lectures, discussions, and periods of relaxation in the south of France, in Italy, and in Germany, Merezhkovskiy did not lessen his literary output. He contributed to French newspapers and journals, publishing articles and essays in the émigré periodical Sovremennye Zapiski (Contemporary Notes), in which his two novels also appeared, the Paris newspaper Obshchee Delo (Common Cause), and the Berlin newspaper Rul' (The Helm). On the whole, however, Merezhkovskiy was as undesirable and unacceptable in the circles of the émigré journals as he had been much earlier in Russia. It is significant in this respect that the majority of his monographs dedicated to the lives of the saints and religious thinkers were not serialized in any periodical, but were published independently. Moreover, Merezhkovskiy's implacable hatred of communism alienated him from the large body of intellectual exiles who could not treat Soviet Russia with the same inflexibility of mind as he did.

Indeed, on his arrival in Paris, Merezhkovskiy immediately embarked on what he then considered to be his main task: to warn the West of the dangers of communism and to arouse Europe to combat it. He had no success in his self-appointed mission. Poland, on which he had laid his hopes, had made peace with the Soviet Union; other European countries failed to intervene, as Merezhkovskiy had desired, and even began to recognize Russia's new government. Merezhkovskiy regarded this to be a short-sighted policy, for he was convinced that he himself perceived the perils more clearly than his European friends and many Russian exiles who had not experienced the Bolshevik regime in Russia, as he had. He struck a prophetic note, one that is being recognized in our own day, when he wrote in 1920:

> Europe craves peace and calm labor. And it deceived itself in thinking that it can attain calm, as long as Russia is strangling under the yoke of the new barbarians. It deceives itself in considering that it can prosper economically, as long as an entire neighboring nation is dying of hunger and in convincing itself that it is immune to internal shocks while the Third International has such a base as Russia. It deceives itself if it shuts its eyes to the religious essence of the International, which reigns in Russia, and to its main principle, which it can repudiate only when it has ceased to exist.
>
> Sooner or later Europe will understand this. We would hope that it will understand before it is too late.[31]

In addition to opposing Soviet communism because it had established the detested rule of the collective, Merezhkovskiy opposed it because it had destroyed the old without creating something worthwhile to replace it. Especially repellent to him, not only as a highly cultured person but as the advocate of universal culture, was the negative attitude of the Bolsheviks toward culture: "The denial of any culture as an unhealthy and perverted complexity—the will to simplification, to 'commonness'—is, in the last analysis, the metaphysical will to savagery."[32] This added to Merezhkovskiy's conviction that bolshevism was absolute evil, and his policy was one of irreconcilability toward it: "It is possible to reconcile oneself with relative evil, but with absolute evil it is impossible. And if there is on the earth the incarnation of Absolute Evil, the Devil, then it is bolshevism."[33] Any reconciliation with this Kingdom of the Beast, as he termed Soviet Russia, meant an unavoidable world catastrophe.

Yet he hoped that communism could be overcome, and he proclaimed that this would be so, for "Revolution is alive as long as Democracy is alive, because both have one soul—Freedom."[34] The means for overcoming communism did not exist in Europe, where the bourgeois was no better than the Bolshevik and where Christ had gone out of historic Christianity. The sole salvation of the world, in Merezhkovskiy's estimation, would be a new, a Third, Russia. The First Russia, autocratic Russia, no longer existed; the Second Russia, Soviet Russia, was based on an atheistic religion, communism. The Third Russia must therefore be religious in order to be victorious; moreover, "in order to get out of this pit, Russia must do what

Europe did not do: it must disclose not only the political and social but also the religious content of Revolution; it must affirm freedom with Christ, the Absolute Individual."[35] Then the Third Russia would unite with Europe (not existing Europe, to be sure, but a new, a Third, Europe) in the Kingdom of the Third Testament:

> Not in the first or the second Christianity, not in Orthodoxy and not in Catholicism, but only in the Third Christianity, in the "Third Testament," which is foretold from Mickiewicz to Ibsen by all prophets of holy Europe, "the land of holy miracles"—only in the Third Testament will the Third Russia and the Third Europe be united. And in this union will break out universal revolution, which will vanquish bourgeois-bolshevik universal reaction; there will blaze up "the threefold shining light"—Liberty, Equality, Fraternity.[36]

Thus Merezhkovskiy expressed his faith in the appearance of a resurrected Russia and a resurrected Europe in the religion that he had long advocated; nevertheless, as he looked at his native land from a distance, he could not help but write with despair, longing, and hope: "Russia does not exist—Russia will exist."[37]

Merezhkovskiy remained a relentless foe of the Soviet Union, and from time to time he warned the West of the threat of communism. Indeed, his antipathy was so profound that it led him in the 1930s to consider Italian fascism and Mussolini as worthy fellow warriors. Drafts of three letters addressed to Mussolini are extant.[38] The first letter, dated 5 February 1934, was essentially a request that the Italian leader facilitate a sojourn of several months in Italy to enable Merezhkovskiy to prepare for two works, *St. Francis of Assisi (Frantsisk Assisskiy)* and *Dante*. His references to Mussolini as the Creative Genius of the New Italy and the Creative Soul of the New Italian Renaissance take on the character of flattery aimed at having his request granted. The second letter, undated but probably written in March 1936, refers to a fifteen-minute interview that Merezhkovskiy had had with Mussolini on 4 December 1935. Once again, praise of Mussolini as a brother to Napoleon and Dante was incidental to his primary concern: an allowance of 30,000 lire to enable him to spend eight or nine months in Italy. The final letter is the most significant of the three. In it Merezhkovskiy thanks Mussolini for inviting him to Italy and poses three questions, through which it is obvious that Merezhkovskiy was seeking to enlist Mussolini as a universal opponent to communism, rather than a purely national one; that he wished Mussolini, as the leader of a nation elect—that is, of Rome—to save the world for a third time by renouncing the concept of nationalism and thus becoming the Pacifier, uniting the earthly laurels of victory with the heavenly olive branch of peace; and finally that, in denouncing the Concordat as a compromise, he was attempting to convince Mussolini to support the concept of an absolute union of Church and state. Merezhkovskiy's efforts to transform il Duce into the epitome of the Hero and the savior of the world, as World War II approached, were ill founded; they remain a stain on the record of one who throughout his life had striven against external coercion, whether that of an autocrat or of a collective. It is perhaps fortunate that in the early 1920s Merezhkovskiy had brought an end to the sociopolitical campaign that had been the basis of his writing for nearly twenty years. Disillusioned by the course of history in Russia, by the failure of his writings prior to the revolution, and by the lack of interest on the part of Europeans with regard to his urgent warnings, he turned his attention from the sociopolitical field and retired once more into the realm of religious contemplation.

In respect to this, Merezhkovskiy's two short novels of the 1920s, *The Birth of the Gods* and *The Messiah (Messiya)*, assume a significance beyond their rather limited merits: they represent the period of transition. They are, of course, thoroughly tendentious; but it is inaccurate to dismiss them out of hand, which one critic does, as being "devoid of all indications of artistic value, filled with the most tedious conversations and hazy prophecies."[39] Inadvertently, the critic has recognized one of the singularities of these novels—the extensive use of dialogue, which had become ever more pronounced in Merezhkovskiy's novels coincidentally with his interest in the dramatic form. In *The Birth of the Gods* and *The Messiah* exchanges of speech far outweigh descriptive passages, not only in ideological importance, but also in sheer bulk. There is just enough description of setting, customs, and costumes to provide a minimum of local and historical color and to reveal the depth of Merezhkovskiy's research into the period and the countries that serve as the background of the novels. The fullness and multitude of details, which enrich *Leonardo da Vinci* and its companion works, are lacking; the postrevolutionary novels are thus closer to *Alexander I* and *December the Fourteenth* in this facet of their composition.

A further similarity to the latter is the fact that *The Birth of the*

Gods and *The Messiah* are less sequels than two parts of one novel. While the action takes place in Crete and Egypt respectively, two of the main characters occupy the central position in both novels; indeed, it is really the story of one of them, Dio, Cretan priestess of the mother-goddess Ma. In *The Birth of the Gods*, Dio rebels against the full integration of the state and its religion, which is represented by the equality of the tsar-beast—the Cretan king wearing the head of a bull—and the high priestess of Ma. The analogy to autocracy and Orthodoxy in Russia is easily recognizable.

Merezhkovskiy was concerned primarily with the religion of Crete. Although he demonstrates that it has been corrupted, it nevertheless admits belief in a trinity of deities: father, son, and, above all, mother. Much of the discussion between Dio and the Babylonian exile Tammuzadad, whose self-sacrifice for love of Dio saves the girl from death on the pyre and serves to emphasize the evils of a religion founded on forced human sacrifice, are used by Merezhkovskiy to point out how widespread and similar were the ancient beliefs in a trinity of gods and the importance of the mother-goddess within it.

Also of some concern to Merezhkovskiy was the question of the blending of male and female in one individual. It is to be seen in the Cretan king, who is purported to be man and woman together.[40] It is visible in Dio, a fact that terrifies Tammuzadad:

> Neither he nor she; she and he together; Lilith! Lilith!
> At times he wanted to ask her directly: "But who are you?" And if he did not ask, it was not only because it was ridiculous. "He who raises the veil from my face will die," says the Babylonian goddess Ishtar, the star of love, of dawn, and of evening, at sunset Woman, at dawn Man—Man and Woman together. He was afraid to learn who she was: to learn is to die.[41]

Similarly, in *The Messiah* it is Akhnaton who resembles a mixture of male and female and thus possesses a godly charm.[42] Yet this union of the masculine and the feminine in one individual, first raised by Merezhkovskiy in the person of Leonardo da Vinci, though increasingly important to him, was still of secondary consequence in his thought at this time.

More significant was his attempting to reveal how the ancient religions presaged the coming of the Messiah and, above all else, how Akhnaton, in reestablishing the supremacy of Aton—the one god, the most ancient god—over Amon, is "the shadow of Him who is to come."[43] The conflict between Aton and Amon is the conflict

154

between the next world and this, between Merezhkovskiy's Third Testament and the Second. Ptamos, high priest of Amon, relates to Dio:

"Everything that was through the centuries will exist in eternity. *He* also existed. His first name is Osiris. He came to us, and we slew Him and destroyed His task. He wished to found His kingdom on the earth of the living, but we drove Him out into the kingdom of the dead, the eternal West—Amenti: that world is His, this is ours. And He will come again, and we shall slay Him again and destroy His task. We have conquered the earth, not He."[44]

In Merezhkovskiy's opinion, therefore, it is man who refuses to part with this earth, the kingdom of Man, for the Kingdom of God. Such, too, is the meaning of the revolution of the beast people (which refers equally to the Bolshevik revolution in Russia) against Akhnaton and his divine purpose and of the reestablishment of the tsar-beast in the person of Tutankhamon.

Through the above-mentioned relating of Akhnaton to Osiris, Merezhkovskiy related the present to the past. But he also sought to relate the present to the future by means of the half-Jewish, half-Egyptian Issachar-Isserker, who links Akhnaton to the far-distant advent of Christ. Such is the superficial analogy; but in the light of Merezhkovskiy's earlier statements, a deeper symbolism is revealed. He is not merely trying to establish a connection between non-Christian dying-rising gods and Christ, but perhaps most of all is attempting to link the First Coming of Christ, historic Christianity, to the future, the Second Coming.

Merezhkovskiy's return to purely religious contemplation was, however, only in its early stages when he was composing *The Birth of the Gods* and *The Messiah*. It was in other, nonartistic works of the postrevolutionary period that he expressed his latest concepts more clearly and more fully.

Although many of his compositions of the 1920s and 1930s were translated into English, French, German, and other European languages, they aroused little comment in the West. This lack of interest in Merezhkovskiy's final work was, and still is, common. One reviewer, while in essence unsympathetic to him, is quite just in pointing out the cause of his unpopularity. While referring specifically to *The Secret of the Three: Egypt and Babylon* (*Tayna Trekh: Egipet i Vavilon*), his words may be applied to the major portion of

155

Merezhkovskiy's literary output of the interwar years: "For some it is an incomprehensible book; for others a daring one! For all (or almost all) who have read it, it is not of its own time; it is either too far in the past or still only in the future, but not in the present."[45] This is perhaps as fair a criticism of Merezhkovskiy's later writing as may be found anywhere; one that is as applicable today as when these works were written; for Merezhkovskiy's volumes, while directed towards the aim of presenting a means of salvation for humanity, seem out of place in an environment that is concerned only with the present and with material values.

Perhaps "bourgeois morality," which Merezhkovskiy opposed from his early Nietzschean period, found his works too daring, for they are most assuredly erotic; almost all of them revolve around sex in some form or other. The preoccupation with sex, which had been growing in Merezhkovskiy from the time when he had sanctioned Bacchic pleasures in his early poetry, finally came to the fore in the writings of these two decades. He was not unaware of the almost complete uniqueness of his position in writing about sex as he did, when he remarked, referring to humanity at large, "We are silent; we are ashamed to speak of it."[46] Nonetheless, he felt obliged to break the bond of silence, for, he explained: "We will never understand that sex is a holy or accursed point, the gates of heaven or hell, but a profundity and not a level. With all its weight our world, our hell, leans upon these gates, lest they open."[47] The problem of sex was therefore of the utmost importance in Merezhkovskiy's religious program, and it was to be dealt with thoroughly in his works.

The primary motif of the majority of his compositions in this period was the presentation of all pagan antiquity, which represented the religion of the flesh, as pointing the way to the coming of Christ. The idea of pre-Christian religions as "pagan Christianity" was not a recent concept; Merezhkovskiy had expressed this equivocal view in *L. Tolstoy and Dostoevskiy*, but at that time paganism was synonymous with Greek and Roman civilization. Stimulated by ever-increasing archaeological discoveries in Egypt and Asia Minor and by the works of V. V. Rozanov on Egyptian and Babylonian religion, Merezhkovskiy's interest in more distant antiquity was aroused. However, he was dissatisfied with the accepted scientific interpretations of antiquity. He believed that pagan religions should be approached with sympathetic religious experience: a method that he could follow, but that was, he thought, beyond the limitations of "godless scholars."[48] Merezhkovskiy was indeed sympathetic to all ancient religions, for he did not agree with the opinion that they were no more than beliefs in nonexistent gods and myths. He accepted myth as fact, declaring that "the truth of the myth is in the mystery; its secret is in the sacrament."[49] The key to pagan mystery was Christian sacrament, and it was in the light of this belief that he examined pagan antiquity, for he was convinced that if Christianity was truth, so was paganism. He agreed with Schelling's statement that mythology was a religion, hence all gods exist; but he was not content to remain at this premise, so he continued his reasoning to the point of declaring that there were no false gods, that all gods were true.

It was his contention that all humanity was under the sign of the cross, and it was with a view to proving this that he examined all pre-Christian antiquity. He discovered deep similarities between the life of Christ and the myth-mysteries of pagan gods who had died and been resurrected:

> History is the mystery, the sacrament of the cross, and all nations participate in it. The way from Bethlehem to Golgotha is already the path of paganism, of pre-Christian humanity. There are many nations, or "tongues," and there are many myths, but there is only one mystery—the mystery of the God who died and was resurrected.
>
> Egyptian Osiris, Babylonian Tammuz, Canaanite-Egyptian Adonis, Attis of Asia Minor, Iranian Mithras, Hellenic Dionysos —in all of them is He.[50]

He was so convinced of the truth of his theory that these gods were indeed precursors of Christ that he formulated the following concept: "In each earthly age, each eon, the dead body of one Man is preserved undecayed; when the new age comes, it rises from the dead, and That Man becomes God; then he again dies, again is resurrected —and so it is for all time. In all ages—in all eternities—he is like the sun in drops of dew."[51]

Merezhkovskiy did not merely base his deductions on the superficial similarity that is most clearly apparent: that Osiris, Tammuz, Dionysos, Mithras, Adonis, and even Quetzalcoatl (whom he later included), as well as Christ, were gods who became incarnate on earth, suffered in order to save mankind, perished, and rose from the dead. He sought more obscure evidence. He found theophagy in the Eleusinian mysteries and in the religion of Osiris. In the latter instance, for example, he decided that since Osiris was the spirit of wheat, then by eating bread the Egyptians ate their god, just as in the Christian Eucharist: "So the shadow comes in contact with the Body: the shadow—Osiris—falls at the feet of the Lord."[52] He also declared that the concept of the shepherd-god extended from Babylon to Israel in the person of Tammuz-Adonis-Adonai (Merezhkovskiy considered these three to be in essence one god, just as he asserted that Tammuz and Osiris were one), and from Israel to the end of time in the person of Christ.[53]

Besides stressing these and other similarities, Merezhkovskiy placed great emphasis on the mystic number three, which was of paramount importance in his own form of Christianity. He sought and found in pagan religions the same trinity of gods that exists in Christian teaching. He ascribed evidences of it to Samothrace in the worshiping of the Father, heavenly Zeus; the Mother, Demeter the earth; and the son of earth and heaven, Dionysos. In a somewhat different order he found it in the Eleusinian cult of Dionysos as the Father, Demeter as the Mother, and Iacchus as the Son. In Canaan they were represented by Baal, Astarte, and Adonis; in Babylon, by Ea, Ishtar, and Tammuz; and in Egypt, by Osiris, Isis, and Horus. These trinities of deities corresponded with the Christian Trinity of God the Father, God the Son, and God the Holy Ghost—Merezhkovskiy's "Mother-Spirit."[54]

Merezhkovskiy was attempting to show, by these analogies, the importance of the Trinity throughout all humanity. He hoped, of course, to attract humanity once more to the Trinity, for he declared that in the past three centuries, and particularly in the preceding twenty or thirty years, man had forgotten the Three in One, although he saw reflections of it in all aspects of life. He stated that man thinks threefold, although he failed to show how this takes place; that space and time are threefold: space because it is made up of length, width, and depth; and time because it comprises past, present, and future. He found the Trinity in physics and chemistry, citing the law of chemical reaction as an example. The biological field also provided indications of it. In this case he pointed out the external symmetry and duality of organs, such as the eyes and ears, and the inner unity of their functions; but even greater was the trinity visible in sex: "two sexes, two poles, and between them is the eternal spark of life."[55]

Merezhkovskiy's attitude toward the importance of sex in religion at this period of his development, as well as his whole concept of the religion of God the Father, closely approached that of Rozanov. Rozanov had preached a natural (one might even term it "phallic") religion since the end of the nineteenth century, even before Merezhkovskiy had embarked on his first pronouncements on sex. At that time, in the early years of the twentieth century, Merezhkovskiy disclaimed any kinship with Rozanov, and he opposed the latter's views on the importance of the family and progeny. So antagonistic had Merezhkovskiy been toward Rozanov that he had seized every opportunity to denounce him in the Religious-Philosophical Society. V. F. Botsianovskiy reported that Merezhkovskiy sought personal quarrels with Rozanov, citing the following instance as an example: " 'We,' Bishop Sergiy interrupted him [Merezhkovskiy], 'are not speaking about Rozanov, but about marriage. . . .' 'No,' Merezhkovskiy persisted, 'we must talk about Rozanov.' "[56] While Merezhkovskiy did not accept Rozanov's teachings as a whole at this later date, his attitude toward his former antagonist altered considerably, to the extent that after Rozanov's death in the Soviet Union in 1919 Merezhkovskiy conceded that he was a great Russian writer;[57] he even quoted frequently from Rozanov's works in his *Secret of the Three*. Like Rozanov before him, Merezhkovskiy now proclaimed the holiness of the phallic religions of pre-Christian antiquity; but while Rozanov merely stated that Christianity, too, should be at least in part based on sex, Merezhkovskiy went further, for he believed that it was originally so and would be again.

Merezhkovskiy was one of the most vehement protagonists of the holiness of sex and its transcendental mystery. Not only did he declare that "sexual craving is the craving for knowledge, curiosity towards the transcendental,"[58] but he also stated: "For man, sex is the only possible flesh-and-blood 'contact with other worlds,' with transcendental essences. Here, in sexual love, is birth, but here also is death, for everything that is born dies; death and birth are two roads to the same place, or one road to and from it."[59] Sex is the godly Trinity in the human body: "Sex is the first, primordial, flesh-and-blood touch of God the Three in One."[60] From it flowed the whole of the Testament of the Father—paganism.

There is little need to examine (as Merezhkovskiy did) all the pagan manifestations of holy sex, from the "divine" prostitution of the worshipers of Ishtar to the "godly" bestiality, which, like Rozanov, Merezhkovskiy felt was one of the secrets of Egypt and was quite permissible;[61] for he not only proclaimed the animal in God but also stated that the animal was closer to God than man was, since the heavenly joy of earth (sex), though extinguished in man, still shone in the animal.[62] Although he found evidence of the holiness of sex in all pre-Christian religions, he continued to maintain that the greatest revelation of it was circumcision. This concept, too, Merezhkovskiy had borrowed from Rozanov: "Circumcision is the flesh-and-blood betrothal of man to God, a Testament of marriage, a conjugal union, the sexual copulation of man with God."[63] Thus sex, the most ardent point of the flesh, was consecrated in God.

Merezhkovskiy did not agree with Rozanov that Christ was a refutation of the Father, and the New Testament a break with the Old. Following up his line of thought that circumcision was the marriage of God with humanity, he decided that Christ, who was circumcised according to Hebrew rites, welded both covenants with the blood of circumcision; he also added his belief in the references to Christ as the bridegroom and the Church as His bride for further justification of this acceptance of sex.[64] He also discovered a new significance in Christ's healing of the woman with the issue of blood: "She approached from behind, because she was ashamed of her illness; she hid it from people, just as all conceal from one another their eternal 'shameful wound'—sex."[65] Merezhkovskiy's interpretation of this act of healing was that by it Christ took on Himself the "shameful wound" of sex and therefore accepted the whole Testament of the Father.

All paganism, Merezhkovskiy asserted, showed the way to resurrection through sex. This was but a further development of his concept that "the secret of love is Resurrection."[66] Not only did he see evidence of this in pagan cults: Osiris resurrected by Isis, Tammuz by Ishtar, and so on; but he also sought to find it in Christianity, in Christ's resurrection. Very significant, in Merezhkovskiy's opinion, was that the resurrected Christ was seen first by a woman, Mary Magdalene. He took this as proof that Mary's love for Christ had been stronger than death, and that Christ's resurrection was a miracle of love.[67] As for human sexual love, he declared:

> Sexual love is the unended and unending path to resurrection. Vain is the striving of the two halves to the whole: they unite and once more fall apart; they wish to, but cannot rise from the dead—they always give birth and always die.
> Sexual enjoyment is the anticipation of the resurrecting flesh, but through bitterness, shame, and fear of death. This

contradiction is the most transcendental in sex; I take pleasure, and I am repelled.[68]

He continued this line of thought, stating his belief that "the wholeness of sex, the wholeness of the personality, is life, and, at the final limit, eternal life is Resurrection."[69]

Before beginning an analysis of Merezhkovskiy's concept of the androgyne as the perfect individual, a concept shared by Solov'ev and Berdyaev, it is first imperative to examine the role of the mother as the third member of the Trinity, for Merezhkovskiy's deductions regarding bisexualism hinge in part on the latter. He had already written on the Holy Ghost as the Eternal Woman-Mother who would save the world. Now he turned his attention to a detailed study of the mother-goddess, whom he found throughout the world, from Babylon (" 'Ishtar Mami'—'Mama,' Babylon lisped in the earliest baby talk, and this will be taken into account for it in the ages and in eternity")[70] through countless Stone Age idols depicting a mother and child—which have been discovered in various parts of Europe, Asia Minor, and Africa—to the Apocalypse: " 'The woman, clothed with the sun, and the moon under her feet, and upon her head a crown of twelve stars. And she being with child' and 'pained to be delivered.' "[71]

This convinced Merezhkovskiy that humanity's first and last thought was about the Mother; he went on to state that "Mother Earth is more ancient than the Heavenly Father."[72] He was certain that God the Mother was an integral part of Christianity, as of all other religions, for God the Father, he argued, could not give birth to the Son without a female divine being. While he attached great importance to the earthly mother of Christ, he regarded her as an earthly symbol that only pointed the way to the heavenly Mother, who alone could complete the Trinity: "The Trinity in God begins and ends with the Mother-Spirit."[73] The basis for his belief in the Holy Ghost as the Eternal Mother was not derived exclusively from his own logic, but from an apocryphal source in which Christ speaks of "My Mother, the Holy Ghost."[74]

God is therefore Father and Mother, male and female—a bisexual Supreme Being. This was one of the two concepts that were responsible for Merezhkovskiy's preoccupation with the androgyne. The other was his belief, derived from Otto Weininger, whose *Sex and Character* influenced both Merezhkovskiy and Gippius,[75] that in each of the human sexes there are traces of the other. "In each man there is the secret woman; in each woman, the secret man. The unearthly charm of man is femininity; of woman—masculinity. Empiric sex is opposed to the transcendental."[76] Bisexualism was a divine state. Not only did Merezhkovskiy find it in pagan deities: Isis and Osiris, Ishtar and Tammuz, bearded Venus, the portrayal of the heads of Hera and Zeus joined to one neck on an ancient coin; but he also believed that the same bisexualism was apparent in the one God of Israel. He seized on the fact that *Elohim*, the Hebrew word for God, is in the plural; and he deduced that this revealed that God was dual—consequently male and female. This was corroborated for Merezhkovskiy by the creation of man in God's image; since God created both Adam and Eve, male and female, then God is two in one: "Elohim, He and She—the Man-Woman";[77] and "two sexes in one being—that is what is meant by 'the image of God' in man."[78] Conversely, since God at first created Adam in his own image, Adam was a divine creature, an androgyne. Merezhkovskiy drew the same conclusion from other myths, and thus decided that in each case the androgyne had been split into two sexes because he rivaled the gods.[79]

The male-female was revealed not only in pagan deities and in the God of Israel, but also in Christ. Merezhkovskiy did not rely on the Gospels for his evidence, for in them Christ is represented as asexual; he once again drew on apocryphal sources to establish Christ's beauty, which he declared to be infinitely greater than any other manifestation of human beauty, since it was neither masculine nor feminine, but a harmonious blending of the two.[80] God the Father was bisexual, and so was God the Son; for in the divine order the Son and Father were one. Merezhkovskiy added:

> If the birth of the Son is not empty abstraction, by which the very dogma of God Incarnate would be destroyed, then the Son is born in the Father of the Spirit-Mother. Or, speaking in our coarse and feeble tongue, all three Countenances of the Divine Trinity unite, giving birth to each other and being born of each other, in the Maternal-Paternal-Filial, ineffably conjugal love.[81]

Christ had to be male and female in order to fit into Merezhkovskiy's concept of resurrection as being the return to the state of the complete individual and the whole sex, the androgyne. As the final proof of the holiness of, and the eventual uniting of, the sexes into one bisexual being, Merezhkovskiy cited Christ's words (found in an apoc-

ryphal source, the writings of Clement of Alexandria) that His Kingdom would come:

> when the two are one . . .
> male is female,
> and there is neither male nor female.[82]

Merezhkovskiy saw traces of this "third sex"[83] in contemporary
humanity in the hermaphrodite and also in unisexual love:

> Men love men, and women love women, because for the former
> the female is visible in the male, and for the latter the male is
> visible in the female. It is as if a golden deposit of initial bisex-
> ualism—of the whole Man, the Androgyne, who is more than
> the present-day man, cleaved into two, into man and woman—
> gleams in the dark ore of two separate sexes.
>
> It is possible that in unisexual love it is something greater
> —the primary whole, the complete—which fascinates "the peo-
> ple of the moonlight."[84]

Plato's influence on Merezhkovskiy's thought and terminology
is evident here. In his *Symposium*, the dialogue on love, Plato puts
forward the myth that in the beginning the sexes were three in number: man, the child of the sun; woman, the child of the earth; and
the man-woman, or androgyne, the child of the moon. For daring to
scale the heavens and attack the gods, Zeus split the androgynes into
two equal parts; and from that time onward the halves have sought
to reunite their original nature, to make one of two, thus healing the
state of man. The halves, male or female, that retain some element
of the original androgynous nature seek fulfilment with the opposite
sex. The ones that are wholly female seek female attachments; those
that are wholly male seek only the male.

However, in contrast to Plato's defense of homosexuality, Merezhkovskiy condemned physical manifestations of unisexual love as
being opposed to spiritual bisexualism. He viewed the openness of
homosexuality, Sodom, with alarm, for he considered it to be the
reflection of divine bisexualism—such as is revealed by his "Christ
the Unknown"—in the devil's mirror. "Europe is Sodom,"[85] he declared, for the spirit of unisexualism predominated. In the East, in
the Soviet Union, communism represented a purely feminine oneness, for all were comrades, neither men nor women, and consequently impersonal and sexless. In the West he found an equal im-
personality and sexlessness in masculine militarism.[86] The result
would be war—the destruction of humanity.

It was with the intention of preventing this destruction, by warning the world of the danger that faced it, that Merezhkovskiy wrote of the first humanity, Atlantis. If one is to adopt a scientific approach to Merezhkovskiy's writings on this subject, then one is apt to dismiss them as of no value, for the author indulged in complicated and extremely speculative theories on the historical existence of Atlantis. He examined myths and legends which he found in Greek, Babylonian, Egyptian, and Hebrew sources; then he correlated them and accepted as fact, reiterating his belief that myth was but a veil for higher truths. He invaded the realm of the archaeologist and the anthropologist in order to justify his claims, drawing conclusions from the vaguest of similarities. He declared, for example, that Mayan pyramids, Babylonian ziggurats, and Egyptian pyramids showed a common Atlantean origin;[87] that the symbol of the snake found among the Aztecs and the Hebrews must also have originated in Atlantis;[88] and that samples of soils brought up from the bottom of the Atlantic Ocean matched the color of the houses of Atlantis as reported in Plato.[89]

Although Merezhkovskiy revealed his belief in the actual existence of this mythical land, it is its symbolic meaning that is of importance, for Atlantis represents antediluvian humanity. Since he contended that man was at first bisexual, it was his contention that the Atlantides were androgynes, living in Paradise in divine love and peace. They were not divine, however, and in their pride considered "that they had reached the summits of wisdom, knowledge, power, greatness, and beauty; in the words of Plato, these unfortunates considered themselves 'all-beautiful'—'men-gods.' Each one of them considered himself to be God and was prepared to sacrifice all to himself alone."[90] War and Sodom resulted, and Atlantis was therefore destined to perish in the Flood. It is interesting at this point to compare the opinion of another Russian exile, G. Golokhovastov, on the same theme. In his narrative poem "The Destruction of Atlantis" (Gibel' Atlantidy) he puts forward the thesis that Atlantis perished because it strove to become androgynous and thus become divine:[91] a view directly opposed to that held by Merezhkovskiy.

Merezhkovskiy's theory was that Atlantis was the origin of Europe and that the first humanity and the second were inextricably linked. In endeavoring to establish the historical truth of his deduction, he again ran counter to more scientific theories, for he stated that the European races moved from west to east, from Atlantis to

Crete, and from there to the rest of the ancient world. Once more it is necessary to overlook Merezhkovskiy's error as a historian and to examine the metaphysical significance of this theory. Atlantis bequeathed to Europe a knowledge of divine bisexualism. Merezhkovskiy saw this clearly in Cretan paintings, in which he could not distinguish man from woman. Yet the greatest link between Atlantis and Europe, in his estimation, was contained in the Gospels, for by His baptism, Christ had become the second Adam: "The former man, the first Adam, as it were, drowns, dies, in the watery grave of the font; and there rises from it, is born, the new man of the new humanity, the second Adam."[92]

The second, and equally important, uniting of the first and second humanities, and also the third humanity, Merezhkovskiy discovered in the Gospels:

> If the myth of the flood, "Atlantis"—the end of the first humanity—is religiously and, perhaps, prehistorically significant, then "the second Adam," Jesus, speaks to the second humanity in the tongue of the first.
>
> In the eleventh century B.C. Aramaic was just as universal as a thousand years later was the vulgar, *Common—Koinê—* Hellenic language of Alexander the Great and the God Dionysos —the shadow of the Sun, of the coming Son. The Gospel unites both universalities into one, both humanities into one: the second and the first into the third. And here again is the thesis, antithesis, and synthesis; the Father, the Son, and the Holy Ghost: the Gospel resounds with the same music of the Trinity, as a shell resounds with the noise of the waves of the sea.[93]

Yet Merezhkovskiy believed that Atlantis also bequeathed the greatest evil of all to Europe—war: "The first humanity began, and the second continues, everlasting war."[94] This was what caused Merezhkovskiy to declare that Europe, the second humanity, was doomed to perish like the first. Consequently, he regarded the approach of World War II with apprehension, for he felt that it would be the end of the world, "the second Flood, no longer of water, but of blood and fire."[95] He saw no salvation in the second humanity; instead he put his faith in the Apocalypse, in the third humanity: "The fearful knot of social inequality, which especially in our time threatens to tighten into a noose of death and to strangle humanity, may be united only in the Third Testament—in the Kingdom of the Holy Ghost."[96]

Perhaps Merezhkovskiy himself realized, at the end of his long and strenuous efforts to present humanity with the means for salvation, that his work was not "of his own time." In spite of his attempts to repeat and proliferate his views in less aphoristic form than in his "third trilogy"—*The Secret of the Three, The Secret of the West (Tayna Zapada),* and *Jesus the Unknown (Iisus Neizvestnyy)*—when writing his biographies of Napoleon, St. Paul, St. Augustine, St. Francis of Assisi, Joan of Arc, Dante, Luther, Calvin, St. John of the Cross, Ste. Theresa of Avila, and Ste. Thérèse de Lisieux, his words remained unheeded. Perhaps he hoped that they would be of value to future generations—to the third humanity of which he wrote.

Merezhkovskiy never relaxed his literary activity, even to the very day of his death. He and Gippius had fled to Biarritz in the spring of 1940, where, despite financial straits and ensuing lodging difficulties, he completed *The Life of St. John of the Cross (Zhizn' sv. Ioanna Kresta),* the first of a projected series to be called *Spanish Mystics (Ispanskie mistiki).* He also worked on *The Life of St. Theresa of Avila (Zhizn' sv. Terezy Avil'skoy)* and the unfinished *Little Theresa (Malen'kaya Tereza).* Yet he could not remain for long away from his beloved Paris, so he sought permission to leave Vichy France, voluntarily facing the rigors of the German occupation of the capital. He was in Paris less than three months when he suffered a fatal brain hemorrhage on the morning of 7 December 1941.[97]

Merezhkovskiy was motivated throughout his life by one desire: to discover the absolute religious truth. A man of complex character and a well-developed individualism, he was too original to accept Christianity in any of its historical forms, which he considered to be either a complete denial of life and human values or, at best, half-measures in an attempt to reconcile natural human needs and spiritual teachings. At the same time he was not presumptuous enough to preach a new form of Christianity, as did Tolstoy. Mentally torn by the basic duality of his nature, which manifested itself in many ways—in his love for Europe and for Russia; in his love for God and for man; in his love for the paganism of Hellas and for the spirituality of Christ—he strove to discover the solution of this duality, which was revealed to him not only in himself but in the world at large.

He sought it first in the Populist ideal of service to the people.

Yet he knew that he was incapable of following such a path, for his individualism and inability to love mankind in individuals made his service to the people nothing more than hypocrisy. He turned to the other extreme, in which he extolled classical virtues and Nietzschean superhumanity as the highest point of human values. In time he could not help but realize that this religion, which in its very essence denied God, was incomplete, for God was as essential to him as man was. He continued his search in an effort to unite his ideals of man and God; and eventually he came to the religion of the Trinity, in which all duality would end.

Merezhkovskiy's religious search was occasioned by the desire, not for personal salvation, but for the salvation of all humanity. For this reason and because of his own rebellion against any form of restraint, he denounced statehood, nationalism, and all other social manifestations, for only after a complete overthrowing of existing orders could mankind succeed in uniting in religious sociality, the Kingdom of the Holy Ghost. Merezhkovskiy exhibited a deep love of humanity as a whole; and his feeling for mankind was not limited solely to that of his own lifetime, but to humanity from its first day on earth to generations yet to come. The entire literary production of the last twenty years of his life testifies to this fact, for he believed that all people had to be saved together. The intention of his whole literary career, therefore, was not only to solve the problem of his own duality, but to offer a means of salvation to the world.

Merezhkovskiy's value as a religious thinker is not limited to his being a representative of one current of religious thought in Russia during the twentieth century. It was he who was largely responsible for the regeneration of interest in religious problems, both by his writings and by his energetic formation of the Religious-Philosophical Society and his active participation in it.

Notwithstanding his importance as a religious thinker, Merezhkovskiy is primarily remembered for his creative literature, which was but a further manifestation of his religious striving. Unfortunately, his poetry is usually dismissed with but brief mention, although he most certainly owed his position as leader of the first generation of Symbolists to this phase of his literary activity rather than to his prose works. It is in connection with his novels, and especially his first trilogy, that he is renowned in the West—not because of their religious overtones, but because they are, despite the minor flaws that are to be found in them, brilliant historical novels in which the author succeeded in accurately reproducing the periods with which he was dealing.

Yet it was not as a historical novelist that Merezhkovskiy wished to be remembered. He was aware in his own lifetime that, although the reception of his works in the West was the opposite of what occurred in his own country, the result was the same. It was with regret that he complained as early as 1905: "In Russia they did not like me and upbraided me; abroad they liked me and praised me; but equally here and there they failed to comprehend 'what is mine.' "[98] This was the greatest of the many tragedies of Merezhkovskiy's life. He had won for himself an undisputed position in the development of Russian literature and in the development of Russian religious thought; but he had failed in his task to give the world the true means for its salvation.

Notes

The following abbreviations are used in the notes:

DSM   Dmitriy Sergeevich Merezhkovskiy

PSS   *Polnoe sobranie sochineniy* (17 vols.; St. Petersburg and Moscow, 1911–1913)

RL   *Russkaya literatura XX veka* (edited by S. A. Vengerov; volume 1; Moscow, 1914)

ZGM   Zinaida Gippius-Merezhkovskaya

CHAPTER 1: FORMATIVE YEARS

1. DSM, "Avtobiograficheskaya zametka," *RL* 1:288.
2. All dates are given according to the Gregorian calendar.
3. DSM, "Starinnye oktavy," *PSS* 15:138.
4. DSM, "Avtobiograficheskaya zametka," *RL* 1:289.
5. DSM, "Starinnye oktavy," *PSS* 15:141.
6. Ibid., 15:144.
7. Ibid., 15:139.
8. Ibid., 15:144–45.
9. DSM, "Avtobiograficheskaya zametka," *RL* 1:290.
10. ZGM, *Dmitriy Merezhkovskiy* (Paris, 1951), p. 43.
11. DSM, "Starinnye oktavy," *PSS* 15:165.
12. DSM, "Avtobiograficheskaya zametka," *RL* 1:289.
13. Ibid.
14. DSM, "Starinnye oktavy," *PSS* 15:203–4.
15. Ibid., 15:141–42.

Я слушал няню, трепетом объятый
И любопытством, полный чудных грез,
От ужаса я <u>Отче наш</u> в кроватке
Твердил всю ночь в мерцании лампадки.

16. Ibid., 15:139.
17. ZGM, *Dmitriy Merezhkovskiy*, p. 11.
18. DSM, "Starinnye oktavy," *PSS* 15:149.
19. Ibid., 15:142.

Всегда один, в холодном доме рос
Я без любви, угрюмый, как волчонок,
Боясь лица и голоса людей,
Дичился братьев, бегал от гостей.

20. Ibid.
21. Ibid., 15:148.
22. Ibid., 15:154–56.
23. ZGM, *Dmitriy Merezhkovskiy*, pp. 10–11.
24. DSM, "Avtobiograficheskaya zametka," *RL* 1:289.
25. DSM, "Starinnye oktavy," *PSS* 15:187. For more detailed reference to Merezhkovskiy's opinions on the school system and the teachers see ibid., 15:183–87, and "Avtobiograficheskaya zametka," *RL* 1:289.
26. DSM, "Avtobiograficheskaya zametka," *RL* 1:290.
27. DSM, "Starinnye oktavy," *PSS* 15:176.
28. ZGM, *Dmitriy Merezhkovskiy*, p. 55.
29. DSM, "Starinnye oktavy," *PSS* 15:179–83.
30. Ibid., 15:177–78.
31. Ibid., 15:188–92.
32. Ibid., 15:193–94.
33. Ibid., 15:200.
34. Ibid., 15:200–201.
35. DSM, "Avtobiograficheskaya zametka," *RL* 1:290.
36. Ibid.
37. Ibid., 1:291.
38. Ibid.
39. Ibid.
40. Ibid., 1:292.
41. ZGM, *Dmitriy Merezhkovskiy*, p. 31.
42. Ibid., p. 44.
43. DSM, "Avtobiograficheskaya zametka," *RL* 1:292.
44. Ibid., 1:291.
45. Ibid., 1:292.

CHAPTER 2: THE POPULIST PHASE

1. Ivanov-Razumnik, "Mertvoe masterstvo," in *Tvorchestvo i kritika* (St. Petersburg, 1911), pp. 152–53.
2. Andrey Belyy, "Nastoyashchee i budushchee russkoy literatury," in *Lug zelenyy* (Moscow, 1910), p. 90.
3. A. Dolinin, "Dmitriy Merezhkovskiy," *RL* 1:300.
4. DSM, "Pushkin," *PSS* 13:322.
5. DSM, "Vera," in *Simvoly* (St. Petersburg, 1892), p. 129.

> Нас верно будут критики бранить
> За смелость рифм, за тон, за выбор темы.

6. ZGM, *Dmitriy Merezhkovskiy*, p. 104.
7. Modeste Hofmann, *Histoire de la littérature russe* (Paris, 1946), p. 237.
8. R. Poggioli, *The Poets of Russia, 1890–1930* (Cambridge, Mass., 1960), p. 82.
9. M. Slonim, *Modern Russian Literature* (New York, 1953), p. 51.
10. Valeriy Bryusov, *Dalekie i blizkie* (Moscow, 1912), p. 58.
11. Ibid., p. 56.
12. See J. H. Billington, *Mikhailovsky and Russian Populism* (Oxford, 1958).
13. DSM, "Geroy-pevets," in *Stikhotvoreniya, 1883–1887* (St. Petersburg, 1888), pp. 9–10.
14. DSM, "Poetu," in *Stikhotvoreniya*, pp. 7–8.
15. DSM, "Korally," in *Stikhotvoreniya*, pp. 11–12.
16. DSM, "Poetu," in *Stikhotvoreniya*, p. 8.

> Поймешь ты красоту и смысл существованья
> Не в упоительной и радостной мечте,
> Не в блестках и цветах, но в терниях
>   страданья,
> В работе, в бедности, в суровой простоте.
> И жаждущую грудь роскошно утоляя,
> Неисчерпаема, как нектар золотой,
> Твой подвиг тягостный сторицей
>   награждая,
> Из жизни сумрачной поэзия святая
> Польется светлою, могучею струей.

17. DSM, "O zhizn', smotri:—vo mgle unyloy," in *Stikhotvoreniya*, p. 73.
18. DSM, "My idem po tsvetushchey doroge," in *Stikhotvoreniya*, p. 124.

Прочь, боязнь!... Упивайся мечтою,
И не думай о завтрашнем дне,
И живи, и люби всей душою,
И отдайся могучей весне!

19. DSM, "Vse grezy yunosti," in *Stikhotvoreniya*, p. 15.

Хочу я творчеством и знанием упиться
Хочу весенних дней, лазури и цветов,
Хочу безумного веселия пиров;
Хочу из нежных уст дыханья аромата
И смеха, и вина, и песен молодых,
И бледных ландышей, и пурпура заката,--
Всей дивной музыки аккордов мировых;
Хочу,--и не стыжусь той жажды упоений.

20. DSM, "Blazhen kto tsel' izbral," in *Stikhotvoreniya*, pp. 32–33.
21. DSM, "Lyubit' narod?" in *Stikhotvoreniya*, p. 23.

И что я дам теперь народу?
Он полон верою святой;
А я... ни в счастье, ни в свободу
Не верю скорбною душой.

22. Ibid., p. 24.

Ужель младенческую душу
Сомненьем жгучим отравлю,
Чтоб он в отчаяньи бесплодном
Постиг ничтожность бытия,
И в мертвой тьме умом холодным
Блуждая, мучился, как я,
Чтоб без надежды в глубь эфира
С усмешкой горькой он взирал
И перед вечной тайной мира
Свое бессилье проклинал!

23. DSM, "Poetu nashikh dney," in *Stikhotvoreniya*, pp. 45–46.
24. DSM, "Don-Kikhot," in *Stikhotvoreniya*, pp. 213–19.
25. DSM, "Poroy, kak obraz Prometeya," in *Stikhotvoreniya*, p. 20.

Могу я страстно ждать свободы,
Могу любить я все народы,
Но людям нужно от меня,
Чтобы в толпе их беспредельной
Под небом пасмурного дня
Любил я каждого отдельно,--
И кто бы ни был предо мной--
Ничтожный шут или калека,

Чтоб я нашел в нем человека...
Не мне бессильною душой,
Не мне принять с венцом терновым
Такое бремя тяжких уз:
Пред этим подвигом суровым
Я не герой -- я жалкий трус...

26. DSM, "I khochu, no ne v silakh lyubit' ya lyudey," in *Stikhotvoreniya*, p. 21.

И хочу, но не в силах любить я людей.
Я чужой среди них; сердцу ближе друзей--
Звезды, небо, холодная, синяя даль
И лесов, и пустыни немая печаль...
Не наскучит мне шуму деревьев внимать,
В сумрак ночи могу я смотреть до утра
И о чем-то так сладко, безумно рыдать,
Словно ветер мне брат, и волна мне
    сестра,
И сырая земля мне родимая мать...
А меж тем не с волной и не с ветром мне
    жить,
И мне страшно всю жизнь не любить никого.
Неужели навек мое сердце мертво?
Дай мне силы, Господь, моих братьев
    любить!

27. DSM, "Sovest'," in *Stikhotvoreniya*, p. 59.

Что мог бы ты сказать измученному миру?
Кому свою печаль ничтожную поешь?...
Твой бесполезный стих--кощунственная
    ложь:...
Разбей ненужную, бессмысленную лиру!...
С людьми ты не хотел бороться и страдать,
Ни разу на мольбу ты не дал им ответа,
И смеешь ты себя, безумец, называть
Священным именем поэта!...

28. See above, p. 4.
29. ZGM, *Dmitriy Merezhkovskiy*, p. 25.
30. Ibid., p. 115.
31. Zinaida Gippius's diaries are in the possession of Professor Temira Pachmuss of the University of Illinois.
32. ZGM, *Dmitriy Merezhkovskiy*, p. 32.

33. DSM, "V sumerki," in *Stikhotvoreniya*, p. 128.
34. DSM, "Odinochestvo," in *Simvoly*, p. 209.

Чужое сердце -- мир чужой,
    И нет к нему пути!
В него и любящей душой
    Не можем мы войти.

. . . . .

В своей тюрьме, -- в себе самом,
    Ты, бедный человек,
В любви, и в дружбе, и во всем
    Один, один навек!...

35. DSM, "Odinochestvo v lyubvi," in *Novye stikhotvoreniya, 1891–1895* (St. Petersburg, 1896), pp. 39–40.

Не виноват никто ни в чем:
Кто гордость победить не мог,
Тот будет вечно одинок,
Кто любит, -- должен быть рабом.

Стремясь к блаженству и добру,
Влача томительные дни,
Мы все -- одни, всегда -- одни:
Я жил один, один умру.

36. DSM, "Ne dumala-li ty," in *Stikhotvoreniya*, pp. 135–36.
37. DSM, "Davno-l' zhelannyy mir," in *Stikhotvoreniya*, p. 137.

Свобода без любви -- угрюмая темница:
Отдам я все, -- и жизнь, и радость, и
    покой,
Но только-б вновь любить с безумною
    тоской,
Страдать, как я страдал, и плакать и
    томиться!

38. DSM, "Volny," in *Simvoly*, p. 212.

Но нет во мне глубокого бесстрастья:
И родину, и Бога я люблю,
Люблю мою любовь, во имя счастья
Все горькое покорно я терплю.
Мне страшен долг, любовь моя тревожна.
Чтоб вольно жить -- увы! я слишком
    слаб...

О, неужель свобода невозможна,
И человек до самой смерти -- раб?

39. DSM, "Proklyatie lyubvi," in *Novye stikhotvoreniya*, p. 38.

И нет свободы, нет прощенья,
Мы все рабами рождены,
Мы все на смерть, и на мученья,
И на любовь обречены.

40. DSM, "Solntse," in *Stikhotvoreniya*, pp. 66–67.
41. DSM, "Legenda iz T. Tasso," in *Stikhotvoreniya*, pp. 285–90.
42. DSM, "Smert'," in *Simvoly*, pp. 5–66.
43. DSM, "Vera," in *Simvoly*, pp. 101–201.
44. DSM, "Imogena," in *Simvoly*, p. 254.

CHAPTER 3: THE SYMBOLIST MOOD

1. E. Anichkov, *Literaturnye obrazy i mneniya* (St. Petersburg, 1904), p. 148.
2. DSM, "Goluboe nebo," in *Novye stikhotvoreniya*, p. 23.

Я людям чужд и мало верю
Я добродетели земной:
Иною мерой жизнь я мерю,
Иной, бесцельной красотой.

3. DSM, "Temnyy angel," in *Novye stikhotvoreniya*, p. 10.
4. DSM, "Izgnanniki," in *Novye stikhotvoreniya*, p. 11.

Есть радость в том, чтоб люди ненавидели,
    Добро считали злом,
И мимо шли, и слез твоих не видели,
    Назвав тебя врагом.

Есть радость в том, чтоб вечно быть
    изгнанником,
        И, как волна морей,
Как туча в небе, одиноким странником
    И не иметь друзей.

5. DSM, "Detskoe serdtse," *PSS* 15:55.
6. DSM, "Smert'," in *Simvoly*, p. 64.

Мы -- дети горестных времен,
Мы -- дети мрака и безверья.

7. DSM, "Semeynaya idilliya," in *Simvoly*, p. 264.
8. DSM, "Vera," in *Simvoly*, p. 127.

9. DSM, "Smert'," in *Simvoly*, pp. 62–63.
10. DSM, "Konets veka," in *Simvoly*, pp. 349–50.
11. Ibid., p. 349.

> Но скорбь великая растет в душе у всех...
> Надолго-ль этот пир, надолго-ль этот
>   смех?
> Каким путем, куда идешь ты, век железный?
> Иль больше цели нет, и ты висишь над
>   бездной?

12. DSM, "Budda," *PSS* 15:65.

> Нет спасенья! Слава, счастье,
> И любовь, и красота --
> Исчезают, как в ненастье
> Яркой радуги цвета.

13. Ibid., 15:67.

> Наши радости мгновенны,
> Как обманчивые сны,
> Как в пучине брызги пены,
> Как над морем блеск луны.

14. DSM, "Tak zhizn' nichtozhestvom strashna," *PSS* 15:52.

> Так жизнь ничтожеством страшна,
> И даже не борьбой, не мукой,
> А только бесконечной скукой
> И тихим ужасом полна,
> Что кажется -- я не живу,
> И сердце перестало биться,
> И это только наяву
> Мне все одно и то же снится.

15. DSM, "Kak letney zasukhoy," in *Stikhotvoreniya*, p. 36.

> Приди ко мне, о ночь, и мысли потуши!
> Мне надо сумрака, мне надо тихой ласки:
> Противен яркий свет очам больной души.
> Люблю я темные, таинственные сказки.
>
> Приди, приди, о ночь, и солнце потуши!

16. DSM, "Poroy, kogda mne v grud' otchayan'e tesnitsya," in *Stikhotvoreniya*, pp. 19–20.
17. DSM, "Dal'," in *Stikhotvoreniya*, pp. 94–95.

18. DSM, "Son," in *Stikhotvoreniya*, p. 249.

> Здесь, даже здесь, увы! нет мира и
>   покоя:
> Все та-же предо мной и здесь, в глуши
>   лесов--
>   Резня чудовищного боя
>   И злоба бешенных врагов!

19. DSM, "Esli rozy tikho osypayutsya," in *Stikhotvoreniya*, p. 118.

> У нее, наставницы божественной,
> Научитесь, люди, умирать,
> Чтоб с улыбкой кроткой и торжественной
> Свой конец безропотно встречать.

20. DSM, "Chto ty mozhesh'," in *Simvoly*, p. 210.

> Если надо,-- покорно вернись,
> Умирая, к небесной отчизне,
> И у смерти, у жизни учись --
> Не бояться ни смерти ни жизни!

21. DSM, "Smert'," in *Simvoly*, p. 21.

> О, я завидую глубоко
> Тому, кто верит всей душой:
> Не так в нем сердце одиноко,
> Не так измучено тоской
> Пред неизбежной тайной смерти:
> Друзья, кто может верить, верьте!...
> Нет, не стыдитесь ваших слез,
> Святых молитв и откровений:
> Кто бремя жизни с верой нес,
> Тот счастлив был среди мучений.
> А мы... во всех дарах земли
> Как мало счастья мы нашли!

22. DSM, "Khristos voskres," in *Stikhotvoreniya*, p. 34.
23. DSM, "Molitva prirody," in *Stikhotvoreniya*, pp. 116–17.
24. DSM, "Iov," in *Novye stikhotvoreniya*, pp. 95–104.
25. DSM, "Khristos, Angely i Dusha," in *Simvoly*, pp. 244–45.

> Она Меня любила,
> Но, клятвы не храня,
> Невеста изменила,
> Покинула Меня.
>
> .   .   .   .   .   .

Она -- во власти тела
И, Господа забыв,
Дары Мои презрела,
Отвергла Мой призыв.

26. DSM, "Prazdnik sv. Konstantsiya," in *Simvoly*, pp. 228–30.
27. DSM, Frantsisk Assisskiy," in *Simvoly*, pp. 67–100.
28. DSM, "Bog," *PSS* 15:5.

БОГ

О, Боже мой, благодарю
За то, что дал моим очам
Ты видеть мир, Твой вечный храм,
И ночь, и волны, и зарю...
Пускай мученья мне грозят,--
Благодарю за этот миг,
За все, что сердцем я постиг,
О чем мне звезды говорят...
Везде я чувствую, везде
Тебя, Господь,-- в ночной тиши,
И в отдаленнейшей звезде,
И в глубине моей души.
Я Бога жаждал -- и не знал;
Еще не верил, но, любя,
Пока рассудком отрицал,--
Я сердцем чувствовал Тебя.
И Ты открылся мне: Ты -- мир.
Ты -- все. Ты -- небо и вода,
Ты -- голос бури, Ты -- эфир,
Ты -- мысль поэта, Ты -- звезда...
Пока живу -- Тебе молюсь.
Тебя люблю, дышу Тобой,
Когда умру -- с Тобой сольюсь,
Как звезды с утренней зарей.
Хочу, чтоб жизнь моя была
Тебе немолчная хвала.
Тебя за полночь и зарю,
За жизнь и смерть -- благодарю!

29. DSM, "Priroda," in *Simvoly*, p. 79.

Ни злом, ни враждою кровавой
Доныне затмить не могли
Мы неба чертог величавый
И прелесть цветущей земли.

30. DSM, "Panteon," in *Simvoly*, p. 216.

> Верю в Тебя, о, Господь, дай мне
>   отречься от жизни,
> Дай мне во имя любви вместе с Тобой
>   умереть!...

31. Ibid., p. 217.

> Где же ты, истина?... В смерти, в
>   небесной любви и страданьях,
> Или, о тени богов, в вашей земной
>   красоте?
> Спорят в душе человека, как в этом
>   божественном храме,--
> Вечная радость и жизнь, вечная тайна и
>   смерть.

32. DSM, "Budushchiy Rim," in *Simvoly*, p. 218.

> Ныне в развалинах древних мы, полные
>   скорби, блуждаем.
> О, неужель не найдем веры такой, чтобы
>   вновь
> Объединить на земле все племена и
>   народы?
> Где ты, неведомый Бог, где ты, о,
>   будущий Рим?

33. DSM, "Poet," in *Novye stikhotvoreniya*, p. 6.

> Посреди ликующих глупцов,
> Я иду, отверженный, бездомный.

34. DSM, "Konets veka," in *Simvoly*, p. 357.

> Но **в**ера в идеал -- единственная вера,
> От общей гибели оставшаяся нам,
> Она -- последний Бог, она -- последний
>   храм!

35. DSM, "Gimn Krasote," in *Simvoly*, pp. 259–60.
36. DSM, "Leda," in *Novye stikhotvoreniya*, pp. 7–9.
37. DSM, "Rim," in *Simvoly*, p. 215.

> Если бы в мире везде дух человеческий
>   пал,--
> Здесь возопили бы древнего Рима
>   священные камни:

"Смертный, бессмертен твой дух; равен
   богам человек!"

38. DSM, "Smekh," in *Novye stikhotvoreniya*, p. 14.

Больше счастья, добра и себя самого,
Жизнь люби, -- выше нет на земле ничего.

39. Ibid.

Смех детей и богов,
Выше зла, выше бурь,
Этот смех, как лазурь --
Выше всех облаков.

40. DSM, "Pesn' vakkhanok," in *Novye stikhotvoreniya*, p. 18.

Один есть подвиг в жизни -- радость,
Одна есть правда в жизни -- смех.

41. Ibid., p. 19.

Мы нектар жизни выпиваем
До дна, как боги в небесах,
И смехом смерть мы побеждаем
С безумьем Вакховым в сердцах.

42. DSM, "Dvoynaya bezdna," *PSS* 15:53.

Ты сам -- свой Бог, ты сам свой ближний.
О, будь же собственным Творцом,
Будь бездной верхней, бездной нижней,
Своим началом и концом.

43. See A. L. Volynskiy, *Kniga velikogo gneva* (St. Petersburg, 1904),
   p. 213; Ivanov-Razumnik, "Mertvoe masterstvo," in *Tvorchestvo
   i kritika*, p. 132.

44. DSM, "Lev," in *Novye stikhotvoreniya*, p. 22.

45. DSM, "Pustaya chasha," in *Novye stikhotvoreniya*, p. 45.

Но хмель прошел, слепой отваги
Потух огонь, и кубок пуст.
И вашим детям каплей влаги
Не омочить горящих уст.

Последним ароматом чаши --
Лишь тенью тени мы живем,
И в страхе думаем о том,
Чем будут жить потомки наши.

46. DSM, "Deti nochi," in *Novye stikhotvoreniya*, p. 5.

> Слишком ранние предтечи
> Слишком медленной весны

47. Ibid.

> Мы -- над бездною ступени,
> Дети мрака, солнца ждем,
> Свет увидим и, как тени,
> Мы в лучах его умрем.

48. DSM, "Smert'," in *Simvoly*, p. 66.

> Мы гибнем жертвой искупленья.
> Придут иные поколенья.
> Но в оный день, пред их судом,
> Да не падут на нас проклятья:
> Вы только вспомните о том,
> Как много мы страдали, братья!
> Грядущей веры новый свет,
> Тебе от гибнущих привет!

49. V. Bryusov, "V mire shirokom, v more shumyashchem," in *Iz-brannye sochineniya* (Moscow, 1955), 1:128.

50. DSM, "O esli by dusha polna byla lyubov'yu," *PSS* 15:54.

> Душа моя и Ты -- с Тобой одни мы оба,
> Всегда лицом к лицу, о мой последний
>   Враг.
> К Тебе мой каждый вздох, к Тебе мой
>   каждый шаг
> В мгновенном блеске дня и в вечной
>   тайне гроба,
> И в буйном ропоте Тебя за жизнь кляня,
> Я все же знаю: Ты и Я -- одно и то же,
> И вопию к Тебе, как сын Твой: Боже,
>   Боже,
> За что оставил Ты меня?

51. DSM, "De Profundis," in *Novye stikhotvoreniya*, p. 44.

> Люблю я смрад земных утех,
> Когда в устах к Тебе моленья --
> Люблю я зло, люблю я грех,
> Люблю я дерзость преступленья.

52. DSM, "V lunnom svete," in *Novye stikhotvoreniya*, p. 64.

Неразгаданная тайна
В чаще леса, и повсюду --
Тишина необычайна...

53. DSM, "Tishina," in *Novye stikhotvoreniya*, p. 64.

Бог -- не в словах, не в молитвах,
Не в смертоносном огне,
Не в разрушеньи и битвах,
Бог -- в тишине.

CHAPTER 4: THE NEW IDEALISM

1. ZGM, *Dmitriy Merezhkovskiy*, p. 44.
2. Gippius gives an account of her husband's lifelong work habits; see ibid., p. 47.
3. Ibid., p. 58.
4. Ibid., p. 59.
5. I. Annenskiy, I. Kholodnyak, "Perevody D. S. Merezhkovskogo," *Zhurnal Ministerstva Narodnogo Prosveshcheniya* 12:237 (1908).
6. ZGM, *Dmitriy Merezhkovskiy*, p. 56.
7. DSM, "O prichinakh upadka i o novykh techeniyakh sovremennoy russkoy literatury," *PSS* 15:211.
8. Ibid.
9. Ibid., 15:212.
10. Ibid.
11. Ibid., 15:213.
12. Ibid., 15:214.
13. Ibid., 15:215.
14. R. E. Matlaw, "The Manifesto of Russian Symbolism," *Slavic and East European Journal* 3:179 (1957). This is an excellent and detailed analysis of *O prichinakh upadka i o novykh techeniyakh sovremennoy russkoy literatury*.
15. DSM, "O prichinakh upadka," *PSS* 15:216. To support his contentions, Merezhkovskiy refers to the isolation of Pushkin, Lermontov, and Gogol'; the enmity between Dostoevskiy and Turgenev, and between Turgenev and Tolstoy; Nekrasov's and Saltykov-Shchedrin's hatred for Dostoevskiy; and Turgenev's instinctive aversion for the poetry of Nekrasov.
16. Ibid., 15:218.
17. Ibid., 15:219.
18. Ibid.

19. Ibid., 15:222–23. In view of his being an opponent of any critical method but his own, it is surprising that Merezhkovskiy attacks only the imitators of Pisarev, and not Pisarev himself. Less startling is his justification of Saltykov-Shchedrin's satiric manner because of his mastery of the popular idiom, a mastery lacking among the critics of the "petty press."
20. Ibid., 15:224. In his article "The Manifesto of Russian Symbolism" (*Slavic and East European Journal* 3:177–91 [1957]), Matlaw rightly points out Merezhkovskiy's own contribution to the growing ignorance by referring to the English writer "Samuel Ben-Johnson."
21. DSM, "O prichinakh upadka," *PSS* 15:224.
22. ZGM, *Dmitriy Merezhkovskiy*, p. 57.
23. DSM, "O prichinakh upadka," *PSS* 15:226.
24. Ibid.
25. Ibid., 15:229.
26. Ibid., 15:231.
27. Ibid.
28. Ibid.
29. Ibid.
30. Ibid., 15:232.
31. Ibid.
32. Ibid., 15:233.
33. Ibid.
34. Ibid., 15:235–36.
35. Ibid., 15:239.
36. Ibid., 15:240.
37. Ibid., 15:241.
38. Ibid., 15:242.
39. Ibid., 15:243.
40. Ibid., 15:247.
41. Ibid.
42. Ibid., 15:248–49.
43. Ibid., 15:248.
44. Ibid., 15:249 (the quotation is from F. I. Tyutchev's "Silentium!").
45. Ibid.
46. Ibid.
47. Ibid., 15:250.
48. Ibid.
49. Ibid., 15:251.
50. Ibid., 15:252.
51. Ibid.

52. Ibid., 15:253.
53. Ibid.
54. Ibid.
55. Ibid., 15:254.
56. Ibid., 15:259.
57. Ibid., 15:261.
58. Ibid., 15:268.
59. Ibid., 15:269.
60. Ibid.
61. Ibid., 15:272.
62. Ibid., 15:274.
63. Ibid., 15:275.
64. Ibid., 15:276.
65. Ibid., 15:281.
66. Ibid., 15:282.
67. Ibid., 15:285.
68. Ibid.
69. Ibid., 15:287.
70. Ibid., 15:295.
71. Ibid., 15:296.
72. Ibid.
73. Ibid., 15:300.
74. Ibid., 15:299.
75. Ibid., 15:303.
76. Ibid., 15:304.
77. Ibid., 15:305.

CHAPTER 5: CHRIST AND ANTICHRIST

1. Ivanov-Razumnik, "Mertvoe masterstvo," in *Tvorchestvo i kritika*, p. 139.
2. DSM, "Dafnis i Khloya," in *Vechnye sputniki* (3d ed.; St. Petersburg, 1910), p. 25.
3. DSM, "Montan'," *PSS* 13:144.
4. DSM, "Akropol'," *PSS* 13:9–10.
5. Ibid., 13:12.
6. DSM, "Pushkin," *PSS* 13:329.
7. DSM, "Akropol'," *PSS* 13:13.
8. DSM, "Mark Avreliy," *PSS* 13:34.
9. DSM, "Kalderon," *PSS* 13:87.
10. DSM, "Maykov," *PSS* 13:275.
11. Ibid., 13:266.
12. DSM, "Kalderon," *PSS* 13:83.
13. DSM, "Pushkin," *PSS* 13:321–22.

14. Ibid., 13:322.
15. Ibid.
16. Ibid., 13:348.
17. DSM, "Smert' bogov: Yulian Otstupnik," *PSS* 1:47.
18. Ibid., 1:49.
19. Ibid., 1:67–68.
20. Ibid., 1:69.
21. Ibid., 1:318.
22. Ibid., 1:317.
23. Ibid., 1:198.
24. Ibid., 1:263.
25. Ibid., 1:33.
26. B. Griftsov, *Tri myslitelya* (Moscow, 1911), p. 103.
27. DSM, "Smert' bogov: Yulian Otstupnik," *PSS* 1:240.
28. Ibid., 1:144.
29. Ibid., 1:25.
30. Ibid., 1:88.
31. Ibid.
32. Ibid., 1:309.
33. Ibid., 1:87.
34. Ibid., 1:149.
35. Ibid., 1:229.
36. Ibid., 1:309.
37. Ibid., 1:25.
38. Ibid., 1:148.
39. Ibid., 1:333.
40. Ibid., 1:335–36.
41. DSM, "Voskresshie bogi: Leonardo da Vinchi," *PSS* 2:25.
42. Ibid., 2:62.
43. Ibid., 2:18.
44. Ibid., 3:254.
45. Ibid., 2:13.
46. Belyy has remarked that Merezhkovskiy's hands were also elegant and small, like a lady's. See A. Belyy, *Nachalo veka* (Moscow and Leningrad, 1933; photo-offset, Chicago, 1966), p. 186.
47. DSM, "Voskresshie bogi: Leonardo da Vinchi," *PSS* 3:28.
48. Ibid., 2:192.
49. Ibid., 3:242.
50. Ibid., 3:248.
51. Ibid.
52. DSM, "Antikhrist: Petr i Aleksey," *PSS* 4:103–4.
53. Ibid., 5:15.
54. Ibid.

55. Ibid., 5:98.
56. Ibid., 4:7.
57. Ibid., 5:28–29.
58. Ibid., 4:145.
59. Ibid., 5:13–14.
60. Ibid., 4:146.
61. Ibid., 5:19.
62. Ibid., 5:98–99.
63. Ibid., 5:226.
64. Ibid., 4:71.
65. Ibid., 5:159.
66. Ibid., 5:186.
67. Ibid.
68. The *Khlysty* (self-styled "People of God") formed an ostensibly Christian sect incorporating many pagan beliefs and rites, which arose in Russia in the mid seventeenth century at the time of the schism in the Russian Orthodox Church. It penetrated even into the monasteries and convents of Moscow, was rooted out in 1733, and then revived and continued into the first half of the nineteenth century before fragmenting into various lesser sects. The foremost belief of the *Khlysty* was the incarnation of God, Christ, the Holy Spirit, the Mother of God, and other figures of Christian faith in worthy individuals. Most frequently such incarnation occurred at *radeniya* through flagellation *(khlyst* is a whip), prayer, and dancing. Merezhkovskiy apparently describes an "exceptional" *radenie* to initiate a new member.
69. DSM, "Antikhrist: Petr i Aleksey," *PSS* 5:245.
70. Ibid., 5:256.
71. Ibid., 5:263.
72. Ibid., 5:264.

CHAPTER 6: THE SECOND COMING

1. DSM, "Ot avtora," *PSS* 1:III.
2. DSM, "L. Tolstoy i Dostoevskiy," *PSS* 7:305. In a sarcastic and unjust parody of Merezhkovskiy's apt terms "seer of the flesh" and "seer of the spirit," Chukovskiy dubbed Merezhkovskiy "seer of the thing" *(taynovidets veshchi).* See K. Chukovskiy, *Ot Chekhova do nashikh dney* (St. Petersburg, 1908), p. 149.
3. DSM, "L. Tolstoy i Dostoevskiy," *PSS* 7:109.
4. Ibid., 7:8.
5. Ibid., 8:24–25.
6. Ibid., 8:38.
7. Ibid., 8:22.

8. Ibid., 8:26.
9. Ibid., 7:211.
10. Ibid., 8:186.
11. Ibid., 8:179.
12. Ibid., 8:29.
13. DSM, "V tikhom omute," *PSS* 12:350.
14. DSM, "L. Tolstoy i Dostoevskiy," *PSS* 7:103.
15. Ibid., 8:12.
16. Ibid., 8:13.
17. Ibid., 8:15.
18. Ibid., 9:139 (the quotation is from John 10:30).
19. Ibid., 7:34. Merezhkovskiy has made a negative of John 6:54: "Whoso eateth my flesh and drinketh my blood hath eternal life."
20. DSM, "L. Tolstoy i Dostoevskiy," *PSS* 9:39.
21. Ibid., 7:52.
22. Ibid., 8:87.
23. Ibid., 8:133.
24. Ibid., 9:42.
25. Ibid., 9:202.
26. Ibid., 9:203–4 (the quotation is from Matthew 19:5).
27. Ibid., 9:204.
28. Ibid., 9:206.
29. Ibid., 9:226.
30. Ibid., 9:238.
31. Ibid., 9:241 (the quotations are from John 1:14 and John 5:25).
32. Ibid., 9:243.
33. Ibid., 9:244.
34. Ibid., 9:245.
35. See S. Kierkegaard, *Papers.*
36. See Kierkegaard, *Concluding Unscientific Postscript to the Philosophical Fragments.*
37. See Kierkegaard, *Papers* and *This Has to Be Said, So Be It Now Said.*
38. See Kierkegaard, *Fear and Trembling.*
39. See above, quotation 22, p. 98.
40. See Kierkegaard, *The Works of Love.*
41. See Kierkegaard, *Either/Or,* vol. 2.
42. See Kierkegaard, *The Concept of Dread.*
43. See Kierkegaard, *Either/Or,* vol. 2.
44. See Kierkegaard, *Repetition.*
45. See Kierkegaard, *On Authority and Revelation.*
46. See Kierkegaard, *Training in Christianity.*

47. See Kierkegaard, *Christian Discourses*.
48. See Kierkegaard, *Either/Or*, vol. 2.
49. See Kierkegaard, *Three Edifying Discourses*.
50. DSM, "L. Tolstoy i Dostoevskiy," *PSS* 7:8.
51. Ibid., 7:251.
52. Ibid., 7:295.
53. Ibid., 9:250–51 (the quotation is from Revelations 22:20).
54. DSM, "Ne mir, no mech," *PSS* 10:20–21.
55. See V. V. Rozanov, *V mire neyasnogo i nereshennogo* (St. Petersburg, 1901).
56. DSM, "Ne mir, no mech," *PSS* 10:21–22.
57. DSM, "Gryadushchiy Kham," *PSS* 11:153.
58. DSM, "Ne mir, no mech," *PSS* 10:13.
59. Ibid., 10:22.
60. Ibid., 10:11.
61. DSM, *Dve tayny russkoy poezii: Nekrasov i Tyutchev* (Petrograd, 1915), p. 111.
62. DSM, "V tikhom omute," *PSS* 12:237.
63. DSM, *Bylo i budet* (Petrograd, 1915), p. 232.
64. DSM, "Bol'naya Rossiya," *PSS* 12:134.
65. DSM, "Lermontov: poet sverkhchelovechestva," *PSS* 10:330.
66. DSM, "Ne mir, no mech," *PSS* 10:123.
67. DSM, "Lermontov: poet sverkhchelovechestva," *PSS* 10:330.
68. Ibid., 10:331.
69. DSM, *Nevoennyy dnevnik* (Petrograd, 1917), p. 74.

CHAPTER 7: THE APPLICATION: SOCIAL AND POLITICAL IDEALS

1. For a contemporary commentary on the new religious awareness, see A. Zakrzhevskiy, *Religiya: Psikhologicheskie paralleli* (Kiev, 1913).
2. ZGM, *Dmitriy Merezhkovskiy*, p. 80.
3. DSM, "Avtobiograficheskaya zametka," *RL* 1:293.
4. Ibid.
5. ZGM, *Dmitriy Merezhkovskiy*, p. 92.
6. Ibid., p. 96.
7. Ibid., p. 98.
8. Ibid., p. 108.
9. Ibid., p. 112.
10. Ibid., p. 113.
11. Editorial note in periodical *Novyy Put'* 2:287 (1904).
12. DSM, "Avtobiograficheskaya zametka," *RL* 1:294.

13. For Belyy's reminiscences of his relationship with Merezhkovskiy and Gippius, see A. Belyy, *Na rubezhe dvukh stoletiy* (Moscow and Leningrad, 1930) and *Nachalo veka*. For Gippius's accounts see A. Krayniy (Z. Gippius), *Literaturnyy dnevik* (St. Petersburg, 1908).
14. ZGM, *Dmitriy Merezhkovskiy*, pp. 147–49.
15. Ibid., p. 159.
16. Ibid., p. 164.
17. Ibid., p. 185.
18. Ibid., p. 186.
19. Ibid., p. 187.
20. Ibid., p. 189.
21. Ibid., p. 196.
22. DSM, "Avtobiograficheskaya zametka," *RL* 1:294.
23. Ibid.
24. ZGM, *Dmitriy Merezhkovskiy*, p. 185.
25. For a brief evaluation of these aspects of *Alexander I* see S. Mel'gunov, "Roman Merezhkovskogo: 'Aleksandr I,'" *Golos Minuvshego* 12:39–80 (1914).
26. V. G. Malakhieva-Mirovich, "Novaya p'esa D. S. Merezhkovskogo," *Russkaya Mysl'* 3:24 (1916).
27. V. Kranikhfel'd, "Literaturnye otkliki," *Sovremennyy Mir* 1:89 (1908).
28. M. Tsetlin, "D. S. Merezhkovskiy," *Novosel'e* 2:53 (1942).
29. Bryusov, "Razgadka ili oshibka?" *Russkaya Mysl'* 3:19 (1914).
30. DSM, "V tikhom omute," *PSS* 12:257.
31. DSM, "Gogol'," *PSS* 10:165.
32. Ibid., 10:167.
33. Ibid., 10:187.
34. Ibid., 10:184.
35. Ibid., 10:191 (the quotation is from Matthew 10:36).
36. DSM, "Gryadushchiy Kham," *PSS* 11:7.
37. Ibid., 11:19–20 (the quotation is from Matthew 7:20).
38. Ibid., 11:8.
39. Ibid., 11:9.
40. See Genesis 9:18–27. Merezhkovskiy does not employ *kham* in its modern sense of "boor" or "cad," but in its original usage. *Kham* is the biblical Ham, son of Noah and father of Canaan, the object of Noah's curse: "A servant of servants shall he be unto his brethren" (Genesis 9:25).
41. DSM, "Gryadushchiy Kham," *PSS* 11:34.
42. Ibid., 11:10.
43. Ibid., 11:10–11.

44. The tramp *(bosyak)* to be found in the early stories of Maxim Gor'kiy ("Chelkash," 1895; "Mal'va," 1897; "Konovalov," 1897) is an elemental protestor who has broken away from the strictures of organized society in order to seek a free life. Independent, proud, and scornful of those who obey the laws and customs imposed by society and tradition, the tramp served Gor'kiy as a means for exposing the faults of Russia. However, Gor'kiy soon realized that the tramp was too much the individualist and anarchist by nature to unite in the struggle for change. He therefore abandoned his romantic hero in favor of the more prosaic, but more socially oriented, worker.
45. DSM, "Gryadushchiy Kham," *PSS* 11:54.
46. Ibid., 11:60.
47. DSM, "Gogol'," *PSS* 10:258 (the quotation is from Gogol', "Spor Ivana Ivanovicha s Ivanom Nikiforovichom").
48. Ibid., 10:286.
49. DSM, "Gryadushchiy Kham," *PSS* 11:34.
50. ZGM, *Dmitriy Merezhkovskiy*, p. 132.
51. DSM, "Gryadushchiy Kham," *PSS* 11:106.
52. DSM, "Prorok russkoy revolyutsii," *PSS* 11:180.
53. DSM, "Gryadushchiy Kham," *PSS* 11:156.
54. DSM, "Prorok russkoy revolyutsii," *PSS* 11:210.
55. Ibid., 11:200.
56. DSM, "Gryadushchiy Kham," *PSS* 11:48.
57. Ibid., 11:96–97.
58. Ibid., 11:99.
59. DSM, "Religion et révolution," in *Le Tsar et la révolution* (together with Z. Gippius and D. Filosofov, Paris, 1907), pp. 159–60.
60. Ibid., p. 194.
61. DSM, "Prorok russkoy revolyutsii," *PSS* 11:181.
62. Ibid., 11:182.
63. DSM, "V tikhom omute," *PSS* 12:267.
64. N. A. Berdyaev, *Dukhovnyy krizis intelligentsii* (St. Petersburg, 1910), p. 102.
65. DSM, "Préface," in *Le Tsar et la révolution*, p. 7.
66. DSM, "Gryadushchiy Kham," *PSS* 11:29–30 (the quotation is from Matthew 5:6).
67. Ibid., 11:31.
68. DSM, "V tikhom omute," *PSS* 12:241.
69. DSM, "Gryadushchiy Kham," *PSS* 11:33.
70. Ibid., 11:121.
71. DSM, "Préface," in *Le Tsar et la révolution*, p. 12.
72. DSM, "Prorok russkoy revolyutsii," *PSS* 11:208–9.

73. Ibid., 11:209.
74. DSM, "V tikhom omute," *PSS* 12:283.
75. DSM, "Religion et révolution," in *Le Tsar et la révolution*, p. 237.
76. Ibid., p. 190.
77. DSM, "V tikhom omute," *PSS* 12:227.
78. Ibid., 12:263.
79. DSM, "Prorok russkoy revolyutsii," *PSS* 11:195.
80. DSM, "Gryadushchiy Kham," *PSS* 11:35.
81. DSM, "Ne mir, no mech," *PSS* 10:8.
82. See Kierkegaard, *On Authority and Revelation: The Book on Adler; Postscript*; and *The Present Age.*
83. DSM, "Ne mir, no mech," *PSS* 10:29.
84. Ibid.
85. Ibid., 10:104.
86. DSM, "Gryadushchiy Kham," *PSS* 11:35.
87. DSM, "Bol'naya Rossiya," *PSS* 12:6.
88. Ibid., 12:28.
89. Ibid., 12:60.
90. Ibid., 12:98.
91. DSM, *Bylo i budet*, p. 157.
92. Ibid., p. 176.
93. Ibid., p. 291.

CHAPTER 8: THE THIRD HUMANITY

1. ZGM, *Dmitriy Merezhkovskiy*, p. 214.
2. DSM, *Bylo i budet*, pp. 258–59.
3. DSM, *Nevoennyy dnevnik*, p. 123.
4. Ibid., p. 142.
5. Ibid., pp. 54–55.
6. Ibid., p. 56.
7. Ibid., p. 57.
8. Ibid., p. 59.
9. Ibid., p. 185.
10. Ibid., p. 188.
11. Ibid., p. 177.
12. ZGM, "Peterburgskiy dnevnik," in *Tsarstvo Antikhrista* (together with Merezhkovskiy, D. Filosofov, and V. Zlobin [Munich, 1921]), p. 39.
13. ZGM, *Dmitriy Merezhkovskiy*, p. 219.
14. DSM, *Perventsy svobody* (Petrograd, 1917), p. 3. The article is dedicated to A. F. Kerenskiy.
15. ZGM, *Dmitriy Merezhkovskiy*, p. 226.

16. ZGM, "Peterburgskiy dnevnik," in *Tsarstvo Antikhrista*, p. 93.
17. Ibid., p. 76.
18. DSM, "Zapisnaya knizhka 1919–1920," in *Tsarstvo Antikhrista*, p. 244.
19. Ibid., p. 243.
20. Ibid., p. 245.
21. ZGM, *Dmitriy Merezhkovskiy*, p. 246.
22. E. Salgaller, "Dmitrij Samozvanets: A Dramatic Fragment by D. S. Merežkovskij," *Slavic and East European Journal* 4:399 (1963).
23. ZGM, *Dmitriy Merezhkovskiy*, pp. 246–47.
24. Ibid., p. 255.
25. Ibid., p. 292.
26. DSM, *Joseph Pilsudski* (translated by H. E. Kennedy; London and Edinburgh, 1921), p. 4.
27. Ibid., p. 17.
28. ZGM, *Dmitriy Merezhkovskiy*, p. 301.
29. Yu. Terapiano, *Vstrechi* (New York, 1953), p. 43. Terapiano, a member of the group, provides interesting recollections of the Merezhkovskiys, their "Sundays," and the Green Lamp (pp. 22–82). Of particular significance are his comments (p. 46) that the salon was one of the liveliest Russian literary centers in Paris and that attempts to emulate it after the deaths of Merezhkovskiy and Gippius ended in failure, leaving a void in émigré intellectual life. Also, on the Green Lamp and the Merezhkovskiys' soirées see T. Pachmuss, *Zinaida Hippius: An Intellectual Profile* (Carbondale and Edwardsville, Ill., 1971), pp. 238–41.
30. Terapiano, *Vstrechi*, pp. 46–47.
31. DSM, "Predislovie," in *Tsarstvo Antikhrista*, p. 5.
32. DSM, "L. Tolstoy i bol'shevizm," in *Tsarstvo Antikhrista*, p. 192.
33. DSM, "Tsarstvo Antikhrista," in *Tsarstvo Antikhrista*, p. 24.
34. Ibid., p. 20.
35. Ibid., p. 30.
36. Ibid., p. 31.
37. Ibid., p. 34.
38. These letters are among the Merezhkovskiy archives in the possession of Professor Temira Pachmuss.
39. *Literaturnaya entsiklopediya*, ed. A. V. Lunacharskiy (Moscow, 1934), 7:197.
40. DSM, *Rozhdenie bogov: Tutankamon na Krite* (Prague, 1925), p. 52.
41. Ibid., pp. 18–19.

42. DSM, *Messiya* (Paris, 1928), 1:102.
43. Ibid., 2:63.
44. Ibid., 1:84.
45. I. Demidov, "D. Merezhkovskiy, Tayna Trekh: Egipet i Vavilon," *Sovremennye zapiski* 28:479 (1926).
46. DSM, *Tayna Trekh: Egipet i Vavilon* (Prague, 1925), p. 327.
47. Ibid.
48. Ibid., p. 20.
49. Ibid., p. 23.
50. Ibid., p. 27.
51. Ibid., p. 297.
52. Ibid., p. 147.
53. Ibid., p. 299.
54. Ibid., p. 39.
55. Ibid., p. 41.
56. V. F. Botsyanovskiy, *Bogoiskateli* (St. Petersburg and Moscow, 1911), p. 148.
57. DSM, "Zapisnaya knizhka 1919–1920," in *Tsarstvo Antikhrista*, p. 238.
58. DSM, *Tayna Trekh*, p. 181.
59. Ibid., pp. 48–49.
60. Ibid., p. 54.
61. Ibid., p. 114.
62. Ibid., pp. 118–19.
63. Ibid., p. 114.
64. DSM, *Tayna Zapada: Atlantida-Evropa* (Belgrade, 1930), pp. 223–24.
65. DSM, *Iisus Neizvestnyy* (Belgrade, 1931), 1:360.
66. DSM, *Tayna Trekh*, p. 169.
67. DSM, *Iisus Neizvestnyy*, 2(1):153.
68. DSM, *Tayna Trekh*, p. 189.
69. Ibid., p. 326.
70. Ibid., p. 346.
71. Ibid., p. 224 (the quotations are from Revelations 12:1 and 2).
72. DSM, *Tayna Zapada*, p. 88.
73. Ibid., p. 369.
74. DSM, *Iisus Neizvestnyy*, 1:102.
75. Pachmuss, *Zinaida Hippius: An Intellectual Profile*, p. 92.
76. DSM, *Tayna Trekh*, p. 187.
77. Ibid., p. 188.
78. DSM, *Tayna Zapada*, p. 343.
79. Ibid., pp. 301–8.
80. Ibid., p. 346; and *Iisus Neizvestnyy*, 1:364.

81. DSM, *Tayna Zapada*, p. 496.
82. DSM, *Iisus Neizvestnyy*, 1:159.
83. DSM, *Tayna Zapada*, p. 199.
84. Ibid.
85. Ibid., p. 201.
86. Ibid., p. 198.
87. Ibid., p. 128.
88. Ibid., pp. 430–31.
89. Ibid., p. 112. Plato describes Atlantis in his dialogues *Timaeus* and *Critias*.
90. DSM, *Tayna Zapada*, p. 150.
91. G. Golokhovastov, *Gibel' Atlantidy* (New York, 1938).
92. DSM, *Iisus Neizvestnyy*, 1:221.
93. Ibid., 1:44–45.
94. DSM, *Tayna Zapada*, p. 184.
95. DSM, *Dante* (Brussels and Paris, 1939), 2:120.
96. Ibid., 2:163.
97. For a more detailed account of the last days of Merezhkovskiy's life see V. Zlobin, *Tyazhelaya dusha* (Washington, D.C., 1970), pp. 116–29.
98. DSM, "Gryadushchiy Kham," *PSS* 11:151.

Selected Bibliography

I. MEREZHKOVSKIY'S WORKS IN COLLECTED FORM

Stikhotvoreniya, 1883–1887. St. Petersburg, 1888.

Simvoly. St. Petersburg, 1892.

O prichinakh upadka i o novykh techeniyakh sovremennoy russkoy literatury. St. Petersburg, 1893.

Novye stikhotvoreniya, 1891–1895. St. Petersburg, 1896.

Smert' Bogov: Yulian Otstupnik. St. Petersburg, 1896.

Vechnye sputniki. St. Petersburg, 1897.

"Ottsy i deti" russkogo liberalizma. St. Petersburg, 1901.

Voskresshie bogi: Leonardo da Vinchi. St. Petersburg, 1901.

L. Tolstoy i Dostoevskiy. St. Petersburg, 1901–1902.

Stikhotvoreniya, 1888–1902. St. Petersburg, 1902.

Lyubov' sil'nee smerti. Moscow, 1902.

Sobranie stikhov, 1883–1903. Moscow, 1904.

Antikhrist: Petr i Aleksey. St. Petersburg, 1905.

Pushkin. St. Petersburg, 1906.

Gogol' i chort. Moscow, 1906.

Gryadushchiy Kham: Chekhov i Gor'kiy. St. Petersburg, 1906.

Prorok russkoy revolyutsii. St. Petersburg, 1906.

Teper' ili nikogda. Moscow, 1906.

Le Tsar et la révolution (together with Z. N. Gippius and D. V. Filosofov). Paris, 1907.

Pavel I. St. Petersburg, 1908.

Makov tsvet (together with Z. N. Gippius and D. V. Filosofov). St. Petersburg, 1908.

V tikhom omute. St. Petersburg, 1908.

Ne mir, no mech. St. Petersburg, 1908.

M. Yu. Lermontov: Poet sverkhchelovechestva. St. Petersburg, 1909.

Sobranie stikhov, 1883–1910. St. Petersburg, 1910.

Bol'naya Rossiya. St. Petersburg, 1910.

Lermontov: Poet sverkhchelovechestva; Gogol'. St. Petersburg, 1911.

Aleksandr I. St. Petersburg and Moscow, 1913.

Polnoe sobranie sochineniy. St. Petersburg, 1911–1913.

Polnoe sobranie sochineniy. Moscow, 1914.

Bylo i budet: Dnevnik 1910–1914. Petrograd, 1915.

Dve tayny russkoy poezii: Nekrasov i Tyutchev. Petrograd, 1915.

Zavet Belinskogo. Petrograd, 1915.

Budet radost'. Petrograd, 1916.

Zachem voskres. Petrograd, 1916.

Nevoennyy dnevnik, 1914–1916. Petrograd, 1917.

Ot voyny k revolyutsii. Petrograd, 1917.

Perventsy svobody. Petrograd, 1917.

Romantiki. Petrograd, 1917.

Chetyrnadtsatoe dekabrya. Petrograd, 1918.

Tsarevich Aleksey. Petrograd, 1920.

Tsarstvo Antikhrista (together with Z. N. Gippius, D. V. Filosofov, and V. Zlobin). Munich, 1921.

Rozhdenie bogov: Tutankamon na Krite. Prague, 1925.

Tayna Trekh: Egipet i Vavilon. Prague, 1925.

Messiya. Paris, 1928.

Napoleon. Belgrade, 1929.

Tayna Zapada: Atlantida-Evropa. Belgrade, 1930.

Iisus Neizvestnyy. Belgrade, 1931.

Pavel, Avgustin. Berlin, 1936.

Frantsisk Assisskiy. Berlin, 1938.

Zhanna d Ark. Berlin, 1938.

Dante. Brussels and Paris, 1939.

Luther. Translated into French by C. Andronikoff. Paris, 1941.

Pascal. Translated into French by C. Andronikoff. Paris, 1941.

Calvin. Translated into French by C. Andronikoff. Paris, 1942.

II. MEREZHKOVSKIY'S WORKS IN PERIODICALS (EXCLUDING INDIVIDUAL POEMS)

"Staryy vopros no povodu novogo talanta." *Severnyy Vestnik,* no. 11 (1888).

"Flober v svoikh pis'makh." *Severnyy Vestnik,* no. 12 (1888).

"Russo." *Russkoe Bogatstvo,* no. 11 (1889).

"Rasskazy V. Korolenki." *Severnyy Vestnik,* no. 5 (1889).

"Don-Kikhot i Sancho Pansa." *Severnyy Vestnik,* nos. 8 and 9 (1889).

"O 'Prestuplenii i nakazanii' Dostoevskogo." *Russkoe Obozrenie,* vol. 2, no. 3 (1890).

"I. A. Goncharov." *Trud,* no. 24 (1890).

"Vera." *Russkaya Mysl',* nos. 3 and 4 (1890).

"Sil'vio." *Severnyy Vestnik,* nos. 2, 3, 4, and 5 (1890).

"Prorok." *Nablyudatel',* no. 12 (1891).

"Frantsisk Assisskiy." *Niva,* no. 3 (1891).

"Sem'ya." *Russkaya Mysl',* no. 6 (1891).

"Smert'." *Severnyy Vestnik,* nos. 2 and 3 (1891).

"A. N. Maykov." *Trud,* no. 4 (1891).

"Mark Avreliy." *Trud,* no. 21 (1891).

"Kal'deron." *Trud,* no. 24 (1891).

"Konets veka." *Russkie Vedomosti.* Moscow, 1892.

"Groza proshla." *Trud,* no. 1 (1893).

"Montan'." *Russkaya Mysl',* no. 2 (1893).

"Pamyati Turgeneva." *Teatral'naya Gazeta,* no. 8 (1893).

"Pamyati A. N. Pleshcheeva." *Teatral'naya Gazeta,* no. 14 (1893).

"Misticheskoe dvizhenie nashego veka." *Trud,* no. 4 (1893).

"Neoromantizm v drame." *Vestnik Inostrannoy Literatury,* no. 11 (1894).

"Noveyshaya lirika." *Vestnik Inostrannoy Literatury,* no. 12 (1894).

"Krest'yanin vo frantsuzskoy literature." *Trud,* no. 7 (1894) and no. 9 (1895).

"Zheltolitsye pozitivisty." *Vestnik Inostrannoy Literatury,* no. 3 (1895).

"Portret iz epokhi Trayana." *Trud,* no. 11 (1895).

"Iov." *Niva,* no. 3 (1895).

"Na novom Zamoskvorech'i." *Niva,* no. 6 (1895).

"Knyazhna Distina." *Niva,* no. 8 (1895).

"Rytsar' za pryalkoyu." *Niva,* no. 52 (1895).

"Otverzhennyy (Smert' bogov)." *Severnyy Vestnik,* nos. 1–6 (1895).

"Pir." *Niva,* no. 8 (1896).

"Nauka lyubvi." *Severnyy Vestnik,* no. 8 (1896).

"Lyubov' sil'nee smerti." *Severnyy Vestnik,* no. 8 (1896).

"Pushkin; Kol'tsov; Maykov." In *Filosofskie techeniya russkoy poezii.* Edited by P. Pertsov. St. Petersburg, 1896.

"Pis'mo v redaktsiyu." *Novosti,* no. 340 (1896).

"Selenie Vinchi." *Cosmopolis,* no. 2 (1897).

"Zheleznoe kol'tso." *Vsemirnaya Illyustratsiya,* nos. 1–3 (1897).

"Prevrashchenie." *Niva,* nos. 7 and 8 (1897).

"Lyubov'." *Zhivopisnoe Obozrenie,* no. 5 (1898).

"Angel." *Zhivopisnoe Obozrenie,* no. 1 (1899).

"Voskresshie bogi: Leonardo da Vinchi." *Nachalo,* nos. 1–4 (1899).

"Ya. P. Polonskiy." *Mir Iskusstva,* vol. 1, nos. 1 and 2 (1899).

"Tragediya tselomudriya i sladostrastiya." *Mir Iskusstva,* vol. 1, nos. 7 and 8 (1899).

"Prazdnik Pushkina." *Mir Iskusstva,* vol. 2, nos. 13 and 14 (1899).

"Pis'mo v redaktsiyu." *Novoe Vremya,* no. 8347 (1899).

"Voskresshie bogi: Leonardo da Vinchi." *Mir Bozhiy,* nos. 1–12 (1900).

"L. Tolstoy i Dostoevskiy." *Mir Iskusstva,* vol. 3, nos. 1–12 (1900); vol. 4, nos. 13–22 (1900); vol. 5, nos. 1–6 (1901); vol. 6, nos. 7–12 (1901); vol. 7, no. 2 (1902).

"Pamyati A. I Urusova." *Mir Iskusstva,* vol. 4, nos. 15 and 16 (1900).

"Pis'mo v redaktsiyu." *Novoe Vremya,* no. 8571 (1900).

"Ottsy i deti russkogo liberalizma." *Mir Iskusstva,* vol. 5, nos. 2 and 3 (1901).

"Otvet Rozanovu na ego stat'yu: 'Seriya nedorazumeniy.' " *Novoe Vremya,* no. 8974 (1901).

"Pis'mo v redaktsiyu." *Novoe Vremya,* no. 9248 (1901).

"O novom znachenii drevney tragedii." *Novoe Vremya,* no. 9560 (1902).

"Sud'ba Gogolya." *Novyy Put',* nos. 1–3 (1903).

"Otvet khudozhniku A.B." *Novyy Put',* no. 2 (1903).

"L. Tolstoy i russkaya tserkov'." *Novyy Put',* no. 2 (1903).

"Iz chernovykh nabroskov k romanu 'Petr i Aleksey.' " In *Severnye Tsvety,* 1903.

"Novyy Vavilon." *Novyy Put',* no. 3 (1904).

"O svobode slova." *Novyy Put',* no. 10 (1904).

"Antikhrist: Petr i Aleksey." *Novyy Put',* nos. 1–5 and 9–12 (1904); *Voprosy Zhizni,* nos. 1–3 (1905).

"Krasnaya smert'." *Vestnik i biblioteka samoobrazovaniya,* nos. 21–23 (1905).

"Teper' ili nikogda." *Voprosy Zhizni,* nos. 4 and 5 (1905).

"O novom religioznom deystvii." *Voprosy Zhizni,* nos. 10 and 11 (1905).

"Umytye ruki." *Vesy,* nos. 9 and 10 (1905).

"O Chekhove (Chekhov i Gor'kiy)." *Vesy,* no. 11 (1905).

"Meshchanstvo i intelligentsiya." *Polyarnaya Zvezda,* no. 1 (1905).

"Gryadushchiy Kham." *Polyarnaya Zvezda,* no. 3 (1905).

"Prorok russkoy revolyutsii." *Vesy,* nos. 2–4 (1906).

"Dekadentstvo i obshchestvennost'." *Vesy,* no. 5 (1906).

"Vse protiv vsekh." *Zolotoe Runo,* no. 1 (1906).

"Starinnye oktavy." *Zolotoe Runo,* nos. 1–4 (1906).

"Makov tsvet" (together with Z. N. Gippius and D. V. Filosofov). *Russkaya Mysl',* no. 11 (1907).

"Revolyutsiya i religiya." *Russkaya Mysl'*, nos. 2 and 3 (1907).
"Posledniy svyatoy." *Russkaya Mysl'*, nos. 8 and 9 (1907).
"Khristianstvo i gosudarstvo." *Obrazovanie*, no. 7 (1908).
"Bes ili Bog?" *Obrazovanie*, no. 8 (1908).
"V obez'yan'ikh lapakh." *Russkaya Mysl'*, no. 1 (1908).
"Khristianskie anarkhisty." *Rech'*, no. 10 (1908).
"Tsvet meshchanstva." *Rech'*, no. 35 (1908).
"Krasnaya shapochka." *Rech'*, no. 47 (1908).
"Eshche odna velikaya Rossiya." *Rech'*, no. 65 (1908).
"Asfodeli i romashka." *Rech'*, no. 71 (1908).
"Reformatsiya ili revolyutsiya." *Rech'*, no. 86 (1908).
"Nemoy prorok." *Rech'*, no. 190 (1908).
"Khristianstvo i kesarianstvo." *Rech'*, no. 196 (1908).
"L. Tolstoy i revolyutsiya." *Rech'*, no. 205 (1908).
"Intelligentsiya i narod." *Rech'*, no. 279 (1908).
"Bor'ba za dogmat." *Rech'*, no. 307 (1908).
"Peterburgu byt' pustu." *Rech'*, no. 314 (1908).
"Pavel I." *Russkaya Mysl'*, no. 2 (1908).
"Lermontov, Otryvok." *Vesy*, no. 1 (1909).
"Lermontov: Poet sverkhchelovechestva." *Russkaya Mysl'*, no. 3 (1909).
"Raskolovshiysya kolokol." *Russkoe Slovo*, no. 288 (1909).
"Prorochestvo i provokatsiya." *Rech'*, no. 3 (1909).
"Elizaveta Alekseevna." *Rech'*, no. 17 (1909).
"Serdtse chelovecheskoe i serdtse zverinoe." *Rech'*, no. 38 (1909).
"Turgenev." *Rech'*, no. 51 (1909).
"Pis'mo v redaktsiyu." *Rech'*, no. 60 (1909).
"Arakcheev i Fotiy." *Rech'*, no. 65 (1909).
"Golovka visnet." *Rech'*, no. 79 (1909).
"Kogda voskresnet?" *Rech'*, no. 86 (1909).
"Sem' smirennykh." *Rech'*, no. 112 (1909).
"Ivanych i Gleb." *Rech'*, no. 188 (1909).
"K soblaznu malykh sikh." *Rech'*, no. 244 (1909).
"Kon' blednyy." *Rech'*, nos. 265 and 266 (1909).
"Tsarstvo Gleba." *Rech'*, no. 279 (1909).
"Vlast' zemli i vlast' neba." *Rech'*, no. 286 (1909).
"Svin'ya-matushka." *Rech'*, no. 300 (1909).
"Zemlya vo rtu." *Rech'*, no. 314 (1909).
"Brat chelovecheskiy." *Russkoe Slovo*, no. 13 (1910).
"Velikiy gnev." *Russkoe Slovo*, no. 108 (1910).
"Noch'yu o solntse." *Russkoe Slovo*, no. 138 (1910).
"Lyubov' k rodine." *Russkoe Slovo*, no. 141 (1910).
"Balagan i tragediya." *Russkoe Slovo*, no. 211 (1910).

"Vostok ili zapad?" *Russkoe Slovo*, no. 217 (1910).
"Zemnoy Khristos." *Russkoe Slovo*, no. 236 (1910).
"Strashnoe ditya." *Rech'*, no. 30 (1910).
"Smert' Tolstogo." *Rech'*, no. 308 (1910).
"Natsionalizm i religiya." *Rech'*, no. 289 (1911).
"Aleksandr I (Otryvki)." *Russkoe Slovo*, April–November 1911; January–December 1912.
"Aleksandr I." *Russkaya Mysl'*, nos. 5 and 6 (1911); 10–12 (1911); 1 (1912); 3 and 4 (1912); 10–12 (1912).
"Pis'mo v redaktsiyu." *Russkaya Mysl'*, no. 5 (1912).
"Novaya p'esa L. Andreeva." *Russkoe Slovo*, no. 289 (1912).
"Dva otrecheniya." *Russkoe Slovo*, no. 293 (1912).
"Chego pozhelat' russkim pisatelyam v 1912 g." *Rech'*, no. 1 (1912).
"Ne solenaya sol'." *Russkoe Slovo*, no. 9 (1913).
"O chernykh kolodtsakh." *Russkoe Slovo*, no. 59 (1913).
"Avtobiograficheskaya zametka." *Russkoe Slovo*, no. 65 (1913).
"Na puti v Emmaus." *Russkoe Slovo*, no. 87 (1913).
"V. Rozanov." *Russkoe Slovo*, no. 125 (1913).
"Gete." *Russkoe Slovo*, no. 144 (1913).
"Nekrasov." *Russkoe Slovo*, no. 183 (1913).
"Sv. Elena." *Russkoe Slovo*, no. 226 (1913).
"Malen'kie mysli." *Russkoe Slovo*, no. 238 (1913).
"Tragediya sovesti." *Russkoe Slovo*, no. 253 (1913).
"Gor'kiy i Dostoevskiy." *Russkoe Slovo*, no. 286 (1913).
"Pis'mo k A. S. Suvorinu." *Novoe Vremya*, no. 13606 (1914).
"Pis'mo k A. S. Suvorinu." *Novoe Vremya*, no. 13607 (1914).
"Suvorin i Chekhov." *Russkoe Slovo*, no. 17 (1914).
"Tayna Tyutcheva." *Russkoe Slovo*, no. 43 (1914).
"Pis'mo v redaktsiyu." *Rech'*, no. 25 (1914).
"Pis'mo v redaktsiyu." *Rech'*, no. 27 (1914).
"Pis'mo v redaktsiyu." *Rech'*, no. 29 (1914).
"Avtobiograficheskaya zametka." In *Russkaya literatura XX veka.* Edited by S. A. Vengerov. Moscow, 1914, 1:288–94.
"Smert' tsarevicha Alekseya: Stseny iz neizdannoy tragedii." In *Russkiy sbornik*. Vol. 1, Paris, 1920.
"Egipet-Oziris." *Okno*, nos. 1 and 2 (1923).
"Taynaya mudrost' vostoka. Vavilon." *Sovremennye zapiski*, nos. 15–17 (1923).
"Vechernyaya pesn'." *Sovremennye zapiski*, no. 17 (1923).
"Rozhdenie bogov." *Sovremennye zapiski*, nos. 21 and 22 (1924).
"1925–1825." *Sovremennye zapiski*, no. 26 (1925).
"Pis'ma v 'Novyy dom.'" *Novyy dom*, no. 2 (1926).
"Messiya." *Sovremennye zapiski*, nos. 27–32 (1926–1927).

"Sud'i Napoleona." *Novaya korabl'*, no. 2 (1927).
"Ryzhaya krysa." *Novaya korabl'*, no. 2 (1927).
"Otvet k Adamovichu." *Zveno*, no. 213 (1927).
"Kotoryy zhe iz vas? Iudaizm i Khristianstvo." *Novaya korabl'*, no. 4 (1928).
"Napoleon chelovek." *Sovremennye zapiski*, no. 35 (1928).
"Atlantida." *Sovremennye zapiski*, no. 41 (1930).
"Otchego pogibla Atlantida." *Sovremennye zapiski*, no. 43 (1930).
"Evropa-Sodom." *Chisla*, nos. 2 and 3 (1930).
"Neizvestnoe Evangelie." *Chisla*, no. 5 (1931).
"Nazaretskie Budni." *Sovremennye zapiski*, no. 48 (1932).
"Tsarstvo Bozhie." *Sovremennye zapiski*, no. 52 (1933).
"Otrechenie Petra." *Illyustrirovannaya Rossiya*, no. 414 (1933).
"Blazhenstva." *Chisla*, nos. 7 and 8 (1933).
"Podenshchik Khristov." *Nov'*, no. 8 (1934).
"Antisemitizm i khristianstvo." *Vstrechi*, no. 1 (1934).
"Mir ili voina." *Mech*, no. 7 (1934).
"Okolo vazhnogo: O 'Chislakh.' " *Mech*, nos. 13 and 14 (1934).
"O khoroshem vkuse i svobode." *Mech*, nos. 17 and 18 (1934).
"Kommunizm bozhestvennyy." *Sovremennye zapiski*, no. 58 (1935).
"Zhizn' Dante." *Russkie zapiski*, no. 2 (1937).
"O Pushkine." *Pushkinskie dni v Shankhae* (1937).
"Zhisn' Paskalya." *Vozrozhdenie*, nos. 5 and 6 (1949); 8 (1950).
"Turgenev." *Vozrozhdenie*, no. 77 (1958).
"Poeziya Tyutcheva." *Vozrozhdenie*, no. 80 (1958).
"Asfodeli i romashki." *Vozrozhdenie*, no. 84 (1958).
"Khlestakov, Chichikov i chert." *Vozrozhdenie*, no. 87 (1959).
"Sv. Tereza Iisusa." *Vozrozhdenie*, nos. 92 and 93 (1959).
"Sv. Ioann Kresta." *Novyy zhurnal*, nos. 64 and 65 (1961); 69 (1962).
"Chto sdelal Paskal'." *Novyy zhurnal*, no. 87 (1967).

III. MEREZHKOVSKIY'S WORKS IN ENGLISH TRANSLATION

The Death of the Gods. Translated by H. Trench. London, 1901.
The Forerunner (The Romance of Leonardo da Vinci). London, 1902. Repeatedly issued, particularly in the translation by B. G. Guerney. New York, 1928.
Tolstoy as Man and Artist, With an Essay on Dostoievski. Westminster, 1902.
Peter and Alexis. London, 1905. Also in a translation by B. G. Guerney. New York, 1931.
Daphnis and Chloe. Translated by G. A. Mounsey. London, 1905.
The Life Work of Calderon. Translated by G. A. Mounsey. London, n.d.

The Life Work of Hendrik Ibsen. Translated by G. A. Mounsey. London, n.d.

The Life Work of Montaigne. Translated by G. A. Mounsey. London, n.d.

The Life Work of Pliny the Younger. Translated by G. A. Mounsey. London, n.d.

The Life Work of Flaubert. Translated by G. A. Mounsey. London, n.d.

The Life Work of Marcus Aurelius. Translated by G. A. Mounsey. London, n.d.

The Life Work of Dostoievski. Translated by G. A. Mounsey. London, n.d.

The Acropolis. Translated by G. A. Mounsey. London, n.d.

Joseph Pilsudski. Translated by H. E. Kennedy. London and Edinburgh, 1921.

December the Fourteenth. Translated and abridged by N. A. Duddington. London, 1923.

The Birth of the Gods. Translated by N. A. Duddington. London, 1925.

Akhnaton, King of Egypt. Translated by N. A. Duddington. London, 1927.

Napoleon: A Study. Translated by C. Zvegintsov. London, 1929.

The Life of Napoleon. Translated by C. Zvegintsov. London, 1929.

Michael Angelo and Other Sketches. Translated by N. A. Duddington. London, 1930.

The Secret of the West. Translated by J. Cournos. London, 1933.

Jesus the Unknown. Translated by H. C. Matheson. London, 1933.

Jesus Manifest. Translated by E. Gellibrand. London, 1935.

IV. WORKS BY OTHER AUTHORS

Abramovich, N. Ya. "O khudozhestvennom risunke v sovremennoy belletristike." In *Tvorchestvo i zhizn.* Book 1. St. Petersburg, 1909.

———. "Literaturnye zametki." *Obrazovanie,* no. 6 (1908).

———. "Posledniy roman Merezhkovskogo." *Novaya Zhizn',* no. 3 (1912).

Achkasov, P. "Pis'ma o literature." *Russkiy Vestnik,* no. 1 (1896).

Adamovich, G. "Literaturnye besedy." *Zveno,* nos. 161 and 198 (1926).

———. *Odinochestvo i svoboda.* New York, 1955.

———. *Kommentarii.* Washington, D.C., 1967.

Adrianov, S. "Merezhkovskiy o L. Tolstom i Dostoevskom." *Vestnik i biblioteka samoobrazovaniya,* no. 11 (1904).

Aldanov, M. "D. Merezhkovskiy. Tayna Zapada." *Sovremennye zapiski*, no. 46 (1931).

Aleksandrovich, Yu. *Istoriya noveyshey russkoy literatury, part I: Chekhov i ego vremya.* Moscow, 1911.

―――. *Posle Chekhova.* Vol. 1. Moscow, 1908.

Amfiteatrov, A. "Russkiy literator i rimskiy imperator." In *Literaturnyy al'bom.* St. Petersburg, 1904.

Anichkov, E. "Poety 'Skorpiona.' " In *Literaturnye obrazy i mneniya.* St. Petersburg, 1904.

―――. "Belye pavliny nashey skuki." *Novaya Zhizn'*, no. 7 (1912).

Annenskiy, I., and Kholodnyak, I. "Perevody D. S. Merezhkovskogo." In *Zhurnal Ministerstva Narodnogo Prosveshcheniya*, no. 12 (1908).

Arsen'ev, K. "Novaya forma staroy mechty." *Vestnik Evropy*, no. 5 (1901).

Arskiy. "Iz zhizni i literatury." *Novosti Dnya*, no. 7895 (1905).

Asheshov, N. "Iz zhizni i literatury." *Obrazovanie*, no. 4 (1904).

Aykhenval'd, Yu. "Merezhkovskiy o Lermontove." In *Otdel'nye stranitsy.* Vol. 2. Moscow, 1910.

Ayvazov, N. "Russkoe sektantstvo." *Vera i Razum*, no. 20 (1906).

Bakhtin, N. "Merezhkovskiy i istoriya." *Zveno*, no. 156 (1926).

Bartenev, B. "Neudachnoe obyasnenie." *Novyy Put'*, no. 7 (1904).

―――. "Iz pis'ma k Merezhkovskomu." *Voprosy Zhizni*, nos. 4 and 5 (1905).

Basargin, A. "Kriticheskie zametki." *Moskovskie Vedomosti*, nos. 52, 59, 66, 73, 80, 83, 87, 94, and 306 (1903).

Bazarov, V. "Khristiane Tret'ego Zaveta i stroiteli Bashni Vavilonskoy." In *Na dva fronta.* St. Petersburg, 1910.

―――. "Bogoiskatel'stvo i bogostroitel'stvo." In *Vershiny.* St. Petersburg, 1909.

Bedford, C. H. "D. S. Merezhkovsky: The Forgotten Poet." *Slavonic and East European Review*, December 1957.

―――. "Dmitriy Merezhkovsky, the Intelligentsia and the Revolution of 1905." *Canadian Slavonic Papers.* Vol. 3. 1959.

―――. "Dmitry Merezhkovsky, the Third Testament and the Third Humanity." *Slavonic and East European Review.* December 1963.

Belov, E. "Literaturnoe utro na beregakh Seny." *Russkoe Slovo*, no. 276 (1907).

Belyavskiy, F. "Nad Bezdnoy." *Slovo*, no. 172 (1905).

Belyy, Andrey. *Lug zelenyy.* Moscow, 1910.

―――. *Arabeski.* Moscow, 1911.

―――. "Merezhkovskiy." *Utro Rossii*, no. 28 (1907).

———. "Simvolizm i sovremennoe russkoe iskusstvo." *Vesy*, no. 10 (1908).

———. "Trilogiya Merezhkovskogo." *Vesy*, no. 1 (1908).

———. "Ne mir, no mech." *Vesy*, no. 6 (1908).

———. "Mirovaya ektaniya." *Zolotoe Runo*, no. 3 (1906).

———. *Na rubezhe dvukh stoletiy.* Moscow and Leningrad, 1930.

———. *Nachalo veka.* Moscow and Leningrad, 1933.

———. *Mezhdu dvukh revolyutsiy.* Leningrad, 1934.

Berdyaev, N. A. *Sub specie aeternitatis.* St. Petersburg, 1907.

———. *Dukhovnyy krizis intelligentsii.* St. Petersburg, 1910.

———. "O novom religioznom soznanii." *Voprosy Zhizni*, no. 9 (1905).

———. *The Russian Idea.* London, 1947.

———. *Samopoznanie.* Paris, 1949.

Bibliolog. "Trilogiya o Khriste i Antikhriste. In *Literaturnyy Vestnik.* Vol. 2, bk. 8, 1901.

Billington, J. H. *Mikhailovsky and Russian Populism.* Oxford, 1958.

Blok, A. "Merezhkovskiy." *Rech'*, no. 30 (1909).

Bogdanovich, A. *Gody pereloma.* St. Petersburg, 1908.

——— (A. B.). "Kriticheskie zametki." *Mir Bozhiy*, no. 9 (1895).

———. "Kriticheskie zametki." *Mir Bozhiy*, no. 7 (1896).

———. "Kriticheskie zametki." *Mir Bozhiy*, nos. 6 and 11 (1901).

———. "Pis'mo k Merezhkovskomu." *Novyy Put'*, no. 2 (1903).

———. "Kriticheskie zametki." *Mir Bozhiy*, no. 3 (1904).

———. "Kriticheskie zametki." *Mir Bozhiy*, no. 7 (1905).

Borskiy, B. (Ivinskiy). "V zelenoy pustyn'ke." *Utro*, no. 11 (1908).

Botsyanovskiy, V. F. *Bogoiskateli.* St. Petersburg and Moscow, 1911.

———. "Ustalye." *Rus'*, no. 31 (1908).

———. "Drama D. S. Merezhkovskogo: 'Pavel I.'" *Rus'*, no. 64 (1908).

———. "Kriticheskie nabroski." *Rus'*, no. 109 (1904).

Brandes, G. *Sobranie sochineniy.* Vol. 19. St. Petersburg, 1913.

Bryusov, V. *Dalekie i blizkie.* Moscow, 1912.

———. "Evropeyskaya literatura v 1904 g.: I Rossiya." *Vesy*, no. 9 (1904).

———. *Izbrannye sochineniya.* Moscow, 1955.

——— (Avreliy). "Vekhi. III. Chort i Kham." *Vesy*, nos. 3 and 4 (1906).

———. "Dve knigi." *Vesy*, no. 6 (1908).

———. "Razgadka ili oshibka?" *Russkaya Mysl'*, no. 3 (1914).

Burenin, V. "Kriticheskie ocherki." *Novoe Vremya*, no. 8592 (1900).

———. "Tsvety novoy poezii." *Novoe Vremya*, no. 9149 (1901).

————. "Kriticheskie ocherki." *Novoe Vremya*, nos. 9163 and 9254 (1901).

Byvshiy chlen Obshchestva. "Isklyuchenie D. S. Merezhkovskogo iz Religiozno-Filosofskogo Obshchestva." *Novoe Vremya*, no. 13610 (1914).

Chekhov, A. P. *Pis'ma*. Vol. 2. Moscow, 1912.

Chubarov, N. "Po povodu prochitannogo." *Russkoe Obozrenie*, no. 7 (1892).

Chudovskiy, V. " 'Russkaya Mysl' ' i romany Bryusova, Gippius i Merezhkovskogo." *Apollon*, no. 2 (1913).

————. "Doklad Merezhkovskogo o Tolstom." *Apollon*, no. 5 (1913).

————. "O Merezhkovskom, Nekrasove i o politike v iskusstve." *Apollon*, no. 7 (1913).

Chukovskiy, K. *Ot Chekhova do nashikh dney*. St. Petersburg, 1908.

————. "O Merezhkovskom." *Rech'*, no. 243 (1907).

————. "Merezhkovskiy i Lermontov." *Rech'*, no. 24 (1909).

Chulkov, G. "Bolyashchiy dukh." In *Nashi sputniki*. Moscow, 1922.

Chunosov, M. "Kto zapolnit bezdnu?" In *Kriticheskie stat'i*. St. Petersburg, 1904.

————. "Kriticheskie eskizy." *Slovo*, nos. 136 and 142 (1905).

Chuzeville, J. *Dmitri Mérejkovski*. Paris, 1922.

Demidov, I. "D. Merezhkovskiy, Tayna Trekh: Egipet i Vavilon." *Sovremennye zapiski*, no. 28 (1926).

Dolinin, A. "Dmitriy Merezhkovskiy." In *Russkaya literature XX veka*. Edited by S. A. Vengerov. Vol. 1. Moscow, 1914.

Ellis. "O sovremennom simvolizme, o 'chorte' i o 'deystve.' " *Vesy*, no. 1 (1909).

Engel'gardt, M. "Merezhkovskiy i russkaya intelligentsiya." *Svobodnye mysli*, no. 48 (1908).

————. "Poklonenie zlu." *Nedelya*, no. 12 (1895).

————. "Klassitsizm v literature." *Novoe Vremya*, no. 10086 (1904).

Erisman, V. "Roman Merezhkovskogo (Rozhdenie bogov)." *Na chuzhoy storone*, no. 11 (1925).

"Eshche o Merezhkovskom." *Novoe Vremya*, no. 13610 (1914).

Evgenev-Maksimov, V., and Maksimov, D. *Iz proshlogo russkoy zhurnalistiki*. Leningrad, 1930.

Eykhenbaum, V., and Nikol'skiy, Yu. "Merezhkovskiy—kritik." *Severnye Zapiski*, no. 4 (1915).

Faresov, A. "Tragediya Shellera-Mikhaylova." *Istoricheskiy Vestnik*, no. 4 (1901).

Florovskiy, G. *Puti russkogo bogosloviya*. Paris, 1937.

Frank, S. *Filosofiya i zhizn'*. St. Petersburg, 1910.

————. "Merezhkovskiy o 'Vekhakh.' " *Slovo*, no. 779 (1909).

Galich, L. "Novye techeniya." *Rech'*, no. 1 (1908).

————. "Mysli." *Rech'*, no. 43 (1908).

————. "Byt' pustu." *Utro*, no. 28 (1908).

Galleriya russkikh pisateley. Moscow, 1901.

Galleriya russkikh pisateley i khudozhnikov. St. Petersburg, 1901.

Germanov, V. "Religiya Merezhkovskogo." In *Khristianskaya Mysl'*. N.p., 1916.

Gershenzon, M. "Literaturnoe obozrenie." *Vestnik Evropy*, nos. 7 and 8 (1908).

Gertsenshteyn, D. "Bogoiskatel'skie razvlecheniya." *Slovo*, no. 42 (1909).

Gertsyk, E. "Bogoiskatel'stvo v tikhom omute." *Zolotoe Runo*, nos. 2 and 3 (1909).

Gide, A. *Journal, 1889–1939.* Paris, 1940.

Gippius, Z. N. "Otkrytomu slukhu." *Pravda Zhizni*, no. 4 (1908).

———— (A. Krayniy). "Vlyublennost'." *Novyy Put'*, no. 3 (1904).

———— (A. Krayniy). *Literaturnyy dnevnik, 1899–1907.* St. Petersburg, 1908.

————. *Sinyaya kniga* (Peterburgskiy dnevnik, 1914–1918). Belgrade, 1929.

————. "Varshavskiy dnevnik." *Vozrozhdenie*, nos. 214–216 (1968).

————. "Pis'mo v redaktsiyu." *Russkaya Mysl'*, no. 5 (1914).

————. *Dmitriy Merezhkovskiy.* Paris, 1951.

Glinskiy, B. *Ocherki russkogo progressa.* St. Petersburg, 1900.

————. "Bolezn' ili reklama?" *Istoricheskiy Vestnik*, no. 2 (1896).

————. "Literaturnaya molodezh'." *Istoricheskiy Vestnik*, no. 6 (1896).

Godlevskiy, S. "Pis'mo v redaktsiyu." *Novoe Vremya*, no. 8972 (1901).

Golokhovastov, G. *Gibel' Atlantidy.* New York, 1938.

Golovin, K. F. *Russkiy roman i russkoe obshchestvo.* 2d edition. St. Petersburg, 1904.

Gol'tsev, V. "Literaturnye otgoloski." *Kur'er*, nos. 24 and 86 (1900).

Gorbov, D. "Mertvaya krasota i zhivuchee bezobrazie." *Krasnaya nov'*, no. 7 (1926).

Gornfel'd, A. "Merezhkovskiy i chort." In *Knigi i lyudi.* St. Petersburg, 1908.

————. "Kritika i lirika." *Russkoe Bogatstvo*, no. 3 (1897).

Govorov, K. *Sovremennye poety.* St. Petersburg, 1889.

Griftsov, B. *Tri myslitelya.* Moscow, 1911.

Grinevich, P. "Itogi dvukh yubileev." *Russkoe Bogatstvo*, no. 8 (1898).

————. "Zametki chitatelya." *Russkoe Bogatstvo*, no. 4 (1900).
Gurevich, L. "Khudozhestvennaya literatura." In *Ezhegodnik gazety 'Rech'.*' St. Petersburg, 1913.
Hofmann, Modeste. *Histoire de la littérature russe*. Paris, 1946.
Homo Novus. "Novyy Put'." *Rus'*, no. 325 (1904).
I. "Novosti literatury." *Russkie Vedomosti*, no. 126 (1901).
————. "Literaturnye novosti." *Russkie Vedomosti*, no. 65 (1903).
I. K. "Tolki v ital'yanskoy pechati o romane Merezhkovskogo." In *Literaturnyy Vestnik*. Vol. 3, bk. 3 (1902).
In Memoriam Dmitry Merejkovsky. Paris, 1944.
Ivanov-Razumnik, P. V. (Ivanov). *Istoriya russkoy obshchestvennoy mysli*. Vol. 2. St. Petersburg, 1907.
————. "Mertvoe masterstvo." In *Tvorchestvo i kritika*. St. Petersburg, 1911.
————. "Literatura i obshchestvennost'." *Zavety*, no. 2 (1913).
————. *Zavetnoe*. St. Petersburg, 1922.
Izmaylov, A. *Krivoe zerkalo*. St. Petersburg, 1908.
————. *Pomrachenie bozhkov i novye kumiry*. Moscow, 1910.
————. "Prorok bezblagodatnykh dney." In *Pestrye znamena*. Moscow, 1913.
————. "Literaturnoe obozrenie." *Niva*, no. 44 (1911).
Kierkegaard, Soren. *Attack upon "Christendom."* Translated by W. Lowrie, Princeton, N.J., 1944.
————. *Christian Discourses; and The Lilies of the Field, and The Birds of the Air, and Three Discourses at the Communion on Fridays*. Translated by W. Lowrie. London and New York, 1952.
————. *The Concept of Dread*. Translated by W. Lowrie. Princeton, N.J., 1957.
————. *Concluding Unscientific Postscript to the Philosophical Fragments*. Translated by D. F. Swenson. Princeton, N.J., 1944.
————. *Edifying Discourses*. Translated by D. F. Swenson and L. M. Swenson. 4 vols. Minneapolis, Minn., 1943.
————. *Either/Or*. Vol. 1 translated by D. F. Swenson and L. M. Swenson; vol. 2 translated by W. Lowrie. Garden City, N.Y., 1959.
————. *Fear and Trembling; and The Sickness unto Death*. Translated by W. Lowrie. Garden City, N.Y., 1954.
————. *Journals and Papers*. Edited and translated by H. V. Hong and E. H. Hong. 2 vols. to date. Bloomington, Ind., 1967, 1970.
————. *On Authority and Revelation: The Book on Adler*. Translated by W. Lowrie. Princeton, N.J., 1955.
————. *Repetition*. Translated by W. Lowrie. Princeton, N.J., 1941.

———. *Training in Christianity, and The Edifying Discourse Which Accompanied It.* Translated by W. Lowrie. Princeton, N.J., 1944.

———. *The Works of Love.* Translated by D. F. Swenson and L. M. Swenson. Princeton, N.J., 1946.

Kniga o russkikh poetakh. Edited by M. Gofman. St. Petersburg, 1909.

Kogan, P. *Ocherki po istorii noveyshey russkoy literatury.* Vol. 3, pt. 3. Moscow, 1911.

Kornilov, A. "Istoricheskiy roman D. Merezhkovskogo: 'Aleksandr I.'" *Sovremennik*, no. 2 (1913).

Korobka, N. "Merezhkovskiy o Tolstom i Dostoevskom." In *Ocherki literaturnykh nastroeniy.* St. Petersburg, 1903.

———. "Itogi Gogolevskoy yubileynoy literatury." *Zhurnal Ministerstva Narodnogo Prosveshcheniya*, no. 5 (1904).

———. "Iz zhizni i literatury." *Obrazovanie*, no. 11 (1901).

Kozlovskiy, L. "D. S. Merezhkovskiy kak khudozhnik i myslitel'." *Zhurnal dlya Vsekh*, nos. 8 and 9 (1910).

Kranikhfel'd, V. "Literaturnye otkliki." *Sovremennyy Mir*, nos. 1 and 11 (1908).

———. "Literaturnye otkliki." *Sovremennyy Mir*, nos. 3 and 8 (1909).

———. "Literaturnye otkliki." *Sovremennyy Mir*, no. 1 (1911).

Kropotkin, P. *Idealy i deystvitel'nost' v russkoy literature.* St. Petersburg, 1907.

Lednicki, W. "D. S. Merezhkovsky, 1865–1941." *Russian Review*, no. 1 (April 1942).

Levin, D. "Nabroski." *Rech'*, no. 70 (1908).

Levitzky, S. "An Unnoticed Anniversary: On Merezhkovsky's Role in Russian Culture." *Russian Review*, no. 27 (July 1968).

Lidin, N. "Chem my interesuemsya?" *Peterburgskaya Gazeta.* 8 December 1902.

Literaturnaya entsiklopediya. Vol. 7. Moscow, 1934.

Loengrin. "Zigzagi." *Odesskie Novosti*, no. 6881 (1906).

Lossky, N. O. *A History of Russian Philosophy.* London, 1952.

Lunacharskiy, A. V. "Tsari na stsene." In *Teatr i revolyutsiya.* Moscow, 1924.

Lundberg, E. *Merezhkovskiy i ego novoe khristianstvo.* St. Petersburg, 1914.

Lur'e, S. "Religioznye iskaniya v sovremennoy literature." *Russkaya Mysl'*, no. 10 (1908).

Luther, A. "Eine Roman-Trilogie." *Die Literatur* 8 (1905).

L'vov-Rogachevskiy, V. "Byt' ili ne byt' russkomu simvolizmu?" *Sovremennyy Mir*, no. 10 (1910).

————. "Khudozhnik-pravdoiskatel'." *Sovremennyy Mir*, no. 5 (1912).

Lyatskiy, E. A. "Sredi novykh knig." *Vestnik Evropy*, no. 4 (1906).

————. "Literaturnoe obozrenie." *Vestnik Evropy*, no. 7 (1906).

Lyatskiy, M. "Merezhkovskiy. Kritiko-biograficheskiy ocherk." In D. S. Merezhkovskiy, *Polnoe sobranie sochineniy*. Vol. 15. St. Petersburg, 1912.

Lyubosh, S. "Duel Merezhkovskogo i Struve." *Slovo*, no. 774 (1909).

Makovskiy, F. "Chto takoe russkoe dekadentstvo?" *Obrazovanie*, no. 9 (1905).

Malakhieva-Mirovich, V. G. "O smerti v sovremennoy poeziya." *Zavety*, no. 7 (1912).

————. "Novaya p'esa D. S. Merezhkovskogo." *Russkaya Mysl'*, no. 3 (1916).

Malover, F. "Prorok i tolpa." *Pravda Zhizni*, no. 7 (1909).

Maslenikov, O. *The Frenzied Poets*. Berkeley, Calif., 1962.

Matlaw, R. E. "The Manifesto of Russian Symbolism." *Slavic and East European Journal*, no. 3 (1957).

Mel'gunov, S. "Zashchita Merezhkovskim Aleksandra I." *Golos Minuvshego*, no. 4 (1913).

————. "Roman Merezhkovskogo: 'Aleksandr I.'" *Golos Minuvshego*, no. 12 (1914).

Mel'shin-Yakubovich (P. Ya.). *Russkaya muza*. St. Petersburg, 1904.

————. *Ocherki russkoy poezii*. St. Petersburg, 1904.

Men'shikov, M. "Kleveta obozhaniya." In *Kriticheskie ocherki*. Vol. 2. St. Petersburg, 1902.

Mikhail, Arkh. "Pis'mo v redaktsiyu." *S-Peterburgskie Vedomosti*, no. 13 (1903).

Mikhaylovskiy, N. K. "Dnevnik chitatelya." *Sochineniya*. Vol. 6. St. Petersburg, 1897.

————. "Russkoe otrazhenie frantsuzskogo simvolizma." In *Literaturnye vospominaniya i sovremennaya smuta*. Vol. 2. St. Petersburg, 1900.

————. "Neskol'ko slov o g. Merezhkovskom i L. Tolstom"; "O g. Merezhkovskom"; "O Dostoevskom i g. Merezhkovskom"; "G. Merezhkovskiy ob ottsakh i detyakh"; and "Zapozdalye schety s g. Merezhkovskim." In *Poslednie sochineniya*. Vol. 2. St. Petersburg, 1905.

————. "'Tolstoy i Dostoevskiy' Merezhkovskogo." In *Polnoe sobranie sochineniy*. Vol. 10. St. Petersburg, 1913.

————. "Literatura i zhizn'." *Russkaya Mysl'*, no. 5 (1892).

————. "Literatura i zhizn'." *Russkaya Mysl'*, no. 4 (1893).

————. "Literatura i zhizn'." *Russkoe Bogatstvo*, no. 9 (1893).

————. "Literatura i zhizn'." *Russkoe Bogatstvo*, no. 4 (1899).

Miller, O. "Nashi sovremennye poety." *Russkaya Mysl'*, no. 1 (1888).

Minskiy, N. "Absolyutnaya reaktsiya." In *Na obshchestvennye temy*. St. Petersburg, 1909.

————. "L. Andreev i Merezhkovskiy." *Nasha Gazeta*, no. 1 (1908).

————. "Vokrug i okolo chuzhikh idey." *Rech'*, no. 91 (1908).

Mirskiy, D. S. *A History of Russian Literature*. London, 1949.

Mirskiy, V. "Nasha literatura." *Zhurnal dlya Vsekh*, no. 10 (1902).

————. "Tekushchaya literatura." *Zhurnal dlya Vsekh*, no. 2 (1902).

Misheev, N. "Russkiy Faust." *Russkiy Filologicheskiy Vestnik*, nos. 1 and 2 (1906).

Mochul'skiy, K. "D. Merezhkovskiy. Frantsisk Assisskiy." *Sovremennye zapiski*, no. 67 (1938).

Morozov, M. "V gipnoze slov." *Obrazovanie*, no. 1 (1909).

————. "Po povodu odnoy knigi." *Obrazovanie*, no. 2 (1893).

Murav'ev, V. "Nevedomaya Rossiya." *Russkaya Mysl'*, no. 1 (1914).

Nadson, S. Ya. "Pis'ma k Merezhkovskomu." *Novyy Put'*, no. 4 (1903).

Nevedomskiy, M. "Modernistskoe pokhmel'e." In *Vershiny*. St. Petersburg, 1909.

————. "80-e i 90-e gg. v nashey literature." In *Istoriya Rossii v XIX v.* Vol. 9. Moscow, 1911.

————. "O 'nav'ikh' charakh i 'nav'ikh' tropakh." *Sovremennyy Mir*, no. 2 (1908).

————. "V zashchitu khudozhestva." *Sovremennyy Mir*, no. 3 (1908).

N. G. "Literaturnyy dnevnik." *Odesskie Novosti*, no. 7731 (1909).

Nikitina, E. F. *Russkaya literatura ot simvolizma do nashikh dney*. Moscow, 1926.

Nikol'skiy, B. "Vechnye sputniki Merzhkovskogo." *Istoricheskiy Vestnik*, no. 11 (1897).

N—v, V. "Iz tekushchey zhurnalistiki." *Volyn'*, no. 34 (1900).

Obolenskiy, L. "Vlechenie k drevnosti." *Nedelya*, no. 10 (1896).

Ovsyaniko-Kulikovskiy, D. N. "D. S. Merezhkovskiy, Vechnye sputniki." *Zhizn'*, no. 8 (1899).

————, editor. *Istoriya russkoy literatury XIX v.* Moscow, 1908–1912.

Pachmuss, T. *Zinaida Hippius: An Intellectual Profile*. Carbondale and Edwardsville, Ill., 1971.

Persky, S. *Les Maîtres du roman russe contemporain*. Paris, 1912.

Pertsov, P. "Literaturnye pis'ma." *Novoe Vremya*, no. 11790 (1909).

———. "Zagadka Lermontova." *Novoe Vremya*, no. 11975 (1909).

Peshekhonov, A. "Sluchaynye zametki. Teoriya g. Maklakova i praktika g. Merezhkovskogo." *Russkoe Bogatstvo*, no. 3 (1914).

Petrishchev, A. "Sluchaynye zametki." *Russkoe Bogatstvo*, no. 6 (1908).

Plekhanov, G. "O tak nazyvaemykh religioznykh iskaniyakh." In *Ot oborony k napadeniyu*. Moscow, 1910.

Poggioli, R. *The Poets of Russia, 1890–1930*. Cambridge, Mass., 1960.

Pokrovskiy, A. "Sovremennoe dekadentstvo." *Russkiy Vestnik*, no. 6 (1904).

———. "Religiya i revolyutsiya." In *O veyaniyakh vremeni*. St. Petersburg, 1908.

Polevoy, N. *Istoriya russkoy slovesnosti*. Vol. 3. St. Petersburg, 1900.

Potresov, S. "Poet i tolpa." *Russkoe Slovo*, no. 277 (1908).

Poyarkov, N. *Poety nashikh dney*. Moscow, 1907.

Protopopov, M. "Pis'ma o literature." *Russkaya Mysl'*, no. 9 (1891).

Pypin, A. N. "Literaturnoe obozrenie." *Vestnik Evropy*, no. 6 (1896).

Red'ko, A. M. *Literaturno-khudozhestvennye iskaniya v kontse XIX i nachale XX vv*. Petrograd, 1924.

Romanskiy, T. "Znayushchie." *Novyy Put'*, no. 10 (1903).

Rosenthal, B. G. "Nietzsche in Russia: The Case of Merezhkovsky." *Slavic Review* 33 (1974).

Rozanov, N. P. *O novom religioznom soznanii*. Moscow, 1908.

Rozanov, V. V. *Uedinennoe*. St. Petersburg, 1912.

———. *V mire neyasnogo i nereshennogo*. St. Petersburg, 1901.

———. "Malen'kaya istoricheskaya popravka." *Novoe Vremya*, no. 8941 (1901).

———. "Sredi inoyazychnykh." *Mir Iskusstva*, nos. 7 and 8 (1903).

———. "'Svoi lyudi' possorilis'." *Novoe Vremya*, no. 11532 (1908).

———. "Tragicheskoe ostroumie." *Novoe Vremya*, no. 11822 (1909).

———. "A. S. Suvorin i D. S. Merezhkovskiy." *Novoe Vremya*, no. 13604 (1914).

Rozhdestvin, A. *Lev Tolstoy v kriticheskoy otsenke Merezhkovskogo*. Kazan, 1902.

Rusakov, V. *Sto russkikh literatorov*. St. Petersburg, 1895.

Sadovskiy, B. "Oklevetannye teni." *Severnye Zapiski*, no. 1 (1913).

Sakmarov, A. "Dnevnik." *Syn Otechestva*, no. 195 (1899).

Salgaller, E. "*Dmitrij Samozvanets*: A Dramatic Fragment by D. S. Merežkovskij." *Slavic and East European Journal*, no. 4 (1963).

Sal'nikov, A. *Russkie poety za sto let.* St. Petersburg, 1901.

Sandro. "Zametki chitatelya." *Russkaya Molva,* no. 109 (1913).

Scanlan, J. P. "The New Religious Consciousness: Merezhkovsky and Berdyaev." *Canadian Slavic Studies,* vol. 4, no. 1 (1970).

Schmourlo, A. de. *La Pensée de Mérejkovski.* Nice, 1957.

Sementkovskiy, R. "Chto novogo v literature." *Niva,* no. 6 (1895).

―――. "Khristos, Antikhrist i g. Merezhkovskiy." *Niva,* no. 5 (1901).

Severak, Zh. "Religiozno-nravstvennye idei v proizvedeniyakh Merezhkovskogo." *Vestnik Znaniya,* no. 10 (1907).

Severov. "Russkaya literatura." *Novosti,* no. 164 (1900).

Shcheglova, L. (V. A. Shch.). *Merezhkovskiy. Publichnaya lektsiya.* St. Petersburg, 1909.

Shestakov, D. "Kriticheskie ocherki." *Torgovo-Promyshlennaya Gazeta,* no. 6 (1900).

―――. "Tikhie mgnoveniya." *Mir Iskusstva,* no. 4 (1904).

Shestov (Shvartsman), L. *Vlast' idey: Apofeoz bespochvennosti.* St. Petersburg, 1905.

―――. "Kniga Merezhkovskogo: L. Tolstoy i Dostoevskiy." *Mir Iskusstva,* nos. 8 and 9 (1901).

Sht―n, S. "Literaturnye otrazheniya." *Slovo,* no. 475 (1906).

Shulyatikov, V. "Novoe iskusstvo." *Kur'er,* no. 345 (1900).

―――. *Iz istorii noveyshey russkoy poezii.* Moscow, 1910.

Sigma (S. Syromyanikov). "Opyt misticheskoy kritiki." *Novoe Vremya,* no. 9050 (1901).

Sipovskiy, V. *Pushkinskaya yubileynaya literatura 1899–1900 gg.* St. Petersburg, 1902.

Skabichevskiy, A. *Istoriya noveyshey russkoy literatury.* St. Petersburg, 1891.

―――. "Zametki o tekushchey literature" and "Kur'ezy i absurdy molodoy kritiki." In *Sochineniya.* 3d edition. Vol. 2. St. Petersburg, 1903.

―――. "Literatura v zhizni i zhizn' v literature." *Novoe Slovo,* no. 9 (1896).

Skriba (Andreevich-Solov'ev). "Chto sey son znachit?" *Novosti,* no. 340 (1896).

―――. "Pis'mo v redaktsiyu." *Novosti,* no. 343 (1896).

Slonim, M. *Modern Russian Literature.* New York, 1953.

Slovar' chlenov Obshchestva Lyubiteley Rossiyskoy Slovesnosti. Moscow, 1911.

Solov'ev, S. "Poslednyaya kniga Merezhkovskogo." In *Bogoslovskie i kriticheskie ocherki.* Moscow, 1906.

Solov'ev, V. S. "Osoboe chestvovanie Pushkina: Protiv ispolnitel'nogo lista." In *Sobranie sochineniy*. 2d edition. Vol. 9. St. Petersburg, 1913.

Spasovich, V. "D. Merezhkovskiy i ego 'Vechnye sputniki.'" In *Sochineniya*. Vol. 9. St. Petersburg, 1900.

Stammler, H. A. "D. S. Merežkovskij—1865–1965: A Reappraisal." *Die Welt der Slaven* 12 (1967).

———. "Julianus Apostata Redivivus: Dmitrij Merežkovskij: Predecessors and Successors." *Die Welt der Slaven* 11 (1966).

Starodum, N. "Zhurnalisticheskoe obozrenie." *Russkiy Vestnik*, no. 5 (1903).

———. "Zhurnalisticheskoe obozrenie." *Russkiy Vestnik*, no. 4 (1904).

———. "Zhurnalisticheskoe obozrenie." *Russkiy Vestnik*, no. 4 (1905).

———. "Zhurnalisticheskoe i literaturnoe obozrenie." *Russkiy Vestnik*, no. 3 (1906).

St—n, A. "Zametki." *Novoe Vremya*, no. 11480 (1908).

Struve, G. *Russkaya literatura v izgnanii*. New York, 1956.

Struve, P. B. "Spor s Merezhkovskim"; "Na raznye temy"; and "Bor'ba za veru i bor'ba za dogmat." In *Patriotica*. St. Petersburg, 1911.

———. "Pochemu zastoyalas' nasha dukhovnaya zhizn'?" *Russkaya Mysl'*, no. 3 (1914).

———. "Religiya i obshchestvennost'." *Russkaya Mysl'*, no. 5 (1914).

———. "Otvet Merezhkovskomu." *Rech'*, no. 47 (1908).

———. "Kto iz nas maksimalist?" *Rech'*, no. 66 (1908).

Student-estestvennik. "Pis'mo po povodu knigi Merezhkovskogo: L. Tolstoy i Dostoevskiy." *Novyy Put'*, no. 1 (1903).

Sumtsov, N. *Leonardo da-Vinchi*. Kharkov, 1900.

S. V. V. "Primirenie dukha i ploti." *Novoe Vremya*, no. 9253 (1901).

Terapiano, Yu. "D. Merezhkovskiy. Pavel i Avgustin." *Sovremennye zapiski*, no. 65 (1937).

———. *Vstrechi*. New York, 1953.

Tereshchenkov, S. "Propovednik kontsa." *Russkaya Mysl'*, no. 3 (1903).

Tkhorzhevskiy, I. *Russkaya literatura*. Vol. 2. Paris, 1946.

Trotskiy, L. "Merezhkovskiy." In *Sochineniya*. Vol. 20. Moscow, 1926.

Tsetlin, M. "O novom romane Merezhkovskogo." *Sovremennye zapiski*, no. 5 (1921).

———. "D. S. Merezhkovskiy. Napoleon." *Sovremennye zapiski*, no. 40 (1929).

————. "D. S. Merezhkovskiy." *Novosel'e*, no. 2 (1942).

Vengerov, S. A. *Osnovnye cherty istorii noveyshey russkoy literatury.* 2d edition. St. Petersburg, 1909.

————. *Sobranie sochineniy.* St. Petersburg, 1911.

————, editor. *Entsiklopedicheskiy Slovar'.* Brokgauz-Efron edition. Vol. 37. St. Petersburg, 1896.

Vengerova, Z. "Russkiy simvolizm v otsenke frantsuzskoy kritiki." *Novosti*, no. 114 (1901).

Vergezhskiy, A. "Oplevanie." *Slovo*, no. 746 (1909).

Vetalis (V. Gol'tsev). "So storony." *Russkaya Mysl'*, no. 5 (1902).

Vlagin. "Malen'kiy fel'eton, Pis'ma A. P. Chekhova i g. Merezhkovskiy." *Novoe Vremya*, no. 13611 (1914).

Volynskiy, A. L. *Russkie kritiki.* St. Petersburg, 1896.

————. "Sovremennaya russkaya belletristika." In *Bor'ba za idealizm*. St. Petersburg, 1900.

————. *Kniga velikogo gneva.* St. Petersburg, 1904.

Voronskiy, A. "Vne zhizni i vne vremeni." *Prozhektor*, no. 13 (1925).

"V religiozno-filosofskom obshchestve." *Rech'*, no. 319 (1910).

Vysheslavtsev, B. "D. Merezhkovskiy. Iisus Neizvestnyy." *Sovremennye zapiski*, no. 55 (1934).

Yablonskiy, A. "Son g-na Merezhkovskogo." *Novosti*, no. 45 (1907).

Zakrzhevskiy, A. *Religiya: Psikhologicheskie paralleli.* Kiev, 1913.

Zenger, A. "Petr." *Rus'*, no. 117 (1905).

Zenkovsky, V. V. *A History of Russian Philosophy.* 2 vols. New York and London, 1953.

Zlobin, V. *Tyazhelaya dusha.* Washington, D.C., 1970.

V. BIBLIOGRAPHIES

Foster, Ludmila A. *Bibliography of Russian Emigré Literature, 1918–1968.* Vol. 2. Cambridge, Mass., 1970.

Istoriya russkoy literatury kontsa XIX–nachala XX veka. Bibliograficheskiy ukazatel'. Edited by K. D. Muratova. Moscow and Leningrad, 1963. Includes a list of Merezhkovskiy's "Letters to Editors."

Literatura velikogo desyatiletiya (1917–1927). Edited by I. V. Vladislavlev. Moscow and Leningrad, 1928.

Russkaya literatura XX v. Edited by S. A. Vengerov. Vol. 2, pt. 5. Moscow, 1915. Includes a list of translations by Merezhkovskiy and a list of Merezhkovskiy's poems that had been set to music.

Russkaya slovesnost' s XI do XIX stoletiya vklyuchitel'no. Edited by A. V. Mez'er. Part 2. St. Petersburg, 1902.

Russkie pisateli. Edited by I. V. Vladislavlev. Moscow, 1924.

Index

Brandes, Georg Morris Cohen, 48
Brittany, 117
Bryusov, Valeriy Yakovlevich, 14, 16, 36, 37, 38, 43, 116, 122
Bugaev, Boris Nikolaevich [pseud. Andrey Belyy], 13, 15, 38, 43, 116, 117, 129, 146, 185 n. 46
Bulgakov, Sergey Nikolaevich, 116, 118
Bunakov, I., 117, 118, 119, 145
Bunin, Ivan Alekseevich, 149
Byronism, 9

Calvin, Jean, 166
Capri, 32, 42
Carlisle, Thomas, 48
Caucasus, 11
Chekhov, Anton Pavlovich, 41, 42, 57
China, 125
Christ and Antichrist (Khristos i Antikhrist), 65–90, 111
Chukovskiy, Korney Ivanovich, 186 n. 2
Clement of Alexandria, 163
Comte, Auguste, 12, 124
Constantinople, 42
Constantius (emperor of Rome), 69, 76
Corfu, 42
Crimea, 8, 11

Dante, 152
Dante Alighieri, 152, 166
Darwin, Charles Robert, 12
Davydov, Karl Yul'evich, 11, 41
Davydova, Aleksandra Arkad'evna, 11, 41
Death of the Gods: Julian the Apostate (Smert' bogov: Yulian Otstupnik), 42, 43, 66, 67–73, 80, 120
December the Fourteenth (Chetyrnadtsatoe dekabrya), 119, 120, 153
Decembrist Movement, 119, 120, 136
Denmark, 104

Dolinin, Aleksandr S., 13
Dostoevskiy, Fedor Mikhaylovich, 9–10, 17, 46, 49, 52, 53, 54, 58, 88, 92, 116, 127, 182 n. 15; his *Brothers Karamazov*, 88
Dudyrev, Ivan I., 148
Dyagilev, Sergey Pavlovich, 113, 115, 116

Ecclesiastical Academy, 114
Elagin Island, 2, 6, 8
England, 45
Eternal Companions (Vechnye sputniki), 61–62
Euripides, 42, 51
Evreinova, Anna Mikhaylovna, 12

Fedotov, G., 150
Fet, Afanasiy Afanas'evich. *See* Shenshin, Afanasiy Afanas'evich
Figner, Vera Nikolaevna, 117
Filosofov, Dmitriy Vladimirovich, 113, 114, 116, 117, 118, 119, 121, 129, 142, 143, 146, 147, 148
Finland, 147
Flaubert, Gustave, 41, 52
Flekser, Akim L'vovich [pseud. Volynskiy], 43, 50
Florence, Italy, 42, 45, 77, 80
Fofanov, Konstantin Mikhaylovich, 15, 57
France, 45, 50, 51, 112, 119, 143, 147, 150

Gapon, Father Georgiy A., 130
Garshin, Vsevolod Mikhaylovich, 12, 56–57; his "Four Days," "Red Flower," and "Attalea Princeps," 56–57
Germany, 45, 117, 143, 144, 150
Ghirlandaio, Domenico, 45
Gippius, Zinaida Nikolaevna (Merezhkovskaya): her biography of Merezhkovskiy, 2, 4, 6, 14, 42, 47; marriage, 22, 23, 41; travels, 42, 116, 117, 118, 119, 142, 147–48, 149, 166; on religion, 107, 114; and literary associations, 113–14, 146; and Filosofov, 116, 117, 118,

216

Europe (Tayna Zapada: Atlantida-Evropa), 166; *Jesus the Unknown (Iisus Neizvestnyy)*, 166

Merezhkovskiy, Ivan Fedorovich (grandfather), 1–2

Merezhkovskiy, Konstantin Sergeevich (brother), 7–8, 11

Merezhkovskiy, Sergey Ivanovich (father), 2–4, 5, 7, 8, 9, 22, 47, 118

Messiah, The (Messiya), 153–55

Michelangelo Buonarroti, 45, 76

Mickiewicz, Adam, 148, 152

Mikhaylovskiy, Nikolay Konstantinovich, 12, 17, 56

Mill, John Stuart, 12

Minsk, 148, 149

Minskiy. *See* Vilenkin, Nikolay Maksimovich

Mir Bozhiy, 11

Mir Iskusstva, 113, 114, 115

Mirolyubov, V. S., 114

Mochul'skiy, K. V., 150

Modernist Movement, 43, 113, 117

Molière, 9

Montaigne, Michel Eyquem de, 22, 61

Moscow, 2, 22, 28, 42, 118

Mussolini, Benito, 152–53

Mystical Anarchism, 38

Nadson, Semen Yakovlevich, 10, 11, 17, 18, 22, 26, 30

Naples, 42

Napoleon (emperor of France), 152, 166

Narodnaya Volya, 16–17

Naturalism, 45

Nekrasov, Nikolay Alekseevich, 17, 55–56, 182 n. 15

Newton, Sir Isaac: his *Commentaries*, 87

Nietzsche, Friedrich Wilhelm, 35, 36, 37, 66, 76, 106, 122, 123, 167

Niva, 43

Normandy, 117

Not Peace, but a Sword (Ne mir, no mech), 118

Novyy Put', 114–15, 116, 117

Obshchee delo, 150

Octaves of the Past (Starinnye oktavy), 3, 4, 5, 6

Old Believers, 65, 82, 87

On the Reasons for the Decline and on New Trends in Contemporary Russian Literature (O prichinakh upadka i o novykh techeniyakh sovremennoy russkoy literatury), 43–59

Orenburg Province, 2, 12

Otechestvennye Zapiski, 10, 11

Pachmuss, Temira, 173 n. 31, 192 n. 38

Paris, 11, 28, 117, 118, 119, 142, 148, 149, 150, 166

Paul I (Pavel I), 118, 119, 120, 121

Pericles, 45

Pertsov, P. P., 114, 115, 116

Peshkov, Aleksey Maksimovich [pseud. Maxim Gor'kiy], 127, 146, 190 n. 44; his *Lower Depths*, 127

Peter the Great, Tsar of Russia, 3, 65, 66, 76, 80, 81–83, 85–86, 88, 89, 93, 129, 130, 137

Pilsudski, Josef, 148–49

Pirozhkov, M. V., 119

Pisarev, Dmitriy Ivanovich, 47, 183 n. 19

Plato, 64, 96, 105, 163, 164, 194 n. 89; his *Symposium*, 163

Pleshcheev, Aleksey Nikolaevich, 11, 41–42

Pobedonostsev, Konstantin Petrovich, 114, 115

Poe, Edgar Allan, 52

Poggioli, Renato, 15

Poland, 148, 149, 150

Polonskiy, Yakov Petrovich, 11, 15

Poppy Flower, The (Makov tsvet), 120–21

Populism, 12, 16–17, 19, 21, 55–56, 57, 166

Populists, 25, 26, 37, 55, 56

Portal, Abbé, 117

Positivism, 58, 123–26

Sophocles, 42, 51, 64
Soviet of Workers' and Soldiers' Deputies, 145
Sovremennye zapiski, 150
Spanish Mystics (Ispanskie mistiki), 166
Spasovich, V. D., 58
Spencer, Herbert, 12
Spinoza, Baruch, 87
Stolypin, Petr Arkad'evich, 119
Strakhov, Nikolay Nikolaevich, 49
Strannik, Ivan. *See* Anichkova, A. M.
Struve, Petr Berngardovich, 118
Suvorin, Aleksey Sergeevich, 42, 114
Switzerland, 11
Symbolism, 5, 25, 26, 41, 43, 50–54, 59
Symbolists, 26, 36, 38, 51, 167
Symbols (Simvoly), 35, 42
Syutaev, Vasiliy Kirillovich, 11

Taine, Hippolyte Adolphe, 48
Tale of Igor's Campaign (Slovo o polku Igoreve), 8
Teatral'naya Gazeta, 41
Terapiano, Yuriy Konstantinovich, 192 n. 29
Ternavtsev, V. A., 114
Teternikov, Fedor Kuz'mich [pseud. Fedor Sologub], 37
There Will Be Joy (Budet radost'), 120
Tiflis, 22
Tolstoy, Aleksey Konstantinovich, 121
Tolstoy, Lev Nikolaevich, 11, 17, 46, 52, 53, 54, 58, 92, 116, 166, 182 n. 15; his *Confession,* 11; *War and Peace,* 17, 54; *Anna Karenina,* 54
Trepov, F. F., 7
Trud, 41
Tsar et la révolution, Le, 118
Tsarevich Alexis (Tsarevich Aleksey), 120, 121
Turgenev, Ivan Sergeevich, 46, 49,
52, 53, 57, 58, 182 n. 15; his *Poems in Prose* and *Bezhin Meadow,* 53
Turkey, 143, 144
Tutankhamon (pharaoh of Egypt), 155
Tyutchev, Fedor Ivanovich, 15, 122

Üxküll, Baroness Varvara Ivanovna, 42
Ufa Province, 12
Ukraine, 1, 119
Urusov, Prince A. I., 42
Uspenskiy, Gleb Ivanovich, 12, 56

Vekhi, 139
Vengerov, Semen Afanas'evich, 10
Venice, 42
Verlaine, Paul, 27, 51
Verne, Jules, 6
Verrocchio, Andrea del, 45
Versailles, 82
Verzhbolovo, 119
Vestnik Evropy, 43
Vestnik Inostrannoy Literatury, 41
Vesy, 116
Vienna, 42
Vilenkin, Nikolay Maksimovich [pseud. Minskiy], 11, 15, 17, 35, 41, 57, 58, 117; his *By the Light of Conscience,* 35
Vilnius, 148
Vodovozov, V. V., 116
Volynskiy. *See* Flekser, Akim L'vovich
Voprosy Zhizni, 116
Vsemirnaya Illyustratsiya, 43

Warsaw, 42, 148, 149
Weininger, Otto: his *Sex and Character,* 161
Westernizers, 93
Wilhelm, Kaiser, 144
World War I, 142, 143–44, 145
World War II, 153, 165

Yasnaya Polyana, 116

Zasulich, Vera Ivanovna, 7

221